SP Pvt. Ltd.

Caste in Modern India
Atrocities Against Dalits

RAMESH JARE
&
SAMPAT KALE
School of Rural Development
Tata Institute of Social Sciences
Tuljapur Campus
Tuljapur – 413601

2017

Studium Press (India) Pvt. Ltd.

Caste in Modern India
Atrocities Against Dalits

ISBN: 978-93-85046-11-7

Published by:

Studium Press (India) Pvt. Ltd.
4735/22, 2nd Floor, Prakash Deep Building
(Near Delhi Medical Association),
Ansari Road, Darya Ganj, New Delhi-110 002
Tel.: + 91-11-43240200-15 (15 lines); Fax: 91-11-43240215
E-mail: studiumpress@gmail.com

Printed in India

Foreword

The present book looks at caste-based atrocities in a calibrated, rather than in an iridescent, staccato manner. It develops multiple perspectives: theoretical as well as empirical, diachronic as well as syncretic and longitudinal as well as contemporaneous. The credentials of Sukhadeo Thorat, the most penetrating mind since B. R. Ambedkar, in analysing Indian society, economy and polity in all their correlates and dynamics, are unexceptionable and unquestionable. His article which forms the first chapter of the book is wide-ranging, insightful, thought-provoking and inspiring. Thorat knows what he says and says what he knows with unparalleled clarity and unswerving audacity.

A word about the authors, Ramesh Jare, an accomplished and acclaimed Social Work teacher, scholar, researcher, and writer par excellence, has, as is his wont, adopted an empathetic, but professional approach to addressing and analysing atrocities against dalits. He pulls no punches in fixiung politicians, policy-makers and administrators in failing the dalits and, thereby failing the Constitution whose protection, in letter and spirit, is their bounden duty.

Sampat Kale is a young but noted sociologist, prolific writer with an uncanny scholarly ability to analyse Indian society in its varied and variegated dimensions and polymorphic transmogrification. His approach to the study in the present book is sensitive sans sensationalism, objective but, at the same time, perceptive.

On the whole, the book throws up insights and inputs for scholars, policy-makers, practitioners and, above all, civil society in new benchmarking a la a dynamic process and parallactic but reassuring manner against the backdrop of the headwinds of socio-economic and political changes taking place in geometric progression and engulfing even the excluded and oppressed.

Despite the massive and bourgeoning literature on caste, the question whether it is a basic structure or superstructure phenomenon still remains unsettled. Similarly, notwithstanding the innumerable multi-pronged attempts at its elimination, it continues to persist, in overt and covert forms. B.R. Ambedkar, the indisputable de rigueur in analyzing Indian societal structure, wrote his magnum opus, Annihilation of Caste in 1936, purporting to eliminate it root and branch. Practically, everyone is openly anti-caste. None-the-less, it remains iron-clad as a social institution with all the unavailing consequences, for the material-base of the caste system is almost intact. Little wonder, then, that, caste, anachronistically, continues to be the fulcrum of Indian social analysis, no matter, the reductionist, class-essentialist scholars make their presence conspicuous across the intellectual spectrum. Caste forms the launch-pad for political mobilization. It is ironical that Ambedkar's disciples themselves are not in favor of annihilation of caste. After all, anything useful and functional seldom vanishes. What is relevant and important in the contemporary context is to focus on the pivotal economic role caste played, and continues to play, in determining:

1. Structure of ownership of property;'
2. Division of labour;
3. Distribution of the social product; and
4. Appropriation of social surplus.

While it is necessary to delve into the ideology undergirding the caste system, it is also unavoidable to take cognizance of the varied forms it assumes under various paradigms with a view to historisisng, contemporizing and theorizing caste. It calls for understanding, though in a staccato /iridescent manner, the impacts of:

1. The Constitution;
2. Planning and rural development;

3. Land Reforms;
4. Green Revolution;
5. Implementation of the recommendations of the Mandal Commission
6. BSP; and,
7. Finally, neo-liberal economic policy.

While pursuing remedies for the continuing atrocities on dalits, focus needs to be placed on the demographic dividend, aspirational mobility, the congenial start-up eco-system in place today and the stand –up India vision. It would also make a few brief observations on the now-familiar term, "dalit capitalism".

The present book deals with caste in modern India with specific focus on atrocities on dalits. It pointedly asks the question, "Why Caste Atrocities Still Persist in India and How to Prevent Them?". (Chapter 1 by Thorat). In fact, all the articles in the volume ask the same question and the seriousness of the persistence of atrocities, in spite of all the Constitutional, legal, administrative, political and social safeguards, is brought into bold relief. Using National Crimes Records Bureau data as well as credible field- level data, analyses are undertaken at both macro- and micro-levels.

Modernism must lead to the negation of primordial values, norms and practices such as caste, race, ethnicity etc and build a new syncretism based on scientism, rationalism, secularism and universalism. However, even in most modern societies, with very few exceptions, these stay relevant (Robinson, 1983; Sanyal 2007) and continue to define civil society and determine human destiny, particularly of those who are marginalized and excluded. This is especially so in India where the ex-untouchables (the dalits) have been the victims of atrocities perpetrated by the upper castes, often with the overt and covert support of a complicitous state. Caste hierarchy, justified and sanctioned by religious ideology, not only wantonly deprives them of the material means of livelihood, but also physically oppresses them and forces them to do menial jobs and manual scavenging. In many a situation, the bond between caste and economic frontiers is seldom broken and the dalits, chafing under exploitation, are forced to engage in low productive and unclean activities depriving them of dignity and self-confidence. Their triple alienation- from wealth, knowledge and power- continues in spite of the innumerable measures of positive discrimination / affirmative actions and, above all, reservation.

Important laws like The Untouchability (Offences) Act, 1955, The Protection of Civil Rights Act, 1976, and The Scheduled Castes and Scheduled tribes (prevention of Atrocities) Act, 1989, have remained a dead letter in the wake of increasing atrocities. A singular feature of this book is that all the papers it is composed of cite the failure of the state in carrying out its Constitutional mandate in protecting the dalits against atrocities. Article 46 of the constitution is cold-shouldered with impunity.

It is instructive to note the observation made, in his inimitable style, by Thorat that "the number of registered crimes against SCs reveal that states like Uttar Pradesh, Rajasthan, Madhya Pradesh and Andhra Pradesh have remained at the top of the country's crime map over the last decade. About two-thirds of the total crimes against SCs are registered in these four states. In recent years, the states of Bihar and Orissa have also been witnessing a significant increase in the total number of crimes." (See, Thorat, infra)

In OBC-ruled as well as in the forward caste-ruled states, atrocities against dalits are a regular feature and are a reprisal against the dalits raising demand for land and wage-increase as well as their assertion for dignity and identity. And now, the conflicts are inevitably between land-owning OBCs and landless dalits. It is shuddering to note that civil society is becoming increasingly neo-casteist and, inexorably, this insidious trend is stalking through party politics, academia and the media. A tell-tale case is Maharashtra, a region which produced social reformers like Mahatma Phule and Shahaju Maharaja and the peerless revolutionary, B.R. Ambedkar. Presently, on the social front, the state is taking a great leap backwards, thereby becoming fastidious and caste-fixated. Districts such as Beed, Latur, Osmanabad and Ahmednagar are reporting increasing numbers of crimes against dalits on a daily basis, and are, thus, by any reckoning, acquiring a staid image. A paradigm shift is worth noting here. Earlier, bright and illustrious dalits were co- opted by the rulers whereas, now, such persons are targeted for attack or, as a concomitant of atrocities, forced to commit suicide as has been explicated by the recent Rohit Vemula incident. (Roderigues, 2016) The position that the state takes from time to time with regard to atrocities against dalits is quaint and ominous giving the impression that it is invariably anti-dalit. After all, state (whether it is controlled by OBCs or Forward Castes, or by left, centrist or right parties) is an instrument of oppression.

(Kannabiran, 2004). State means power; and power is used by the strong against the weak. Of course, dalits do have participation in the state. But participation is not the crucial factor here; the crucial question is who controls the state. The ruling classes control the state whose primary duty is to protect property and the propertied class. Obviously, the propertyless, oppressed social groups find themselves at the receiving end. Dalits do not need more icons; they need iconoclasts. For them, there cannot be a better intellectual-cum-social compass than Romila Thapar's assertion: "To Question or Not to Question, That is the Question." (Thapar, Ibid, ix).

The dalit question is not a development question. It is a resource question. Whether through state-sponsored reform or a market-mediated program, building the resource-base of the dalits is the lasting solution for caste atrocities against them. After getting the resource-base in place, they must end the dependence on state-patronage, give up "the comforts of conforming" (Thapar, 2015, 40) and thenceforth, like others, compete in the neo-liberal economy, make the most of the opportunities and benefit there from, not by fits and starts but steadily. There should emerge dalit Tatas, dalit Birlas, dalit Ambanis and dalit Adanis. This will put the society culturally on an even keel, resulting, once-and-for-all, in the deracination of the tap-root of atrocities against the dalits.

References

Leo Panich et al. (ed), Regstering Class. (2014): Socialist Register. "See, particularly, Vivek Chibber, "Capitalism, Class and Universalism: Escaping the Cul-De- Sac of Post-Colonial Theory" and Bryan D. Palmer, "Reconsiderations of Class: Precariousness as Proletarianisation." In line with Bryan, it is instructive and insightful to characterize the dalits as precariat, rather than proletariat.

Sanyal.Kalyan (2007): rethinking Capitalist development. Routledge.

Thapar. Romila (2015): The Public Intellectual in India. Aleph Book Company. "To Question or Not to Question, That is the Question" is the title of the Nikhil Chakravary Memorial Lecture delivered by Romila Thapar on 26October 2014 at the function organized by the Book Review Literary Trust. The book cited here is a "revised and expanded "version of the Lecture along with essays by Sundar Sarukkai, Dhruv Raina, Peter deSouza, Neeladri Bhattacharya and Javed Naqvi

Robinson, Cedric. (1983): Black Marxism. Zed Press.

Kannabiran, K.G. (2004): The Wages of Impunity: power, Justice, and human Rights. Orient Blackswan.

Roderigues, Valerian. (2016): "A new idiom of Dalit Assertion". The Hindu, Saturday. November,19.

Prof. M Kunhaman
Tata Institute of Social Sciences, Tuljapur Campus,
Maharashtra, India.

List of Contributors

Anjali Thomas: Ph.D. Scholar, Tata Institute of Social Sciences (TISS), Mumbai.

Arvindkumar S. Mardan: Gujarat University, Ahmedabad.

Bhat Iqball: Department of Sociology and Social Work Central University of Jammu, Jammu.

Nagaraju Vadapalli: Department of Political Science, Kakatiya University, Warangal, Telangana,

Pradeep Jare: Center for Studies in Rural Development (CSRD), Ahmednagar.

Rajesh Lakum: Centre for Study in Society and Development, School of Social Studies, Central University, Gandhinagar.

Rajnikant Parmar: Ph.D. Scholar, Tata Institute of Social Sciences, Mumbai

Raju Adagale: Ph.D. Scholar, Tata Institute of Social Sciences (TISS), Mumbai.

Ramesh Jare: Tata Institute of Social Sciences (TISS), Tuljapur Campus, Tuljapur.

Sampat Kale: Tata Institute of Social Sciences (TISS), Tuljapur Campus, Tuljapur.

Sanjaykumar Kamble: Savitribai Phule Pune University (SPPU), Pune.

Saumya Uma: Maharashtra National Law University (MNLU), Mumbai.

Sharvani Navangul: Law Students, National University of Study and Research in Law, Ranchi.

Sudhir Maske: Department of Social Work, University of Delhi, New Delhi.

Sukhdeo Thorat: Indian Council of Social Science Research (ICSSR), New Delhi.

Trupti Ratnaparkhi: Tata Institute of Social Sciences (TISS), Tuljapur Campus, Tuljapur.

About the Editor(s)

Dr. Ramesh Jare (M.A. TISS), Ph.D. in Social Work) he is with School of Rural Development, Tata Institute of Social Sciences (TISS) as a Associate Professor. He is the Academic Convener and Programme Convener of MA Social Work with Specialization in Rural Development. He has extensively worked with rural communities on different issues *i.e.* land, water, sustainable agriculture and watershed management particularly for the rights of Women, Dalits and Tribal communities. He has written several articles, two book, some papers in national and international journals. He has presented his work at various conferences and seminars at national and International level. He has visited Gavale University-Sweden, Kabul University, Afghnistan and presented papers as well.

Areas of Interest: Organization of Dalits, Tribal and other Marginal Communities, Local-Self Governance, Participatory Governance, Micro/Participatory Planning, Land, Water and sustainable Agriculture, Food Security, Rehabilitation and Resettlements and Disaster Management.

Specialization: (A) Teaching, Training and Community Mobilization in Professional Social Work and local self governance; (B) Policy advocacy on local self Governance and Participatory Democracy; (C) Studies on issues of Dalit ans women rights, Land and water rights; (D) Studies on development of tribes, nomadic and de-notified tribes.

TISS Tuljapur Campus, *E-mail*: rameshjare@tiss.edu

Dr. Sampat Kale (M.A., Ph.D. in Sociology) is with School of Rural Development, Tata Institute of Social Sciences (TISS) as a Senior Assistant Professor. He is the Programme Convener, MA/M Sc in Sustainable Livelihoods and Natural Resources Governance. He is the in charge of the Social Protection Office of the Tuljapur campus. He is a Life Member of the Indian Sociological Society and the Marathi Samajshastra Parishad. He has written more than two dozens of articles, several books and some papers in national and international journals. He has presented his work at various conferences and seminars at national level. He has visited Karachi-Pakistan, Stockholm-Sweden and presented papers as well.

Areas of Interest: Sociology of Development and Change, Sociology of Marginal groups, Rural Development, Voluntary Organization - NGOs, Social Movements, Public policy and Advocacy, Participatory Governance, Good Governance, Transparency and Accountability, Rurban Livelihood and Marginalized, Governance of Natural Resources-Land, Water, Forest & Work, Food Security, Displacement & Development.

***Specialization*:** (A) Teaching, Training and Capacity building in local self governance, Rurban livelihoods; (B) Policy advocacy on livelihoods and natural resources; (C) Studies on issues of land rights, water rights, forest and drought; (D) Studies on development of tribes and nomadic tribes and food security; (E) Studies on NGOs and Social Movements.

TISS Tuljapur Campus, *E-mail*: samkale@tiss.edu

Preface

The book is an outcome of National conference on Atrocities against Dalits in India, Organised by Tata Institute of Social Sciences, Tuljapur Campus, and Indian Council of Social Science Research (ICSSR), New Delhi in June 2015. The issue of Caste Atrocities on Dalits is the age old phenomenon in Indian society. The book has several chapters on atrocities, caste-based humiliation, and discrimination on dalits. Some chapters discusses the theoretical and conceptual importance as Pan-Indian category. Caste and untochability exist in different forms in Modern India,and it has it different facets. At one side society is becoming the modern and progressive but at other side the mindset of the higher caste is not yet changed hence caste atrocities are increasing and persist in society. The following articles reflects and analyses the aspects of caste based contradictions in Modern Society of India.

The article by Sukhdeo Thorat on Why Caste Atrocities Still Persists and How to prevent them? He raises critical question, *i.e.* why higher castes continue to deny the untouchables the equal citizenship rights despite legal provision? Why the higher castes do used violent methods to deny them equal rights? What is purpose of high caste in denying the rights to untouchables, and what do they gain from this denial? Are the gains material and economic? Or are the gains related to social privileges and high social status? Secondly important question is: what are the roots and sources of this antagonistic behavior? What role do religious and social ideas play in persistence of caste discrimination and violence?

The analysis of his paper reveals that despite the provisions of the law, SCs have failed to receive equal rights in the social, economic, cultural, religious and political spheres. Any attempts by the SC to secure these equal rights often meet with violence of various types. The erstwhile peaceful opposition by higher castes to the attempt by SCs to secure equal rights has now been taken over more by violent forms by higher castes. According his observation earlier atrocities were individual based in the recent period, the violence is perpetrated by the community, whole or by more than one community. Similarly the commitment of more than one atrocity at a given point of time has also increased. More importantly, the incidence of atrocities and sexual violence against SC women has been increasing and assuming various forms- hearting the honor, where it heart most.

This indicates that laws are a must, but they have their limitations in bringing about social change. They can, at best, provide some safeguards. The caste-based discrimination in our society is rooted in the ideology of caste and customary rules, which still continue to exercise a strong hold on the social behavior of the higher caste Hindus.

The article by Ramesh Jare, on Caste Violence in post-colonial period observed that after post colonial period there is wide range of social changes that have happened in the Indian society but the caste structure as remained is static and has not changed much. In Indian caste structure, the Dalits are always the victim of the upper caste society. New forms of issues and problems are emerging in the country. Atrocities and caste violence has been increasing and and it's taking new shape/nature along with the "development" of the country. However, Prevention of atrocities act have been failed due to lack of support of judiciary and police.

This article attempts to address two interrelated issues. First it tries to conceptulise nature and dimension of the "violence-linked to caste Deprivation" of the socially disadvantage groups particularly the dalits in post-colonial era. In those efforts it elaborates the concept and meaning of caste based exclusion, and its implications for development of excluded groups. Secondly, in this theoretical back drop it tries to provide empirical evidence on the caste based violence and discrimination and denial of rights to Dalits – in civil, social, culture political and economic spheres- leading lack of income earning capital assets like agriculture land, employment, education and social needs like housing water, electricity.

The article by Sampat Kale on Violation of Civil Rights and Atrocities Against Dalits based on the case study of *Kharda* village of Maharashtra. The aim of the present article is to understand the issues involved in violation of civil rights in the era of modern and modernity in our country and to examine and analyze causes and its aftermath. Author has selected a case of kharda village where the boy was brutally killed by the upper caste Hindus. In his article he raises the issues that though Maharashtra being a progressive sate, has a history of Shau, Phule and Ambedkar's thought, but it seems that it has not percolated to a large share of citizen of our country. Caste, Class, Gender, Religion, and Minority based discrimination, humiliation, exclusion, inequality and injustice is still prevalent in the society of India.

There have been violations of civil and human rights irrespective of strong legislations and affirmative measures in India and Maharashtra. Why this has been increasing in modern society? Why the dalit youths are targeted and brutally killed on the issues of caste? This shows that Government has failed in protecting the rights of marginalized sections of the society. This article argues about the dream of anti-caste movement or casteless society and its meaning on the context of whether it is a myth or reality? Technological developments and the dream of superpower country will not be achieved unless and until we establish the safety and security of the most vulnerable and marginal used life without fear for their empowerments country.

The article by Saumya Uma on Atrocities and Discrimination Against Dalits: A Critical Examination of the Response of the Law , this article argues that discrimination and atrocities against Dalits are two sides of the same coin – both are entrenched in the caste system that perpetuates inequality. Impunity for atrocities emboldens the perpetrators not only to commit atrocities on Dalits, which are patent in nature, but to continue to subject Dalits to various latent forms of discrimination in the social, cultural, economic and political arena. On the other hand, the absence of an effective legal intervention against discrimination could, potentially, function as a build up towards commission of atrocities.

The article by Kamble Sanjaykumar on The Scope of Contemporary Caste Struggle, Violence and Exploitation in Maharashtra' narrates that the caste and gender are oppressive factors in Indian society. In this article, detailed note has been taken of the important caste conflicts in India and the related literature. Often, higher castes claim that the Dalits themselves are responsible for the crimes against them. The news is false and that the cases are purposely filed. Therefore, it is also important to understand some basic issues like 'What is abuse?', 'How is it related to caste?', 'What role does gender play in this?' etc. We must also realize that in the influence of caste and male dominance, the issues of Dalits, tribal and women folk subtly affect every aspect of their lives. That is why it is essential to understand this question in its historical context and then think of it in the contemporary social setting. For this, it is also necessary to see how the nature of injustice and abuse against the Dalits is changing in the modern globalized world, and how the social system is undergoing a change while also maintaining its basic nature. Analysis of caste related issues *i.e.* renaming of the Marathwada University in Maharashtra during the late 70s, the conflict between upper castes and Dalits in Khairlanji, the issue of 'honour killing' is also taken into account. Also, effort has been made to understand Structural violence and community violence in the light of the Ranveer Sena of the upper classes and the violent struggle of landless Naxalite Dalits in Bihar. This will help realize that 'there is no resistance without organization, no protection without resistance and no self-confidence without protection.

The article by Pradeep Jare on 'Development Under the threat of Caste atrocities in Post- Colonialism, analyses the rise in awareness level and the enhancement in educational status among Dalits challenged the orthodox nature of caste system with the support of protective measures which are imbibed in constitution of India. Hence, the tension and social interaction between Dalits and non Dalits has become more complicated as Dalits have started asserting their rights. These complications lead to harmful activities by upper caste communities to save their prestige in society. This article explores the impact of atrocities on the development of Dalits in rural Maharashtra. The series of atrocities in the form of killing has become threat for Indian democracy in progressive state like Maharashtra. The atrocities not only affects the victim but whole Dalit community in particular village. Hence, in these article author tried to explore the impact of these atrocities on other members of Dalit community. It will also focus on the issues related to the social interactive patterns among Dalits and Non-Dalits in post-colonial and neo-liberal era and its impact on availing their basic human rights.

The article by Iquball Bhat and Sudhir Maske, on Anti-Oppressive Social Work Theory and Practice: Contextualising the caste dabate in Indian Social Work Education

The article by Bhat Iqball and Sudhir Maske on Anti-Oppressive Social Work Theory and Practice: Contextualising the Caste Debate in Indian Social Work education.

They criticize the Indian social work education which has remained silent or resistant to adapt many novel approaches like Anti- Oppressive social work theory for practice domain in Indian social settings. Anti- oppressive social work approach has been very influential in analysing and understanding the racial issues in many western countries. According to them Social work education in India has remained very status co-ist with its focus just on the very individualistic approaches. The Indian social work education has been very suspicious of applying Anti-oppressive social work theory to understand and analyze the caste debate in India. This paper particularly makes an effort to show how social work education has remained silent and indifferent to the issue of caste not only in generating the discourse but also to the practice domain of the profession. This paper argues that anti oppressive social work theory overcomes the blame of social work being a historical and apolitical in its pedagogy. The dismal picture that they arrive in this paper with regard to social work profession in India should be cause of concern for all of us and it assume that it would generate the debate for further exploration.

The article by Raju Adagale on Denial of Access to Water Caste and Other Factors, Case Studies of Atrocities against Dalits in Beed District of Rural Maharashtra. The research article is based on a theoretical framework rooted in Phule-Ambedkarian perspective which is different from both Brahmanical perspective and Marxian perspective. According to Phule-Ambedkarian perspective, India is caste-ridden and it is the caste based rules that often determine everything in everyone's every day social life, including control over water. Therefore, access of water becomes the basic human rights. The article argued that unless the state prevents the caste Hindus from preventing the Dalits from accessing water through appropriate legal measures, the Dalits would never get access to water with due respect and dignity. The water-caste conflicts is therefore nothing but a conflict between the power of caste laws that stand by the side of the upper castes and the power of Constitutional laws that stand by the side of the Dalits guaranteeing them their right to water.

The article by Dr. Nagaraju Vadapalli on Social Hegemony and Atrocities against Scheduled Castes of Andhra Pradesh- Human Rights Perspective in this article he writes that In India, the status of an individual is religiously determined by birth in a caste, and it resulted in that some human beings are sacred and others are not, suits for Indian Hindu ethos. Scheduled Castes are one of the marginalized and neglected sections of the Indian society. Indian constitutional provisions accepted fundamental principles of democratic values, but Scheduled Castes of India are have not been permitted to enjoy such democratic principles Equality, Liberty, Justice and Fraternity whenever Scheduled castes tried to get such socio-political values they were attacked by so-called upper (dominant) castes in the name of socio-religious sanctions. As Balladeer, Gaddar said in his song 'every song has its own saga' it suits for Scheduled Castes position in Andhra Pradesh. Every incident/movement has its own cause and every attempt leads to atrocity and every atrocity leads to protest movement. In this context, this article is aimed to discuss to how Scheduled Castes are becoming victims of caste society despite of human rights in their struggles.

The article by Rajnikant Parmar on Social Exclusion, Mobility Strategy and Atrocities against Dalits in Gujarat Untouchability is now practised in hidden forms and surnames have become an important tool of translating social relations in urban areas. Because of caste revealing surnames can result in social exclusion of Dalits from institutional and non-institutional resources. Middle class Dalits, in order to access the mainstream urban life, increasingly attempt to pass as *non-untouchables* or as caste-Hindus by changing surnames. Dalits thus have to hide their caste to access the caste-ridden mainstream urban India. Besides, there are also risks and uncertainties embedded in changing surnames. Dalits after changing surname access to housing and education institutions, but after their revelation as Dalits, they become the victim of unprecedented atrocities from the caste-Hindus.

This article thus tries to and explores the phenomenon of changing surnames among middle class Dalits and its implications. It unveils the social exclusion and atrocities Dalits face after revelation of real Dalit identity in mainstream urban society. This is a case study of the urban middle class Dalits of Gujarat who have undergone critical experiences social exclusion and atrocities in field of education, housing etc after changing their surnames.

The article by Arvindkumar Marden on explains the situation of Gujarat state in the this article entitled 'Exclusion of Dalits and atrocities in celebrating Hindu Rituals, he argues that the caste based atrocities against dalits have been increased not in particular state, but also it has been seen in all over India. According to him there is no difference of cruelty and nature of atrocity between the developed state and less developed states. Gujarat being a economically developed state, also believed the model state of India is not an exception in dalit atrocities. The atrocities were related with social norms and behavior of traditional caste structure. The members of dalit were trying to access such rights and they were obstructed and attacked. The Incidents of atrocities showed that Discrimination and untouchability still prevalent in Gujarat state and tried to continue exclusion of dalit. This research article tried to find out relation between 'exclusion of Dalits and atrocities in celebrating Hindu Ritulas.

The article by Sharvani Navangul on Caste-Less India? Atrocities and Dalit Activism, criticises that the laws and policies have been framed in order to protect the community from atrocities of what is well-known as the 'Creamy Layer'. The marginalised among the dalits been deprived of the basic fundamental rights of education, health, housing, religion and equal treatment before the law. At various instances violence has been inflicted upon this class due to the apparent low societal status they bear. According to unofficial estimates, more than 1.3 million Dalits are employed as manual scavengers to clear human waste from dry pit latrines without proper protection against toxic substances and various allied infections.

The article by Anjali Thomas on Changing Discourses and Experiences of Caste based Discrimination in Higher Education. This article argues that caste and caste dynamics in the urban metropolitan institutions of higher education have increasingly become subtle and harder to trace. The Scheduled Caste participants' social background, especially the educational and cultural capital of their parents influenced their consciousness of caste dynamics and caste based discrimination. Social and cultural capital when associated with Ambedkarite philosophy made the participants from Scheduled Caste communities more aware, confident and assertive about their rights, experiences, challenges, and needs.

In her observation the Upper Caste participants vehemently deny practicing casteist prejudices but were not averse to voicing discourses against reservations and upholding ideas of merit and eligibility. "Deserving" was one term which was frequently used in these narratives. The Upper Caste discourse often expressed resentment against the provisions, services and facilities being made available to Scheduled Caste students during school, college, employment, and promotions in government jobs and services.

The article by Rajesh Lukum on Mapping the Movements and Atrocities: A Study of Dalit Subject in Gujarat attempts to critically examine the notions of movement and atrocities on Dalits subjects in Gujarat. The Dalits face the day to day humiliation as socially excluded and marginalized. How the Caste operates within the modern privilege of discrimination and protected ignorance of movement and atrocities? In difference form of discrimination of the growing human rights violence apart the society and a menace to the unity and integrity of the Indian people. Caste violence to examine the atrocities incident and their relation to response with the state and society that the result in multiple victimizations of Dalit at historical and structure levels. Thus, emerging protest movements for security of Dalits. As a perspective of rights based on political economy that the measures of exclusivityof the growth of development. Understanding agrarian relations of a region and analysis of economic behavior, it power grown up of dominant castes has been use weapons against Dalits.

The article by Ms. Trupti Ratnaparkhi on Castiest Media and Atrocities on Dalits, observed that in India, even today media are overwhelmingly populated by the upper castes. The present article attends to focus on the domination of casteism of Indian media and uninstituted control by the upper castes and their reflections in the coverage of the atrocities on dalits. The presence of dalits and adivasis is negligible in the decision making posts in the media. The lack of dalits and adivasi reperesentation is a serious issue demanding some examination and analysis. This lacuna has resulted in the one-sided, highly partial, prejudiced and casteist presentation of the issues related to dalits and adivasis. The unlimited and uncontrollable power exercised by the upper castes on Indian media results in the unequal balance of power. This has been reflected, so far, in the insensitivity towards dalit issues in media and their (intentional) lack of understanding the issues. Prejudiced presentation of the dalit and adivasi issues ranges from negligible coverage to misinterpretation of the issues.

Ramesh Jare
Sampat Kale

Acknowledgements

The book consists of papers which were presented at a conference on the issues of caste based discrimination and caste as a everyday practice in Indian society held in Tuljapur in June 2015. The issue of Caste Atrocities on Dalits is the age old phenomenon in Indian society. At one side society is becoming the modern and progressive but at other side mindset of the people, particularly higher caste is not yet changed hence caste atrocities are increasing and persist in society. The present volume deals with this issue of caste atrocities in various forms such as social, political, cultural, educational, and economic phenomenon of the Dalits in contemporary society. The papers in this book were presented in the National Conference on Atrocities against Dalits in India held at TISS Tuljapur Campus.

We are indebted to every participant in the conference and have contributed by eminent personalities, academicians, experts and research scholars across India. We would like to thank the writers and eminent personalities who helped us to shape the book. We also thank to all those who directly or indirectly rendered their help and cooperation in making this endeavor a success. We would like express our deep sense of gratitude to the authors who contributed their articles and without whose support this book would not have become complete. Special thanks are owed to Professor Sukhdeo Thorat and several students of TISS for their help in academic and non-academic.

We are very grateful to the renowned scholar and thinker Professor M. Kunhaman (TISS, Tuljapur), who kindly accepted our request to write the Foreword for this book. We must thank the eminent personality Professor and Chairperson of ICSSR, New Delhi Professor Sukhdeo Thorat for Inaugural address and presented paper at the National Conference at Tuljapur.

At the Tata Institute of Social Sciences, We would like to thanks Professor Abdul Shaban, Deputy Director, TISS, Tuljapur for motivating and supporting the National Conference on Atrocities against Dalit and to publish the book. Our special thanks goes to Professor S Parasuraman, Director, TISS without his immense support, guidance, encouragement for completing this book. We would not have reached at this stage of our life without his cooperation and support. We would like to thank all our faculty colleagues and students of TISS Tuljapur Campus. Last but not least we would like to express our deep thanks to our family members for their encouragements in all our achievements.

December 10, 2016

Ramesh Jare
Sampat Kale

Table of Contents

Chapter 1

Why Caste Atrocities Still Persist and How to Prevent Them?

SUKHADEO THORAT[1]

1. INTRODUCTION

The caste system, the social organization of Hindus is based on ideas and customary rules. Two features of the caste system are quite unique in nature. It divides the Hindus into social groups called castes and fixes the rights-economic, social, cultural, religious and political of each caste in advance, make them hereditary not, subject to change. The assignment of rights to each of the five castes is unequal and graded. The higher castes have more rights than the lower castes, and as one goes down the caste hierarchy from the high to the low castes, the entitlement to various rights also reduces. As a result, the untouchables, who are located at the bottom of the caste hierarchy, have much fewer rights. Besides, the untouchables are also treated as inferior social beings and considered as impure and polluting people, which pushes them into social and physical isolation and exclusion. The second most important feature of the caste system is that it provides for a community level mechanism for enforcement that include numerous punishments, in the form of

[1] Jawaharlal Nehru University, E-mail: chairman@icssr.org

penalties that carry economic and social boycott and physical and other violence for violation of the rules of caste behavior by untouchables. The social ostracism as a community level mechanism of enforcement of the caste system tends to be more effective and powerful than even formal law. Thus the denial of equal rights, particularly to the untouchables, with restrictions on change and the prescription of the mechanism of social ostracism to enforce the system are the two prime features of the caste system, which render unimaginable harm to the untouchables.

Recognizing the problem of caste discrimination, the Indian Constitution provides for necessary provisions and safeguards for the discriminated group of untouchables, In Article 15(1) on Fundamental Rights, the Constitution states: "The State shall not discriminate against any citizen on grounds only of religion, race, caste, sex, place or birth or any of them". In Preamble, it promised the State shall endeavor to eliminate inequalities in status facilities and opportunities, not only amongst individuals but also amongst groups of people. Directive Principles of State Policy in Article 46 state: "The State shall promote with special care the educational and economic interests of the weaker sections of the people, and in particular, of the Scheduled Castes and the Scheduled Tribes, and shall protect them from social injustice and all forms of exploitation".

The constitutional provisions were converted into laws to provide legal safeguard against the practice of caste discrimination and untouchability. The enforcement of any disability arising out of 'untouchability' is thus an offence punishable by law. The Anti-untouchability Act called the Untouchability (offences) Act was first enacted in 1955. More than two decades later, in 1976, the 1955 Act was reviewed in order to make it more stringent and effective and it was renamed the "Protection of Civil Rights (PCR) Act".

2. THE PCR ACT AND THE POA ACT

The PCR Act provides for penalties for refusing admission to hospitals, educational institutions, hostels, temples, shops, restaurants and places of public entertainment, wells, tanks, public bathing places, roads, and places of public resort, for demanding unlawful compulsory labour from the untouchables, like scavenging, sweeping, removal of carcasses, flaying animals, or removing the umbilical cord or any job of a similar nature.

In 1989, the Government enacted another Act, namely the Scheduled Castes (SC) and Scheduled Tribes (ST) Prevention of Atrocities (PoA) Act in order to prevent atrocities against the SCs and STs. The need for this additional Act was felt because under the circumstances, the PCR Act and normal provisions of the Indian Penal Code (IPC) had been found to be inadequate for providing safeguards to SCs and STs against the physical and other violence by higher castes in their attempt to seek citizenship right. The PoA Act specifies penalties for the following 18 types of atrocities perpetrated against the SCs and STs: forcing the eating of obnoxious substances; dumping waste matter on land; intimidation during voting; mischievous litigation; false information; public humiliation; denudation; wrongful occupation of land; dispossession; bonded labour; outrage of modesty; sexual exploitation; fouling of water resources; obstruction of entry to a place of public resort; eviction of habitation; mischief with explosive; destruction of building; and suppression of evidence.

The PCR Act thus offers legal safeguards for the SCs against denial of equal citizenship rights, (and provides protection against the first regressive feature of the caste system, namely denial of equal rights to the untouchables). On the other hand the PoA Act provides legal safeguards against the second feature of the caste system, namely, the community level mechanism of social ostracism practiced by the higher castes against the untouchables. Together these two Acts intend to provide legal safeguards against denial of citizenship right and violent opposition by higher castes against the efforts by untouchables to seek equal citizens' rights.

The protection of these two acts has bought some changes in many spheres in regard to access of untouchables to public spheres, and it also served as a deterrent for the high caste against violence. However, while there has been a positive change in many spheres, the denial of access or access with differential treatment in many other public spheres continues, and the use of violent methods by higher caste still practice. This implies that laws have their limitations in eliminating caste discrimination. They appear to, at best, provide some safeguards but are unable to shake off the sources of discrimination and caste violence. The caste–based discrimination in our society is rooted in the structure of the caste system, traditional social and religious ideas, norms and customary rules, which still continue to exercise a strong hold on the thoughts and social behavior of the higher caste Hindus. The old customary rules and ideas continue to influence their behavior even in contemporary society.

The critical questions, therefore, are: Why do higher castes continue to deny the untouchables the equal citizenship rights despite legal provision? Why do the higher castes use violent methods to deny them equal rights? To put it differently what is the purpose of high castes in denying the rights to untouchables, and what do they gain from this denial? Are the gains material and economic? Or are the gains related to social privileges and high social status? Secondly an important question is: What are the roots and sources of this antagonistic behavior? What role do religious and social ideas play in persistence of caste discrimination and violence?

In the keynote address I wish to reflect on these difficult questions. The discussion is organized into three sections. In the first section we present the empirical evidence on the caste discrimination (legally banned under PCA, 1955) and atrocities and violence (legally banned un PoA, 1989), at all India and at the state of Maharashtra levels: In the second section we discuss the insights from the theories about as to why high caste deny equal right to untouchables and what the sources, or what induces higher castes to deny the equal rights to untouchables and also to use violence to stop untouchables? The last section will summarize the position on these two points and make some suggestions for addressing the issue.

The analysis is based on both quantitative and qualitative evidence drawn from multiple sources which include registered cases of crimes against SC provided by the National Crime Records Bureau, primary studies.

3. DISCRIMINATION UNDER PUBLIC SPHERES UNDER PCR ACT 1955.

Graph 1 presents the cases registered under the PCR Act. According to the NCRB data, during 1995 and 2013, a total of 10,536 cases were registered by the SCs for denial of access to public spaces and facilities. Over a period of time the number of reported PCR crimes has declined from 1528 in 1995, 672 in 2000, 291 in 2005, 143 in 2010, and only 62 in 2013. Further, the average number of annual cases registered under PCR crimes against SCs during the decade of 1990 were 785, which decreased to 411 during the 2000s. The significant decrease in the number of PCR crimes against SCs is primarily attributed to a shift in the registration of cases from the PCR Act to the PoA Act.

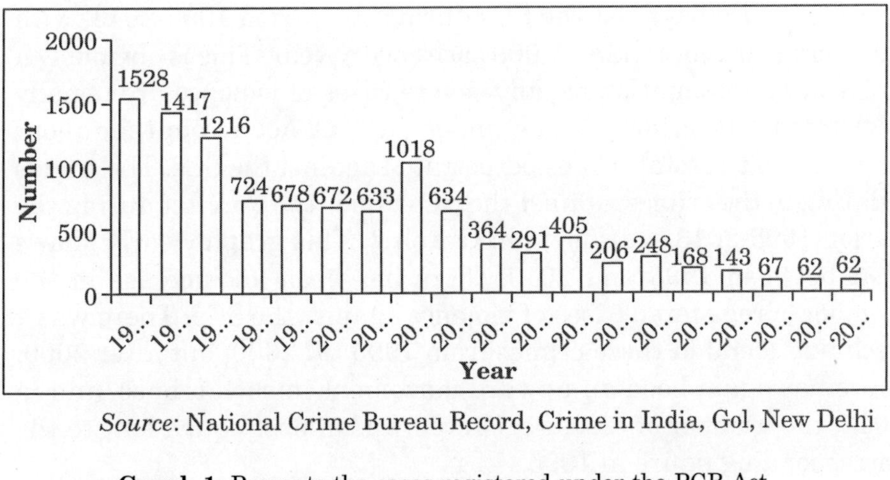

Source: National Crime Bureau Record, Crime in India, GoI, New Delhi

Graph 1: Presents the cases registered under the PCR Act.

The decline in the number of registered cases against the SCs does not mean that the practice of caste discrimination has reduced, as we shall see, instead it only means that more and more cases are now registered under the Atrocity Act. Evidence from the numerous empirical studies based on a primary survey highlights the widespread practice of discrimination against the SCs. They continue to face restrictions in access to various public services which are availed of by others. Any assertion of these rights is often met with further discriminatory and oppressive resistance from the dominant castes. The violence is perpetrated against the SCs in various forms including social boycotts, damage to property, threats to life, humiliation, torture and other heinous crimes. The magnitude and pattern of such violence, based on macro level data provided by the National Crime Record Bureau (NCRB), are discussed in the next section.

4. ATROCITIES AND CASTE VIOLENCE AGAINST SCHEDULED CASTE UNDER POA AND ACT

The data on atrocities provides details of the number of cases registered under the Atrocity Act, 1989. An analysis of the data on crimes provided by the NCRB showed that about 5.79 lakh crimes were registered against the SCs during the period 1995-2013, with an average of more than 30,000 cases every year. This is obviously a gross under-estimation as only severe cases of violence are usually registered. The crimes falling under the PoA Act account for about one-third of the total crimes perpetrated against the SCs. The trends relating to the crimes against the SCs under the PoA Act during the period 1995-2013 are shown in Graph 2. This graph clearly shows that between 1995 and 2013, there has been an increase in the number of registered cases of violence against the SCs. There was a declining trend in these crimes from 1995 till 2000, but after 2000, there has again been an upward movement in such crimes, and in 2013, the number of cases registered was almost equivalent to the corresponding figure in 1995.

Among the reported cases of crimes, the perpetration of hurt/ physical injury constitutes the highest proportion, followed by rape

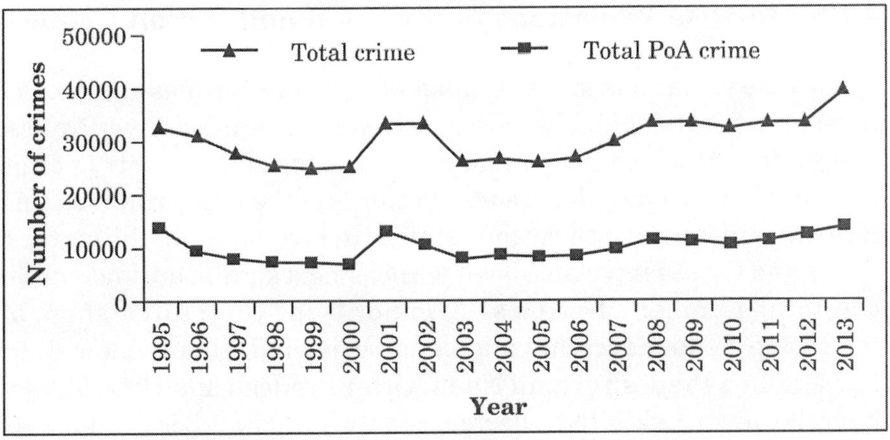

Source: Based on data, Crimes in India, 1995-2013, NCRB, Government of India

Graph 2: Trends of the total and PoA crimes against the Scheduled Castes

and murder. According to the NCRB data, rape cases have shown a steady increase over the years (Table 1). Their number increased from 1083 in 1995 to 2073 in 2013, indicating a rise in the number of rape cases against SC women. The number of kidnapping and abduction cases also showed an increase from 268 in 2000 to 628 in 2013, No significant changes have, however, been observed in the number of cases of murder and physical hurt whereas cases of robbery, dacoity and arson indicate a decreasing trend.

Table 1: Trends of various forms of crimes against scheduled castes during 2000-2013

Crimes/Year	*2000*	*2005*	*2010*	*2013*
Murder	526	669	570	676
Rape	1083	1172	1349	2073
Kidnapping and Abduction	268	258	511	628
Robbery and Dacoity	146	106	117	107
Arson	290	210	150	189
Hurt/Physical Assault	3497	3847	4376	4901

Sources: Crimes in India, Various Years, NCRB, Government of India.

4.1 State-wise Variations in the Total and in PoA Crimes

State-wise variations in the number of registered crimes against SCs reveal that states like Uttar Pradesh, Rajasthan, Madhya Pradesh and Andhra Pradesh have remained at the top of the country's crime map over the last decade. About two-thirds of the total crimes against SCs are registered in these four states. In recent years, the states of Bihar and Orissa have also been witnessing a significant increase in the total number of crimes. A majority of the states show an increasing trend in the total number of registered crimes. A few states like Madhya Pradesh, Tamil Nadu, Uttar Pradesh and Uttarakhand have, however, exhibited a decrease in the total number of registered crimes over the period 2001-13 whereas in other states like Andhra Pradesh and Gujarat, there have not been any significant changes. In recent years, the ratio between the numbers of crimes per an SC population of one lakh reveals that some states like Madhya Pradesh, Uttar Pradesh, Rajasthan, Andhra Pradesh, and Haryana, which have a higher concentration of SC population, exhibit a higher ratio of crimes.

The percentage share of PoA crimes to the total number of crimes against SCs after the year 2010 is considerably higher than the national average in states like Bihar, Himachal Pradesh, Jharkhand, Karnataka, Orissa and Tamil Nadu. Other states like Uttar Pradesh, Andhra Pradesh and Uttarakhand have also registered a relatively higher percentage share of PoA crimes. Further, the data on different forms of crimes reveals that in recent years, states like Uttar Pradesh, Madhya Pradesh and Rajasthan have been accounting for most of the heinous crimes like murder and rape against SC women. A comparative assessment of rape cases against SC women reveals a relatively higher number of cases in Uttar Pradesh, Bihar, Haryana, and Madhya Pradesh.

The discussion in Table 2, which is based on macro level data, highlights some patterns in the total crimes and PoA crimes. However, an analysis of micro level data indicates an emerging feature in the nature of caste violence and atrocities, which is that

Table 2: State-wise number of total crimes and PoA crimes registered against scheduled castes in major states during 2001-2013

Sl. no	*States/*	*Total crimes*				*PoA crimes*			
	Year	*2001*	*2005*	*2010*	*2013*	*2001*	*2005*	*2010*	*2013*
1.	Andhra Pradesh	2933	3117	4321	3270	950	1244	1509	695
2.	Bihar	1303	1824	3516	6721	513	1141	2548	5584
3.	Chhattisgarh	501	454	340	242	164	115	95	2
4.	Gujarat	1242	1307	1008	1190	356	434	220	212
5.	Haryana	229	288	380	493	33	73	131	14
6.	Himachal Pradesh	110	55	101	148	41	18	72	82
7.	Jharkhand	158	277	577	978	35	64	245	479
8.	Karnataka	1621	1780	2505	2566	983	1108	1292	1380
9.	Kerala	499	345	583	756	121	41	35	73
10.	Madhya Pradesh	4212	4356	3374	2945	435	344	13	2
11.	Maharashtra	625	865	1132	1678	146	258	319	277
12.	Orissa	1734	1439	1710	2592	645	639	1224	1785
13.	Punjab	134	140	115	126	49	72	50	13
14.	Rajasthan	4892	3795	4979	6475	295	415	103	112
15.	Tamil Nadu	2336	1206	1631	1845	682	829	1255	1334
16.	Uttar Pradesh	10,732	4397	6272	7078	4885	1623	1328	1847
17.	Uttarakhand	168	99	35	34	84	50	25	10
18.	West Bengal	10	12	63	115	5	5	27	35

Sources: Crimes in India, Various Years, NCRB, Government of India.

such acts of atrocity constitute collective and organized violence by the higher castes as against an act of violence by an individual, as also the multiple dimensions of violence and growing of the incidents of different types of violence against SC women.

The motive behind such collective behaviors of dominant caste perpetrators is to create a fear psychosis among the SCs not only in the former's pursuit to hold on to social power in their respective localities and but also to exhibit their dominance in the everyday lives of the people living there. This also shows the continuing influence of customary caste law in regulating the behavior of higher caste.

Micro level data has also revealed a rising trend in violence against SC women, which assumes the form of verbal abuse, physical assault, restrictions on the use of public resources, rape, and other forms of sexual violence. The fact finding report and case studies provide evidence to show that SC women are more susceptible to all forms of violence including rape, sexual assault/harassment, and other sexual abuses than the higher caste women. The incidence of women from among the SC communities being victims of violence is also remarkably high, especially where crimes like verbal abuse, kidnapping, and threats of physical assault are concerned. It has also been observed that SC women often become soft targets of the perpetrators of violence because of their position at the bottom of both the gender and caste hierarchy. The Hyman Rights Watch Report (1999) reveals that SC women are easy targets for any perpetration of violence because upper castes consider them to be 'sexually available', as they are largely unprotected by the State machinery. On the basis of interviews with SC women victims and their families, Barnhardt (2010) identified two main factors that lead to the perpetuation of violence against SC women: *"Firstly, SC women are intentionally victimized because they lack the social position to stand up for their rights individually and because assaulting or raping them reinforces the subordination of the entire SC community to the dominant caste. Secondly, SC women are not aware of their rights and are individually too powerless to hold the judiciary and the executive accountable for enforcing protective laws "*.

Other micro level studies reveal that SC women are more vulnerable to collective violence (Pal, 2012; Pal and Lai, 2011). The violence against SC women is deliberately promoted to impose 'caste hegemony', as a woman is always associated with the honour of the family and the community. Sexual violence perpetrated by a group is considered to be a tool by the dominant castes to reinforce caste domination, but used where it hurts and humiliates most.

Violence against SCs has also increasingly become multidimensional. In a majority of the cases, different forms of violence are committed simultaneously. As has been often observed, many cases of heinous crimes like rape and murder are preceded by other forms of crimes like physical assault, harassment, and kidnapping. An analysis of the fact-finding reports reveals that in about 40 per cent of the cases, SCs face dualistic forms of violence, whereas in about 20 per cent of the cases, they are even subjected to more than four forms of violence at a single time. Moreover, there is a clear–cut gender difference in the incidence of such violence, indicating the higher vulnerability of women to such multiple forms of violence as compared to men. The perpetration of both 'collective' and 'multiple' forms of violence against SC women, the urgent need to deal with it, therefore, remains one of the greatest challenges to the judicial system in a civil society.

5. DISCRIMINATION BY INSTITUTIONS ENGAGED IN DELIVERY OF JUSTICE

How has the State machinery dealt with such human rights violations? What has been the status of the disposal of registered cases of crimes at the administrative and judiciary levels? The NCRB data clearly show that the disposal of such cases of violence, particularly by the courts, has not been satisfactory. As shown in Graph 3, at the all-India level, on an average, about 81 per cent of the cases remained pending for trial in courts at the end of the each year during 2001-13.

Graph 3: Average rate of disposal of cases by the police and court during 2001-13

Pendency	23
Charge Sheet	91.7
Pendency	80.6
Conviction	29.7

Sources: Based on data, Crimes in India, 2001-2013, NCRB, Government of India.

Among the cases concerning all crimes for which trials were held, including under both the Acts, the accused were convicted in less than one-third of the cases. No significant changes have been noticed in the conviction rates over the last one decade (Graph 4). The average conviction rate for the PoA crimes is still lower as compared to the rate of overall crimes against SCs.

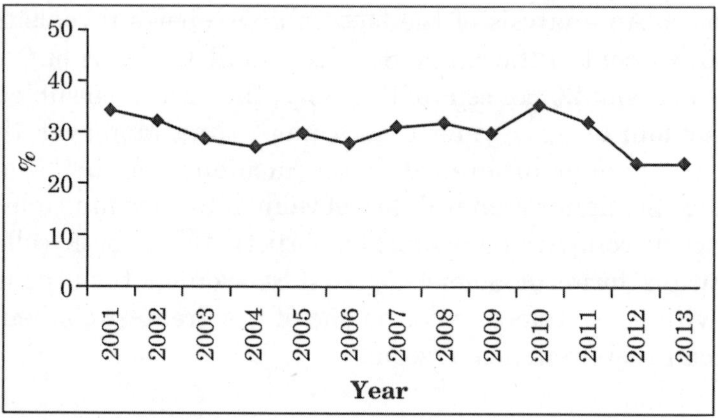

Source: Based on data, Crimes in India, 2001-2013, NCRB, Government of India

Graph 4: The Trend for Conviction Rate during 2001-2013

The reasons for such a low conviction rate are believed to be multifarious. These include delay in the framing of charge sheets, the submission of inappropriate and inadequate evidence against the accused to the court, non-availability of eye witnesses, the recording of contradictory statements in the depositions by witnesses, and delay in court trials, among other things. A significant issue of concern is that the delay in disposal of cases often becomes a potential cause of violence. The poor response of the judiciary to the registered cases of violence also dilutes the applicability of the PoA Act, which, in turn, results in the denial of justice to the victims of violence.

6. CONSEQUENCES OF DISCRIMINATION AND CASTE VIOLENCE

The perpetration of caste-based atrocities and violence have a number of adverse consequences for the SCs. Caste violence also has larger socio-psychological consequences on the lives of both the SC victims as well as other members of their community (Pal, 2011a,b). The most common are feelings of 'helplessness' and 'insecurity', The continued harassment that the latter face during investigation and court proceedings, and finally the acquittals of many of the accused often cumulatively produce a 'repelling effect' on many victims. They become vulnerable to depression and desolation, which, in turn, makes them fall prey to 'unnatural justice' achieved through negotiation and compromise. As observed in a case of murder, "due to the frequent threats from the dominant castes as well as from other influential persons, the deceased family preferred to withdraw the case rather than taking the risk of inviting more troubles". Evidence from the analysis of case studies reveals that the sufferings of the victims often continue to persist in anticipation of further 'atrocity-producing situations' mainly due to the hostile social attitude of the dominant castes.

"As a victim-survivor views 'the major impact of any terrified attack remains in the mind is fear and trauma, there has been an emergence of new violent society.' In another case of group violence, 'the fear of further atrocities, insecurity and lack of confidence in the administrative and judiciary machineries forced several Dalit families to migrate to other localities even with the loss of properties to avoid the cycle of violence perpetuated on their families. The victims express their feelings by saying that they will live in penury, put up with the heat, even forget about everything back home but they will never go back"

The serious social impact of such violence is also manifested in prolonged social tension and disharmony. The issuance of constant threats and weakened interpersonal relationships in the community induce feelings of social insecurity, helplessness and poor 'social well-being'. Often, several mechanisms are used by the dominant castes to impose and enforce social boycotts on the victims' families and the community as a whole, generally in the form of denial of labour, access to basic amenities and other restrictions in the public space (Navsarjan Trust, 2009). Such restrictions and social boycotts also impinge upon the daily lives of the targeted families or communities, causing them loss of livelihood. There is also evidence of linkages between social boycott and 'forced migration' Or symbolic migration that the SCs have been forced to undertake to maintain their self-respect and dignity following instances of social boycott and constant humiliation by the dominant castes The SCs prefer to migrate to rebuild their lives elsewhere instead of living in constant fear in their native places. Often, social distance is thus inflicted even within SC community. The following are findings from the case studies of caste violence:

"The relationship between a victim's family and community was strained with the feeling that the victim family had conflict with dominant castes, but it affected the relationship of Dalit community with dominant castes, and in turn their socio-economic lives'. Similarly, in another case, the incident led to no support to victim family from its own community. As a result, the victim's family lived with social insecurity and lack of confidence in taking the case further, and finally being under pressure, turned to compromise the case,

An elderly Dalit victim of arson says, "The government can provide higher compensation / reliefs but what will the Dalits do when another community constantly opposes their rights to live". Other villagers complement this by saying that "the incident has scarred us forever and it as threatened our livelihood"

The critical issue, however, is that the laws have overlooked the challenges that Dalit victims normally face after incidences of violence and their further vulnerability, leading them to fall into the vicious cycle of caste violence. The experiences of the aftermath of caste violence may vary, depending upon its nature but the matter that needs to be seriously addressed is the overall 'well-being' of the victims, their families and community members, and the larger consequences of incidents on their livelihood. In this context, the social intervention measures by the local administration, people's representatives, local leaders and members of civil society organisations assume a great deal of significance.

This analysis reveals that despite the provisions of the law, SCs have failed to receive equal rights in the social, economic, cultural, religious and political spheres. Any attempts by the SC to secure these equal rights often meet with violence of various types. The erstwhile peaceful opposition by higher castes to the attempt by SCs to secure equal rights has now taken over more violent forms by higher castes. This is clearly reflected in a decline in the number of cases registered under the Protection of Civil Rights Act and an increasing number under Prevention of Atrocities Act. Unlike earlier period where atrocities were individual based in the recent period, the violence is perpetrated by the community, whole or by more than one community. Similarly the commitment of more than one atrocity at a given point of time has also increased. More importantly, the incidence of atrocities and sexual. Violence against SC women has been increasing and assuming various forms hurting the honor where it hurts most.

This indicates that laws are a must, but they have their limitations in bringing about social change. They can, at best, provide some safeguards. The caste-based discrimination in our society is rooted in the ideology of caste and customary rules, which still continues to exercise a strong hold on the social behavior of the higher caste Hindus.

Changes in Caste Relations: Evidence from Maharashtra: 1958-2000

These yearly figures do not provide us an idea about the changes in the behavioral practice of high caste which is embedded in dense social relations that form the humiliating and painful experiences of the untouchables on a regular day to day life. The qualitative studies bring out the actual nature and forms of behaviors of high caste persons which are offensive and prohibited under the two Acts. The study of primary studies conducted at regular interval provides some idea about the nature of change

Maharashtra is such a state where we can build a temporal picture about the change from the regular survey on untouchability. The first survey was conducted in Wai Taluk in 1958, three years after enactment of Anti-untouchability act in 1955, and Gokhale Institute survey, in 1962. Ten years later Harijan Sevak Sangh survey, Pune conducted a survey in 1970;

followed by another survey by Harijan Sevak Sangh and Gokale Institute survey in 1970. Ten years later Marathwada Region College of Social Work, Bombay, conducted a survey in 1991; and final untouchability study, was conducted in 2000, by Action Aid, Delhi. Thus, from first survey in 1958 to last survey in 2000, together these surveys have covered more than forty two years after the enactment of anti-untouchability act in 1955, at a regular interval of ten years and provide excellent data base to capture the change in practice of untouchability.

The obvious trend is the positive change in so far as untouchables have now begun to gain an access to the various public spheres, amenities and institutions–government and public. However the nature of access and participation varies across the public and private spheres. At the risk of over generalization, one could indicate changing nature of caste discrimination in three loosely defined patterns.

The first thing that emerged quite clearly from the studies is that, there are still some spheres where complete or near complete exclusion of the untouchables from having an access/participation or interrelations was of high magnitude. This mainly includes the continuing practice of endogamy, (marriage within the caste), residential segregation, separate burial grounds and social isolation through minimum interpersonal relations through visits at homes of high caste persons or interdining at home. There has been much less change in these spheres of communal life in the village. As is clear these are private spheres.

The second feature that also emerged quite clearly is that in many other public spheres, unlike the first one, an outright denial for access and participation was less common and the untouchables had gained access, but with discriminatory treatment in various forms and shades. These include public spheres such as village restaurants, places of drinking water, and worship, the services of the barber and washermen, use of public road, participation in village religious/ cultural activities and community dinners. These are the spheres the untouchable had gained access, but the participation was marked with varying degree of the differential or discriminatory treatment, which takes various humiliating and dreaming forms.

The third feature that emerged is access and participation either without discrimination and/or accompanied by milder forms of differential treatment in some public spheres. These mainly include those institutions which are run by the government or government approved agencies such as a fair price shop, post offices, polling booth, police station, public transport, public road, panchayat office, and primary health centers. The difference between the second and third is often of degree of differential treatment to the untouchables. In most of these public institutions the untouchables enjoy access and participation without any differential treatment. Yet in some institutions the untouchables faced differential treatment although in lesser number of institutions and in a milder form.

Empirical evidence indicates that caste system as an institution has undergone a change from its original form. The caste relations of high caste towards untouchables are characterized by a complex pattern, which could be described as, "continuity in some spheres characterized by less access to untouchables particularly the private domain to access with discrimination in various modified forms (or differential treatment) in some spheres, and ultimately equal access without much differential treatment in some selective spheres."

WHY DO HIGHER CASTES DENY EQUAL RIGHTS TO UNTOUCHABLES AND WHY DO HIGHER CASTES USE VIOLENT METHODS?

Why does the higher caste oppose the untouchables to have equal access to the citizenship and economic and political rights in many spheres, if not all? Why higher caste use violent methods to stop untouchables from having equal rights? For seeking explanation, we try to draw some insights from the theoretical efforts on the part of economists and sociologists/psychologists.

Way back in mid-1950's Baker argued that people discriminate because they have test for discrimination from which they derive utility and satisfaction. The test for discrimination emanates from prejudices that a group holds against other group, in Baker's case the other groups were black and women (Baker, 1993). The other approach, known as Belief based theory postulates that people discriminate, not because of test for discrimination, but because they perceive that others, on average, have low skills. Due to imperfect information, the employer make hiring and wage decision based on the averages productivity of the individual from particular group, which may not be the case and thus may result in discriminatory outcome. In belief perspective, the discrimination is based on a set of belief about others (Arrow, 1973).

Recently Akerlof and Kranton (2010) argued that while discrimination still persists, the test and belief based theories cannot help to understand many patterns. They brought identity into play. They bring the influence of social context into economic decision by the individuals. The social categories and their norms constitute the identity Individual pecuniary and non-pecuniary motivation, tests and preferences are influenced by social context and norms. In so far as Identity theory brings the social context (that is who they are) and norms (and how should they behave or relate with others) in economic decisions making by individuals, this changed the old economic presumption that tests and preferences are individuals characteristics independent of social context. The identity theory maintained that, the social categories, and their norms would decide how someone in that social category would behave. According to the authors this "socially framed conception of individual decision making should help economists working at various levels to construct sturdier account of the economy (Akerlof and Kranton, 2010: pp 13–20). In its application to race and poverty identity theory explains the racial discrimination in terms of what authors call "Oppositional Identity". The behaviour of whites towards blacks is determined by different codes or norms, which perpetuate a distinction between "us' and 'them". Thus white Americans think of black Americans as 'them' rather than include in "us all" (p. 100). This division of "us and them" based on the norms, what authors call "oppositional identity" with expression of opposition and differences results into discrimination that explains the high poverty of blacks.

Both in Test and Identity theory, the Prejudice serves as source of discrimination Darity examined the source and role of prejudice drawing on two prominent writers on subject of discrimination. (Darity 2014) One approach to the study of prejudice is by Gordon Allport's (1954) The Nature of Prejudice–treats prejudice primarily as a matter of personal psychology. A psychology of prejudice, in turn, produces stereotypical (false) beliefs about the others, which translate into discriminatory behavior towards the subordinate group. It is this view of prejudice that is consistent with Gary Becker's (1957) taste-based approach to discrimination, observed Darity.

However, Herbert Blumer (1958) questions Allport's construction of the theory of prejudice, as a set of individual feeling. Blumer argued that"... race prejudice exists in sense of group position rather than in a set of feelings which members of one racial group have toward members of another racial group". (Blumer, 1958; p. 3), Darity observed that, *Blumer shifts the locus of origin of prejudice from individual beliefs to attitudes of group about the relative status and material benefits associated with membership in the group harbouring stereotypical beliefs toward the "other". Relative group position as the basis for prejudice directs attention to intergroup dynamics and differentials in power and resources between racial / ethnic groups. The extent to which the dominant groups perpetuate advantage for their own and disadvantage for subordinate groups is a key factor for group outcomes.*

Darity quotes Blumer (1958, pp. 3-4) observed:

'The body of feelings which scholars today are so inclined to regard as constituting the substance of race prejudice is actually a resultant of the way in which given racial groups conceive of themselves and of others. A basic under–standing of race prejudice must be sought in the processes by which racial groups form images of themselves and of others. This process...is fundamentally a collective process—to

characterize another racial group is, by opposition, to define one's own group, or defining their positions each other. It is the sense of social position emerging from this collective process of characterization which provides the basis of race prejudice."

According to Blumer, there are four basic types of feeling or attitude that seem to be always present in (race) prejudice in the dominant group: "(1) a feeling of superiority, (2) a feeling that the subordinate race is intrinsically different and alien, (3) a feeling of proprietary claim to certain areas of privilege and advantage, and (4) a fear and suspicion that the subordinate race harbors designs on the prerogatives of dominant race" (Blumer, 1958; p. 4). At the cost of space it is useful to reproduce Blumber's elaboration on these four feelings that represent prejudice:

(a) *In race prejudice there is self-assured feeling on the part of the dominant racial group of being naturally superior. This is commonly shown in a disparagement of qualities of the subordinate racial group.*

(b) *The second feeling ,that the subordinate race is an alien and fundamentally different stock—they are not of our kind is a common way in which this is likely to be expressed— the combination of these two feelings of superiority and distinctiveness can easily give rise to feelings of aversion and even antipathy.*

(c) *The third feeling, the sense of propriety claim, is of crucial importance. It is the feeling on the part of the dominant group of being entitled to either exclusive or prior rights in many important areas such exclusive rights may be wide, covering the ownership of property such as choice lands and sites; the right to certain jobs, occupations, or professions; the claim to certain kinds of industry or lines of business; the claim to certain positions of control and decision-making as in government and law.*

(d) *Again, however this, feeling of superiority, feeling of distinctiveness and feeling of proprietary claims does not explain race prejudice—the remaining feeling essential to race*

> *prejudice is a fear or apprehension that the subordinate racial group is threatening, or threatens the position of the dominant groups. Thus, acts or suspected acts that are interpreted as an attack on the natural superiority of dominant group, or an intrusion into their sphere of group exclusiveness, or enchainment on their property claims are crucial in arousing and fashioning race prejudice* (Bulmer, 1956; p. 4).

Blumer shifts the axis of prejudice away from individual sentiments toward collective interests in maintaining a relative group position. Prejudice becomes an operative, mobilizing instrument for preserving the advantaged position of the dominant group. There are real (material) interests at stake in the efforts of the dominant group to preserve its privileged position, and also the more intangible, and psychic benefit of a status advantage. Darity views these two types of benefits, material and psychic benefits of social status, need not be mutually exclusive and generally go hand in hand. Status advantage is performed by displays of the fruits of the proprietary claim; proprietary claim is conferred by the status advantage (Darity, 2014; p. 13).

I now switch over to Ambedkar. As we shall see below Ambedkar's contribution to this issue expands and enriches Blumber's highly insightful articulation of prejudice. It also enriches Darity's notion of identity and how it produces stratification to serve material interests of dominant group. Equally important view of Darity is the mutually sub serving role of social status, and material interest, both ultimately serve the interest of dominant group of Blumer. However the four senses of group position at constitute prejudice. In first places are formed, as an issue where more clarity is necessary? In Blumer's view, formation of group position is clearly an historical product. Ambedkar's exposition of the issue in the context of caste may help to unfold the aspect of formation of the prejudice. How do the norms that create, preserve and galvanised the feelings that constitute prejudice are formed? Ambedkar delves on the processes that lead to the formation of dominant and subordinate groups and prejudice which serves both the social status and material interest of dominant group. In the context of caste Ambedkar fetches the role of religious and social ideology in formation of group position and prejudice.

Before we discuss this issue, it is useful to discuss Ambedkar's interpretation of caste system to understand his position on prejudice. Ambedkar recognised five main features of caste system. First the caste system involves division of Hindu people in to five groups called castes. These five castes are socially exclusive as endogamy (or marriage within each caste with restriction for inter–caste marriage) made it impossible for members of one caste to join another caste by marrying into it. It then proceeded to assign rights and duties, economic, education and civil and religious, for each of the castes-but the rights and duties are assigned in unequal manner across five castes. The rights are also allocated in graded manner, such that, as one goes down in caste hierarchy the entitlements to rights reduce. Graded inequality implies that, every caste except the Brahmin who are at the top of caste hierarchy, suffers from lack of rights in some degree. But the untouchables who are placed at the bottom of caste ladder suffered the most virtually without any rights, economic, civic, and religious. The principle of "graded inequality" becomes the bedrock of the caste system. The caste system in terms of rights and status is fixed and hereditary, without any possibility of change. In effect then the caste system turns out to be an unfree economic and social order. In Ambedkar's view these are the "essential features of caste system" (Ambedkar, 1987b).

Ambedkar also refers to 'unique feature' of caste system, which other scholars failed to recognise in clear terms (Ambedkar, 1987c). The unique feature of the caste system relates to the unlimited freedom and power to the dominant caste, the Brahmin, who are placed at the top of hierarchy. We have seen that the various castes lack freedom in the choice of occupation or other economic and social rights. While, the castes other than Brahmin do not enjoy freedom of occupations and other rights, an exception is made for Brahmin. For instance in the scheme of caste, in case of occupation (or property rights), the Brahmin is assigned occupation of teaching, the

Kshatriya, the military, Vashya, the mercantile or trade and shudra agriculture and the untouchable the service of four castes above them. There is no freedom for castes other than Brahmin to switch over to occupation of other castes. However the exception is made for Brahmin, they could take the occupation of other castes, if they wish so. Ambedkar quotes Manu Smriti:

Yet Brahmin, unable to subsist by his duties (which is teaching religion), may live by the duty of solider for that is the next rank. If unable to get subsistence by either of these employment (teaching and solider) the answer is, he may subsist as mercantile man, applying himself into tillage and attendance on cattle" (Ambedkar, 1987a; p. 60).

Thus Brahmins as highest caste were given over whelming power to take any occupations. The endogamy, the marriage within caste is the core feature of the caste system which makes the caste exclusionary in nature .However some exception was made for the Brahmin. The justification is Ambedkar quotes:

On account of his pre-eminence, on account of superiority of his origin, on account of his observance off particular rule and on account of his particular sanctification, the Brahmin are the lord of (all) Castes (Ambedkar, 1987a; p. 60).

Ambedkar further quotes,

"Brahmin is (here by) declared (to be) the creator (of the world), the punisher, the teachers (and lone) a benefactor (of all created being) (Ambedkar, 1987a; p. 62).

Similar exception is made in civil, social, and legal rights Ambedkar concludes. The centre of the ideal [of Hinduism] is neither individual nor social. It is a class; it is a class of supermen called Brahmins. Anything which serves the interests of this class is, alone, entitled to be called good" (Ambedkar, 1987a; p. 72). In creating and serving this class of 'supermen', the dominant group of Blumer is all over with massive power, superiority and dominance, brilliantly articulated through religious doctrine and ideology.

Related aspect of the social philosophy of Hinduism is that, there is no distinction between legal philosophy and moral philosophy, as in Hindu social order there is no distinction between legal and moral, legal being also moral. Further the morality of Hindu social order is also social. Both, the law and ethics are concerned with the same things namely regulating the conduct of the lower caste to subserve the end of high caste Hindus. Ambedkar therefore concludes that inequality in other societies has grown as result of historical circumstances. For social Hinduism inequality is a religious doctrine adopted and conscientiously preaches as a sacred dogma. 4 (Ambedkar 1987 a).

Returning to essential feature of the caste system, the story does not end with the features mentioned above. There are two more features which make the system rigid, static and less amenable to change. The idea of caste provides for a community level mechanism in the form of social ostracism, with economic and social penalties for deviation from the prescribed norms and customary rules. Community level action and the penalties for any deviation from the customary rules of caste act as restraints for change in caste system. The high caste community serves as police force to enforce the laws related to caste.

The last and equally important feature of the caste system is the philosophical support to the caste system by Hindu religion. The caste system is a Hindu Social organisation with roots in Hindu religious philosophy. After a careful analysis of the philosophy of Hinduism Ambedkar observed: *In Hinduism inequality is a religious doctrine, adopted and conscientiously preached as ascribed dogma. Inequality for Hindus is a divine prescribed way of life as religious doctrine. It has become incarnate in Hindu society and is shaped and moulded by its thoughts and its doing (Ambedkar, 1987a; p. 63).* Beside, the doctrine of Karma (or deed or work), soul and rebirth are developed in such a manner that they led support and justification to the caste system.

Thus the mechanism of social ostracism (for any attempt to violate the rules and norms of caste) and philosophical support in religion provide enough solidity and abiding strength to the caste system. Unlike other religions, inequality does not enter in to caste system as indirect consequence, or as a side effect, rather the principle of graded inequality is constituent of its foundation on which the structure is erected, sanctified by Hindu religious moral, ethical and legal philosophy, argued Ambedkar (Ambedkar, 1987a)

In Ambedkar's framework, Blumer's notion of four feelings which constitute prejudice gets shaped by religious and social ideology. Social–religious Ideology serves source of group position and the prejudice articulated, and codified as social, moral and legal framework solidified for society to follow. In essence, therefore, the caste system, according to Ambedkar, was developed to serve the material and status interests of dominant higher castes. In its outcome, the system serves the economic and social ends of the dominant group of high castes. And in turn it has denied and restricted occupational choice, education, and civil rights to the subordinate group. In this context Ambedkar observed: *"The Hindus are the only people in the world whose social relation, relation of man to man and economic order–the relation of workman to workman–Is consecrated by religion and made sacred, eternal, and inviolate" (Ambedkar, 1987a; p. 129).*

It is quite clear how Blumer's four feeling, namely feeling of superiority, distinctiveness, proprietary rights and fear of other group challenging the superior position of dominant group are met in their entirety in the scheme of caste system. In so far as, the higher castes considered themselves to be superior to low castes. It meets the condition of superiority, treating the lower caste as distinct and inferior. It meets he condition of distinctiveness, exclusive economic rights and high social status, and at the same time denial of same to the low castes. It meets the condition of proprietary right, and finally use of mechanism of social ostracism and religious ideology, against any deviation from the rules of castes to provide complete protection from any kind of fear of encroachment on the right of dominant caste. It also provides rich evidence on the Darity's important postulate on mutually sub serving role of social status and the material purpose.

For every attempt to lend higher social status to the dominant caste of Brahmin is intertwined with the purpose of tangible material gains.

The caste prejudice is ideologically grounded, to serve the material interest and social status for high castes. Ambedkar is aware about the historicity of processes which develop prejudice and argued that, it is quite likely that, ideal is first created and then enforced ,(or borrowed as in the case of Nepal wherein the society was loosely governed by Buddhists ethics, was systematically converted by importing a Brahmin from India to enforce the caste system by framing series of laws and governance structure by the King), or alternatively there was an emerging stratification which was idealised and the ideal was enforced through laws , ethics and morality. However what Blumer possibly could not imagine and predict that the dominant caste of Brahmin, will have a such a foresight or ingenuity to provide strong social safe guards in the form of social ostracism (involving economic, social and violent penalties) and justification from the religious philosophy, to avoid any possibility or fear of encroachment on their rights. Both the social ostracism and religious sanctity would provide solidity to the caste system so that their superior position is not in jeopardy and that they continue to enjoy position of privilege, economic and social. It seems possible to assume that Blumber's conceptualisation of prejudice, its substantiation by Darity and its substantiation in Indian situation by Ambedkar's interpretation of caste provides tool to comprehend contemporary responses by the dominant groups of higher castes towards the efforts by untouchables in their efforts to seek equal rights economic and social.

How to Deal with Prejudice?

We go back to the two questions that were raised in the beginning. Why do higher castes continue to deny the untouchables the equal citizenship rights despite legal provision? Why do the higher castes use violent methods to deny them equal rights? What is the motive of high caste in denying the rights to untouchables, and what do they gain from this denial? Are the gains material and economic or are the gains related to social privileges and high social status or both? What are the sources of this antagonistic behavior?

Ambedkar-Blumer-Darity (even Akerlof-Kantom) perspective and the empirical evidence provide insights into these questions.

This perspective implies that group consciousness of higher castes and the group action on their part is clearly motivated by economic interest and high social status. The economic and social privileges could be acquired only by denying rights to the untouchables and opposing the attempts by untouchables for equal rights, which the high castes see as threat to their propriety rights as Blumer has argued.

Thus economic and social privileges are at the core of the caste prejudices. The religious and social ideology and code of life is brought into play to justify the privileges of the higher caste. The social ideology and codes justify the superior position of higher castes which entitle them for exclusive economic and social rights at the cost of denial of the same to the untouchables due to their inferior status. The caste prejudice thus becomes an instrument in preserving the group advantage for those on the top of caste hierarchy, at the cost of the lower castes who are at the bottom of hierarchy. Discrimination becomes a function and instrument in the hands of higher castes for holding on to the privileges, by denying any space to untouchables.

The same social ideology and Hindu codes also provide the instrument of social ostracism, with penalties physical, economic and social in the hands of higher castes for the untouchables who attempt to seek equal right and economic and social space. Any efforts by the low castes to get equal rights which others enjoy is seen as a threat to the loss of hereditary economic and social rights of higher caste. The penalties are prescribed in the religious and social text of Hindus.

It is clear that the motive behind the customary rule of the caste system is economic and social–superior economic rights and high social status. The high social status is also used for economic gains in various ways.

This leads us to second question: what enables the higher caste, first to preserve the customary rule of caste and secondly to enforce them in practice, which are contrary to the provisions in the constitution and the country's law. There are reasons why forces of change are weak. Ambedkar provides three reasons: one is the lack of efforts on the part of higher castes to change the customary rule of castes, as they serve their economic and social interest, therefore the old customs continue to govern the thoughts and actions of high caste. The second reason is the limited success of untouchables for their efforts for equal rights. There are two constraints for a limited, success to untouchables efforts. One that untouchable's is in minority, while high castes are in majority. Secondly the untouchables' are completely dependent on high castes for employment and survival on the same high castes. The untouchables being in minority and dependent on the high caste for their economic survival in village economy, it is easy for the higher castes to suppress the attempts by untouchables with violent methods. It is the contest between the Hindus who are economically and demographically strong and the untouchables who are economically poor and numerically small. It is imbalance that leads to higher caste to crush the attempts by untouchables for equal rights. In the villages the alternative is to break this nexus, that is break the economic dependence of untouchables on the high castes and make them economically independent of higher castes.

There are few measures which are necessary to counter the atrocities by the high caste on the untouchables. The first task of policy is to eliminate the economic or material base of the caste order and make the untouchables economically independent of high caste. It will demand improvement in ownership of resources agricultural land and enterprises and business. Equally important is the focus on education to improve employability for regulated salaried jobs These are the measures which are necessary compensate for denial of economic and social rights for long times and to break the economic nexus between intouchables as wage labour and high caste employers.

The discrimination also persists in the present in different spheres, despite provision of the laws. Therefore the discriminated group of untouchables needs protection from the discrimination in economic and social opportunities in the present times. Central to this view is the exposition that discriminated groups face discrimination in market and non–market channels and in institutions of governance. Two measures are used and need to be used, where they are absent. One is the legal safeguards against discrimination in the form ant-discrimination laws, such as ant-untouchability Act of 1955 and Prevention of Atrocities act of 1989), so that in the event of discrimination, the discriminated person could seek the protection of executive and judiciary. Secondly the persistence of discrimination demands set of measures to ensure fair share to the discriminated groups in various spheres, such as ownership of assets, education, employment, political participation and governance. These measure by providing a fair share in ownership of assets, education and employment, also empower the discriminated groups for economic enhancement. The last point in this category of measures includes policy for fair share and participation in governance, which would include adequate representation in legislature, policy making implementing and monitoring of policies and programs socially inclusive governance generally make the implementation of the legal measures, and policies more effective.

These are some of the measures which are necessary for correcting the material consequences of caste and to eliminate their material base. The private sector in India is excluded from the legal and safeguards against discrimination in the form of legally provided reservation policy. There is a lot more to be done on the front of private economic and social sector in India.

However, there is also need to deal with the caste prejudice itself. In so far as the discrimination still continues some forms, the unlearning of ideas related to caste and inequality and the learning of the alternative ideas of equality and justice among the peoples have become necessary. The fact that the caste discrimination still persists in economic and social spheres is reflective of the fact that traditional values and norms continue to govern the economic and social behaviour of high caste/despite the adoption of idea of equality. The ideas about the caste prejudices are developed among the children in family and society. Unlearning of the undemocratic ideas, norms, customs which are picked by children early in the life is a major challenge. Efforts are needed on both fronts, the education and civil society engagement and activism. The education, school and higher education, can play an important role in socialization of the children and adults, as most of the children and majority of the adults pass through educational institutions at various stages in their life. The education in schools and higher educational can serve as an important channel and instrument where unlearning and learning can happens and mould the thought and action of children and adults. This would necessarily mean education for citizenship learning. The civic learning in the educational system would instil the values of non–discrimination, equality, democracy and justice among the children and adults in thought and action and make them better citizens.

In addition to importance of education, the civil society can play an important role. There is a need for the engagement of civil society to change the norms and prejudices that shape the undemocratic behaviour of the people. The experience shows that, it is the civil right movement by people which has brought significant changes in curriculum, teaching and policies for discriminated group such as women, dalit, tribal and similar groups.

Note: Empirical analysis on the PCR and PoA is based on the Working paper Access to Justice, by G.C. Pal for Indian Institute of Dalit Studies, 2014.

REFERENCES

Akerlof, George and Krantom (2012). Identity Economics: How Our Identities Shape Our Work, Wage, Princeton University Press.

Allport, Gordon (1954). The Nature of Prejudice, New York: Perseus Books, New York.

Aloysius, I.S.J., Mangubhai, J.P. and Lee, J.G. (2006). Dalit Women Speak Out: Violence against Dalit Women in India, Vols. I and II, Chennai and New Delhi: IDEAS, NCDHR and NFDW.

Ambedkar, B.R. (1936). "Annihilation of Caste" *In*: Vasant Moon (*ed.*), 1979, Dr. Babasaheb Ambedkar: Writings and Speeches. Education Department, Government of Maharashtra.

Ambedkar, B.R. (1989a). Philosophy of Hinduism in, Dr. Babasheb Ambedkar Writings and Speeches, Vol. 3, Department of Education, Government of Maharashtra, Bombay.

Ambedkar, B.R. (1989b). The Essential Features of Hindu Social Order, Dr. Babasheb Ambedkar Writings and Speeches, Vol. 3, Department of Education, Government of Maharashtra, Bombay.

Ambedkar, B.R. (1989c). The Unique Feature of Hindu Social Order in, Dr. Babasheb Ambedkar Writings and Speeches, Vol. 3, Department of Education, Government of Maharashtra, Bombay.

Arrow, Keneth (1973). The Theory of Discrimination, *ln*: Orley and Albert, Rees (*eds.*), Discrimination in Labour Market, Princeton University Press.

Barnhardt, S. (2010). "Atrocities against Scheduled Caste Women: Notes from the field', Gender and Policy Network, Princeton University. Available at: *http://www. princeton.edu/gender/Field/BamhardtFieldNotes. Html*

Becker, Gary (1993). The Economics of Discrimination, Chicago: University of Chicago Press, Chicago.

Blumer, Herbert (1958). "Race Prejudice as a Sense of Group Position". *The Pacific Sociological Review*, 1(1): 3–7.

Constant, Amelie, Lillya, Gataullina and Zimmerman, Klaus F. (2009). "Ethnosizing Immigrants". *Journal of Economic Behaviors and Organizations*, 69(3): 274–287.

Darity, William (2014). The economics of the dispossessed. *Journal of Social Inclusion Studies*, Voll, No 1 July -December, 2014

Darity, William Jr. (2001). "The functionality of market-based discrimination". *International Journal of Social Economics,* 28:10/11/12 pp. 980–986.

Darity, William Jr. (2005). "Stratification Economics: The role of intergroup inequality". *Journal of Economics and Finance*, 29(2): 149–153.

Darity, William Jr. (2009). "Stratification Economics: Context Versus Culture and the Reparations Controversy" Kansas Law–Review 57 pp. 795–811.

Darity, William Jr., Mason, Patrick L. and Stewart, James B. (2006). "The Economics of identity: The origin and persistence of racial identity norms". *Journal of Economic Behavior and Organization* 60(3): 283–305.

Forbes, H.D. (1997). Ethnic Conflict: Commerce, Culture and the Contact Hypothesis New Haven: Yale University Press.

Human Rights Watch (HRW) (1999). "Broken People: Caste Violence against Untouchables". New York: HRW.

National Commission for Scheduled Castes/Scheduled Tribes (1998). Special Report Submitted to the President of India, Government of India, New Delhi.

National Crime Records Bureau (NCRB) (1995-2011). "Crimes in India", Ministry of Home Affairs, Government of India, New Delhi.

Navsarjan Trust (2009). "Legally Immune mom of Discrimination: Report on Socio–economic Boycotts of Dalits in Gujarat". Ahmedabad, India.

Pal, G.C. (2011a). "Psychosocial Correlates and Consequences of Caste Atrocities: Need for Promoting Social Justice and Security'. Paper presented in International Conference on Social Justice and Human Development, 18–20 December 2011, Allahabad University, Allahabad.

Pal, G.C. (2011b). "Psychological Dimensions of Caste Atrocities and Poverty". Paper presented at an International Workshop on Non-Monetary Dimensions of Poverty, Institute for Rural Management, Anand (IRMA), Gujarat, 3 March.

Pal, G.C. (2012). "Mapping Caste-based Atrocities in Uttar Pradesh". Project Report No. 49, Indian Institute of Dalit Studies, New Delhi.

Pal, G.C. and Lai, L.D. (2011). "Mapping Caste-based Atrocities in India with a Special Focus on Dalit Women". Project Report No. 41, Indian Institute of Dalit Studies, New Delhi.

Pal, G.C., Sukumar, N. and Lai, L.D. (2010). "Atrocities against Dalits: Emerging Trends", Project Report No. 37, Indian Institute of Dalit Studies (IIDS), New Delhi.

Stewart, James B. (2008a). "Africana Studies and Economics: In Search of a New Progressive Partnership". *Journal of Blacks Studies*, 38(5): 495–805.

Stewart, James B. (2008b). "Stratification Economics" in the International Encyclopaedia of the Social Sciences Farmington Hills: Cengage.

The Hague Report (2006). "Human Rights and Dignity of Dalit Women". Report of the Conference in the Hague, 20-25 November, Netherlands.

The Protection of Civil Rights (PCR) Act (1976). "Act No. BC.12013/2/76-SCT-V, dated 15 September 1977". Ministry of Social Welfare and Empowerment, Government of India, New Delhi. Also available at: *http://www.socialjustice.nic.in/pcr-act.php*.

The Scheduled Castes and Scheduled Tribes (Prevention of Atrocities) Act (1989). "Act No. 33, dated 11 September 1989", Ministry of Social Welfare and Empowerment, Government of India, New Delhi, Also available at: *http://www.socialjustice.nic.in/ pronearea.php*.

The Untouchability (Offences) Act (1955). "Notification No. S.R.O.1109". The Official Gazette, Government of India, New Delhi.

Thorat, Sukhadeo (2103) Unlearning Undemocratic Values, The Hindu.

Thorat, Sukhadeo and KatherinrNewmen (2010). Blocked By Caste: Economic Discrimination in Modern India, Oxford, New Delhi.

Prof. Sukhadeo Thorat, Chairman, ICSSR, New Delhi, M.Phil/Ph.D in Economics from Jawaharlal Nehru University, New Delhi and Diploma in Economic Planning, Main School of Planning Warsaw, Poland. He was the Chairman, UGC from February 2006 to February 2011 prier to that he was Faculty Member, Jawaharlal Nehru University, New Delhi w.e.f. 1980 onwards. He has Published 21 Books, 81 articles and completed 28 Research Projects. He has visited USA, Poland, Sweden, Denmark, Germany, Netherlands, UK, Italy, China, Iran, Nepal, Finland, South Africa, Japan, Ethiopia, Thailand, Phillipines, Sri Lanka, France, Northern Ireland, Canada and Czech for participation in Conferences, Lectures and Research Collaboration. He has been Honour and Awards received Padamshree award from the Government of India in 2008.

Chapter 2

Caste Violence Against Dalits in Post-Colonial Period

RAMESH JARE[1]

1. INTRODUCTION

Caste violence in post-colonial India has taken a different format which leads to threats and insecurity among Dalits. Though post-colonialism brought freedom and liberty to the country yet there is a large section of about one section of the total population of 1225 millions (175 millions) is still for from any sense of being free. Dalits are the most victimized sections of the society due to various discriminatory practices which are still rampant. Violence is one of the brutal forms bilaterally and painfully experienced by Dalits after Indian independence. While going deeply into the roots of these acts of violence one can find that caste based discrimination is the only cause which leads to such acts. According to Thorat (2015) the caste system is the social organisation which is based on partisan and discriminatory ideas and customary rules in Hinduism. Therefore, the violence against Dalits is also linked to customary rules of Hinduism. However, the forms of customary rules and practices have been changing due to the process of modernization. Thus, the nature

[1] Tata Institute of Social Sciences, Tuljapur campus, Tuljapur - 413601

and practice of untouchability and caste base discrimination has taken different shapes. The practice of untouchability in Hinduism has been based on the caste status of the individuals. This has marginalised Dalits from mainstream development process. The overall development of the country after Independence has seen incredible changes as it grows from nothing. Along with socio-economic and infrastructural development, individual liberty and freedom based on basic human rights were some of the major change which has taken place in post-colonial period. Indian constitution has played a major role to provide basic human rights to the citizen of independent India. However, Dalits have always been at the verge of all these developmental processes. As Sen argues that real development will never take all, the place are individual people do not enjoy freedom. People should be free from all kinds of tyranny, they should enjoy the socio-economic and political freedom and their basic human rights should be secured. Nevertheless, all these aspects have been neglected as far as the Dalits in India are concerned.

The socio-economic and political development of the Dalit community has still remained stunted. The weakening of the dalit movement has resulted in a new phenomenon of caste atrocities. Atrocities are essentially human rights violations with the added association of unbridled cruelty in human brutality and embittered inhumanness. There may be a combination of factors and aberrations that leads to such behaviour, but the foremost is the conviction that what one is doing is right. The perpetrators of the crime believe that they are justified. Religious ideology, culture and tradition could be the sources of such a conviction. But, however self-righteously a person develops the belief that it is right to inflict harm on others, it is a pre-requisite that he or she should also be in a position to overpower the other. The relative weakness of the other reassures the perpetrator that he can commit the atrocity. If this equation is broken, the atrocity cannot materialize. Atrocities are thus also enabled by the prevailing judicial process the perpetrators operate on the assumption that, by virtue of their caste standing, the police investigation and the trial in court will be weighted in their favour - the crime may indeed not even be deemed cognizable as an offence

(Teltumbade, 2010). The person belonging to the Dalit Communities have always been influenced by their "low status" in society. The marginalisation process from development, new forms of discriminatory practices and changing nature of violence are complex in nature which are interdependent on each other. This article process to describe the changing nature of caste based violence and discriminatory practices. It also focuses on the impact, of caste violence on development process of Dalit community. The article tends to explore the communication pattern of victims and other members from the same community, the nature of support provided by their own caste members that is the members of the Dalit. Finally it desires to focus on the discussion of the political dimensions of caste-based violence.

2. HISTORICAL BACKGROUND OF CASTE BASED VIOLENCE DURING COLONIAL PERIOD/BEFORE INDEPENDENCE

In order to understand the nature and various practices of caste based violence, one need to understand the historical process of violence based on the caste status of the individuals. The Indian population is bound together by the age old caste-system and the network of caste has various peculiarities, and one of them is the practice of untouchability. As per the Hindu mythological theory, Dalits were the "last sections" of the structured society. As these people were assigned all kinds of dirty work in society they were treated as untouchables. The reason behind this was that this dirty work was considered as polluted work. Therefore, untouchables then were denied various rights such as entry into temples, entry at public places, offices, and they were not allowed to touch the high caste men and women. Moreover, Dalits were treated as polluted sections of the society, people from other communities used to practice untouchability with Dalits.

Two features of the Indian caste system are quite unique in nature. It divides the Hindus into social groups called castes and fixes the rights-economic, social, cultural, religious and political–of each caste in advance makes them hereditary, not subject to change (Thorat, 2015). The Caste system not only divides them but it makes them fight with each other and puts them into the positions have where they always remained socially and economically unequal. Dalits, earlier known as "untouchables", before independence, were always treated as impure sections of the society as they were involved into "dirty" jobs.

The segmental division of the society was based on the occupation of each caste. This distribution of occupation was based on the theory of Varna. The Brahmins, Kshatriya, Vaishya and Shudra were four major varnas in Hindu society whose duties were preaching, security, business and cultivation respectively. There was another section which was out of this varna system called as Ati-shudra, which was mainly involved into the serving the above four varnas. Their main job was to clean the places, remove all dirty things and carry out dead cattle from the villages. Each varna has a set of castes and sub-castes. The higher castes have more rights than the lower castes, and as one goes down the caste hierarchy from the high to the low castes, the entitlement to various rights also reduces. As a result, the untouchables (Shudras and Ati-Shudras), who are located at the bottom of the caste hierarchy, have very few rights (Thorat, 2015). They are described in Hindu religious scriptures as Chandala, Ati-Shudra, Antyaja or Namashudra, Panchama and Avarnas. They are treated as Untouchables even today many parts of India. They were Broken Men and Protestant Hindus according to B.R. Ambedkar, and Harijans, according to Mahatma Gandhi. They have been recognized as Scheduled Castes (SCs) in the Constitution of India. They have been termed as a 'Dalits' by Dalit Panthers. According to Ramaiah they can be grouped under two major categories: untouchability and powerlessness. (Ramaiah, 1998) Jodhka (2012) viewed from the 'below', the most critical feature of caste is the experience of untouchability. The line of pollution, which divided the 'untouchables' from the rest, has been historically a critical point of distinction.

The enforcement of any disability arising out of 'Untouchability' shall be an offence punishable in accordance with law. However, the Untouchability was practiced in many parts of the country (Jodhka, 2012). According to Pai (2014) question or challenge is the unequal hierarchal caste structure and the resisting of norms of purity and pollution provided in the Manusmriti–a part of the Hindu Dharmshastras–that have placed the Dalit or ex-untouchable at the bottom, below the line of pollution. The practice of untouchability and discrimination was attached with the strong punishments based on the laws made by the Manu. Ambedkar repeatedly used the phrase of "illegal laws of the Hindus" to describe not merely bahishkar (boycott) but caste society connects him to important discussions about law and violence (Rao, 2010). These laws were only applicable to the "untouchables". Therefore one can say that, violence in pre-independence India was attached with the practice of untouchability. Moreover, in order to maintain status-quo of the violence, discrimination and untouchability practices these were legitimized by the religious sanctions based the laws of Manu. As Max Weber defined the state through its monopoly on the exercise of "legitimate violence," a violence that cannot be name as such because it appears in another guise, preserving violence is helpful here. Similarly, we can see the violence against Dalits was legitimized with the various laws of Manusmriti.

Teltumbde (2010) observed that the pre-colonial closed loop production system of a typical village since everyone followed his or her calling under the divine authority of religion, there were atrocities of the nature we experience in the saner age of globalisation today. If anyone questioned or defined this system, the religious code provided for the punishment. In this scheme, it was more important to fortify the religious control on populace than physically taming them to comply. Although the emphasis was on the enslavement of mind, physical punishment did exist as contingency measure. Atrocities on the dalits today are essence of a physical punishment for their act of forsaking the bondage.

Ambedkar has raised the issues of atrocities and violence against Dalits in the 'Bahishkrit Bharat and Muknayak', on different issues. In the issue of 3rd April, 1927 he has reported that a chamar person who has adopted Satnami sect in Madhya Pradesh was killed by Brahmins and Rajputs because he has put on the sacred thread. During the famous Mahad Satyagraha in Maharashtra held on 19th and 20th March, 1927, to exercise the human rights, more than 100 dalits were brutally beaten up by the upper-caste Hindus, while they were returning to their homes after the Satyagraha. In Nilopada village of Dindori block in Nasik District (Maharashtra) Mahars (dalits) were called by the Gaon Nayak at night at 10 'O' clock and even they were beaten most brutally. They suspected that the Mahars were killing their animals through unidentified poison.

Another incident reported in Bahishkrit Bharat in Issue of 23rd December, 1927 that two persons namely Doma and Kanhu Gedam from Kishi (Chimur) village in Varoda block of Chanda district belonging to the Mahanubhav sect were beaten up with their wife and a child because they had worshipped the god from last step of the temple. The reason was that the family could not give the Dakshina (fees to priest) to the priest of temple.

3. CASTE-BASED VIOLENCE IN POST-COLONIAL PERIOD

a) From Untouchability to Atrocities

Untouchability is linked with the concept of purity and pollution which is linked to Hindu religion. To practice purity and pollution there are many rules and regulations which are imposed on ex-untouchables but due to the modern education and awareness among the youths these young dalits of the next generation have refused to practice these rules. Due to the reservation policies the youths are able to take education, get jobs in Governments and representation in political Institutions, this change in socio-economic and political situation has made them revolt against the rules imposed on them.

They are ready to assert themselves against the traditional practices, whenever Dalits have tried to organise themselves or assert their rights, there has been a backlash from the feudal lords resulting in mass killings of Dalits, gang rapes, looting and arsoning, and deliberate attacks on Harijan [Dalit] basties [villages] (National Commission for Scheduled Caste and Scheduled Tribe)

Dalits, as the habitual target of insult, humiliation, injury and sexual abuse by the high caste people have been the structural victims of gross violence since the inception of the caste system. Since these acts were an integral feature of dalit life, and moreover were in keeping with the moral code of caste society, neither dalits nor anyone else took any note of them. When dalits were not held to be worth treating as human, there was no question of 'human rights' or their violation (Teltumbde, 2012).

Thorat (2007) reported through a survey of primary studies conducted in Maharashtra in 1960, 1970 and 1990 in three different decades which provides some idea about the nature of change in the practice of Untouchability. The first study was conducted in Wai Taluk in 1958, in 17 villages; Three years after enactment of Anti-untouchability Act in 1955. This study was conducted by the Gokhale Institute, Pune. In 1962, Harijan Sevah Sangh, Pune conducted a survey in 25 villages. In the year 1970 Marathwada Abhyas Mandal (Marathwada Study Centre) conducted a survey in 192 villages and survey of 95 villages. Similarly, in the year 2000, Kruti Sahayya Samity conducted such a survey ten years later, Marathwada Region College of Social Work, Bombay, conducted Thwada Region Study Centre survey in 1991; and final untouchability study was conducted in 2000, by Action Aid, Delhi. Thus, from first survey in 1958 to last survey in 2000 the survey of 50 villages was regularly conducted at frequent intervals. These surveys covered more than forty two years after the enactment of anti-untouchability act in 1955, at a regular interval of ten years and these surveys provide excellent data base to capture the change in the practice of untouchability. It was observed the positive change in so far as untouchables have now begun to gain an access to the various public spheres, amenities and institutions-government and public. According to him, Maharashtra is such a State where we can build a temporal picture about change from the regular survey on untouchability.

The 1997 report issued by the National Commission for Scheduled Castes and Scheduled Tribes underscored that "untouchability" the imposition of social disabilities on persons by reason of their birth in certain castes–was still practiced in many forms throughout the country. The report described a number of social manifestations of caste-based discrimination in the 1990s: scheduled-caste bridegrooms were not permitted to ride a mare in villages, a marriage tradition; scheduled castes could not sit on their charpoys (rope beds) when persons of other castes passed by; scheduled castes were not permitted to draw water from common wells and hand-pumps; and in many tea-shops and dhabas (food stalls), separate crockery and cutlery were used for serving the scheduled castes. The prevalence of "untouchability" practices was also noted by the United Nations Committee on the Elimination of Racial Discrimination in 1996, while reviewing India's tenth to fourteenth periodic reports under the Convention on the Elimination of All Forms of Racial Discrimination:

From the empirical evidences and different reports, one finds that there are positive changes taking place in the country due to education and awareness in the country. The various public spaces, amenities and institutions–government and public spaces dalits are getting access. However, Jodhaka (2012) reports that the untouchability does still very much exist in the private spheres. A study that collected data by I.P. Desai in Gujarat from more than 500 villages reported that almost everywhere the rural settlements are divided on caste lines, particularly so in relation to the ex-untouchables. Almost everywhere they live away from the main settlements and the dominant/upper castes continue to impose restrictions on their visits to the main village. The ex-untouchable communities were often not allowed access to the common water source of the village. Similarly, in around one-third of the villages, the local teashops and restaurants used separate utensils for customers from ex-untouchable communities. More than 70 per cent of the villages imposed restrictions on inter-dining with the ex-untouchables and they were also not allowed entry into upper caste houses. In more than 60 per cent of the villages, they were not allowed entry into temples. In around one-fourth of the villages, they had no choice but to 'stand up' in the presence of an upper-caste person (Ibid). While the practice of untouchability had indeed declined in some parts of India and in some spheres of social life, the incidence of its continuity is also quite significant.

Teltumbade, (2010) has observed that such crimes were committed in earlier times as a matter of routine, with an assumption of absolute right in mistreating their victims and with no sense of wrongdoing. Atrocities are now committed with a sense of the loss of that right, with a sense of being wronged. Earlier, atrocities were committed in the arrogance of impunity, for untouchables had no means of resistance; now they are committed in vengeance against the dalit assertion. Earlier, atrocities were a manifestation of contempt; today they are a manifestation of the deep resentment of the 'privileges' Scheduled Castes get from the state. Notwithstanding these differences, what lies at the root of atrocities in any period or point of time is a gross asymmetry of power which precipitates either as routine, when it is legitimated as in earlier times, or in the event of social crisis, as it does now. There is also a difference between the nature of atrocities earlier and now. Previously they were committed as an integrated part of the interaction between *Savarnas and Avarnas,* and hence tended to be casual, more humiliating than injurious. Today, they are far more violent, more physically destructive and more brutal than before.

Earlier caste violence was mostly committed by individuals in a fit of rage. Now it is carried out collectively, in a loosely planned manner, as a spectacle of demonstrative justice. The increasing number of atrocities against dalits in recent years has been alarming enough, but this change in their intensity also needs to be noted.

b) State's Initiative in Reducing Caste-based Violence

Although constitutional provisions (Article 17) and legal texts exist to abolish untouchability and to protect the members of the scheduled castes and tribes, and social and educational policies have been adopted to improve the situation of members of the scheduled castes and tribes and to protect them from abuses, widespread discrimination against those people, and the relative impunity of those who abuse them, points to the limited effect of these measures.

Article 15(1) on Fundamental Rights, the Constitution states: *"The State shall not discriminate against any citizen on grounds only of religion, race, caste, sex, place or birth or any of them"*. In Preamble it promised the State shall endeavor to eliminate inequalities in status, facilities, and opportunities, not only amongst individuals but also amongst groups of people.

The Constitutional provisions were converted into laws to provide legal safeguard against the practice of caste discrimination and untouchability. The enforcement of any disability arising out of 'untouchability' is thus an offence punishable by law. The Anti-untouchability Act, called the Untouchability (offences) Act was first enacted in 1955. More than two decades later, in 1976, the 1955 Act was reviewed in order to make it more stringent and effective, and it was renamed the "Protection of Civil Rights (PCR) Act".

The PCR Act provides penalties for refusing admission to hospitals, educational institutions, hostels, temples, shops, restaurants and places of public entertainment, wells, tanks, public bathing places, roads, and places of public resort, for demanding unlawful compulsory labour from the Untouchables, like scavenging, sweeping, removal of carcasses, flaying animals, or removing the umbilical cord or any job of a similar nature.

In 1989, the Government of India, enacted another Act, namely the Scheduled-Castes (SC) and Scheduled Tribes (ST) Prevention of Atrocities (PoA) Act in order to prevent atrocities against the SCs and STs. The need for this additional Act was felt because under the circumstances, The PCR Act and provisions of the Indian Penal Code (IPC) had been found to be inadequate for providing safeguards to SCs and STs against the physical and other types of violence by higher castes in their attempt to seek citizenship right. The PoA Act specifies penalties for the following 18 types of atrocities perpetrated against the SCs and STs: forcing the eating of obnoxious substances; dumping waste matter on land; intimidation during voting; mischievous litigation; false information; public humiliation; denudation; wrongful occupation of land dispossession; bonded labour; outrage of modesty; sexual exploitation; fouling of water resources, obstruction of place of public resort; eviction of habitation; mischief with explosive; destruction of building; and suppression of evidence.

Despite a large body of legislations and administrative agency mandates assigned exclusively to deal with the plight of Dalits, the persistence of caste–based prejudices and the denial of access to land, education, and political power have all contributed to an atmosphere of increasing intolerance and violence against Dalits in their communities.

c) Dalits *Versus* the Backwards

According to Pai (2014) identity assertion has led to increased discrimination and violence at the grassroots against Scheduled–castes (SCs) by the upper and middle castes in many parts of the country, particularly in the rural areas. While this has been a pervasive feature from the colonial period, some new features have characterized crimes against SCs since the late 1970s. First, the numbers of caste-based crimes against SCs have increased sharply in the 1980s and 1990s. Second, discrimination based on various forms of ritual untouchability has been largely replaced by caste atrocities such as rape, not allowing SCs to caste their votes, burning of houses, parading naked women in village streets, and breaking or removing Ambedkar statues. Third, most of these crimes are perpetrated by the traditionally dominant, landowning middle or backward castes such as the Jats, Gujjars, and Yadavs in the Hindi heartland, and Thevars and Gounders in Tamil Nadu who today constitute to be the direct oppressors of the SCs and try to humiliate and suppress attempts by them to improve their social and economic conditions. Atrocities against dalits by backward castes are also increasing in the progressive state like Maharashtra by Dhangars, Vanjari, Kunbi and Marathas to a large extent. Basically, in the changing socio-political scenario the atrocities on Dalits are committed by land owning castes in rural areas (Jare, 2009). However, there are many OBCs, VJNT and Buddhist groups in *Maharashtra and Chamars (SCs) and OBC groups i.e., Shakyas and Kushavas of Uttar Pradesh and Bihar developing alliances towards the movement call 'Chalo Buddha ki Ore' or 'Walk towards Buddha'.*

d) Linkages Between Development and Atrocities on Dalits

Development in other terms means expanding the freedom (Sen, 2003) in which state should make efforts for developing citizens by enlarging their freedom. Indian social reality has always been biased about the marginalized sections in general and Dalits in particular. Dalits in India have always been the victims of caste based atrocities in the development sphere. Due to meager intervention by the state, Dalits have started empowering themselves based on the constitutional measures. In this process of empowerment they have started raising their voices in democratic forums by challenging the upper caste hegemony.

Assertion at the grassroots level is taking place in areas where dalits have attempted to challenge upper caste domination. This is seen in the installation of Ambedkar statues, formation of Dalit Organisations in the villages and cities, circulation of Dalit literature in the form of small books and pamphlets in the countryside, revolt against atrocities by savarna Hindus, and anger and violence against the practice of untouchability (Pai, 2013). Wearing new and stylish clothes by Dalit youths is considered an assertion by the upper castes in the backward region of Marathwada in Maharashtra State.

e) Social Boycott as Act of Organised Atrocities Reflections from Evidences

One of the most popular methods of dealing with Dalit assertion and teaching them a lesson' has been the social boycott of the entire ex-untouchable community by the dominant castes in the village. Social boycott means banning all the services to Dalits with village resolutions. These services include, no employment within the village, all shops including grocery shops are banned for them. They are also prohibited from using the village commons, which had traditionally been used by the poor for collection of fodder and firewood. They may even face hardships in sending children to the local schools. If the boycott continues for a long time, it has far-reaching negative consequences for the subordinate communities. Such boycotts have been reported from different parts of the country and in some cases they have continued for over a year (Jodhka, 2012; pp. 97-98),

Social boycott is age-old phenomenon from the colonial period, this practice was banned by Government of India Act, 1919. However, Social boycott has also become a recurrent aspect in the contemporary period. One such boycott is recently imposed in Marathwada region of Maharashtra:

A Case Study of Ansurda Village, Osmanabad District

In April 2015 one such boycott has taken place in Ansurda village, Osmanabad District of Maharashtra state. On the day of Ambedkar birth anniversary, after the procession of Dr. Ambedkar's statue, Dalits had gathered for prayer. All of a sudden some youths from upper-caste community started throwing mud on Ambedkar's photo, when the Dalit asked them why this was done, they were brutally beaten up by the upper-caste people. Dalits had registered a case in the police station. The Marathas in the village became angry with the dalits, how can they go to police station? They decided to teach the lesson to Dalits. The next day after the Ambedkar birth anniversary day upper-caste people (mostly Marathas) organised a

Gram Sabha (village meeting) and passed a resolution for imposing social boycott on Dalits in the village meeting. Everything was banned for Dalits including, daily wages on their agriculture land, they were not allowed the collection of fire woods, ban on grocery shops, ban on grinding flour mill, they were also not allowed drinking water on common facility for more than one month. No one had any knowledge of this incident out of the village. After twenty days, the local newspaper reported this matter in the newspaper. The dalits were even banned to use vehicles (auto rickshaws and cars) on hire.

Dalits of Ansurda village approached the District Administration, to provide them place nearer the district headquarter, so that they are protected from the further tragedy. The District administration has neglected their requests. However, Dalits of Ansurda are not ready to stay in Ansurda village. This is how in most of the time social boycott incidents forced the migration of Dalits from their village to other places.

Whether caste clashes are social, economic, or political in nature, they are premised on the same basic principle: any attempt to alter village customs or to demand land, increased wages, or political rights leads to violence and economic retaliation on the part of those most threatened by changes in the status quo. Dalit communities as a whole are summarily punished for individual transgressions; it is observed that the reason for frequently imposing social boycott is an easy way of getting out. They (upper caste people) believe that direct attacks on dalits may lead them to face the police and judiciary. In social boycott, most of the times, no 'single individual' is held responsible for the incident. The entire village community supports every one else and no individual is punished. It is also very easy for not having any proof against the community because all the members of the non-dalit communities are together to teach lessons to dalit. No one talks against their own community members. Ansurda is not the only village where social boycott has taken place in Marathwada region. The empirical evidences show that every year during the celebration of Ambedkar Birth Anniversary the tension and fear among dalits is evident and prevalent.

The social boycott is reinforced when the village council levies fines against caste Hindus who refuse to participate in it. In villages of Karnataka state, upper castes are generally fined Rs. 501 (US $12.53) for giving employment to Dalits during a social boycott (Broken People, 1999).

Apart from collective social boycott, the ex-untouchables also encounter direct violence, often directed against the entire community including those who do not participate in Dalit assertion movements 'extravagant revenge' (Mendelsohn and Vjcziany, 2000; Gorringe, 2005). Reports of such violence have increased over the years. One of the earthest cases of large-scale violence against the Dalits was reported in December 1968 from a place called Kilvenmani located in the Thanjavur district of Tamil Nadu where forty-two Dalits were burnt to death because they had decided to organize themselves and protest against the low wages. They were all locked up in a hut and that hut was set on fire. In a similar incident in the year 1977, in the village of Dharampura in Bihar, the landowners killed four 'untouchable' sharecroppers because they were unwilling to give up their legal claim over the land they had been cultivating for decades. Dalits are not always attacked for economic reasons. While violence in some cases has been overtly economic in origin, there have been other cases in which violence has been the result of "Untouchable" challenges to the traditional ritual norms' (Joshi, 1982: 976; Jodhka, 2012: 98-99)

In a place called Karamchedu in Andhra Pradesh seven Dalits were killed by the dominant Kammas in 1985 because the Dalits protested against the upper castes washing their cattle in the village tank from where the Dalits obtained their drinking water. In another incident in 1991, in the state of Andhra Pradesh, nine Dalits were killed by the local landlords for some trivial reason. In 2006, in a place called Khairlanji in Maharashtra the entire family of a Dalit farmer was brutally murdered by a group of dominant caste men because he had complained to the local police against them for harassing and physically assaulting him (Mohanty, 2007). Apart from these 'spectacular' cases the ex-untouchables also experience everyday violence and humiliation of various kinds, ranging from physical beating of individuals to rape, murder, and mental torture of various kinds. There are young dalit men who have been victimized of honour-killings', In Ahmednagar District of Maharashtra state 18 years dalit boy was killed by the upper-caste family due to his alleged love affair with a Maratha girl. Similarly a Dalit boy was killed in religious place of Shirdi in November 2015; the boy was killed because he had a song on Dr. B.R. Ambedkar as his ring tone in his cell phone. This shows the modernity and development of Dalits are not accepted by the other non-dalit communities all over the country.

In Anupama Rao's book on Dalits, 'The Caste Question: Dalits and the Politics of Modern India', it has been argued that there has been an unprecedented increase in the violence against Dalits after independence than in the pre-independence era.

The report of National Crime Records Bureau, states that the trends of atrocities against the Scheduled-caste communities are increasing every year. The Atrocities on Dalit were recorded to be 33,655 in 2012, 39,408, in 2013, 47,064 in 2014. The increasing rate of crimes between 2012 and 2013 and between 2013 and 2014 is around 20 percent is quite hiked as compared to previous years. Despite having many legislations and government machinery the crime rate is increasing is a matter of grave concern and tremendous worry for Dalits.

4. WHY DO HIGHER CASTES DENY EQUAL RIGHTS TO UNTOUCHABLES? WHY DO HIGHER CASTES USE VIOLENT METHODS?

It is difficult to give a unique answer to the question of what precipitates an atrocity. How do people turn into beasts that kill defenseless fellow beings? How do they become such brutes so as to gangrape women in the most gruesome ways? The gouging out of eyes, the hacking off of limbs and burning alive or stoned to death are the routine happenings in the atrocities perpetrated against dalits. What drives people to commit such inhuman crimes? (Teltumbade, 2010).

The perpetrators of the crime believe that they are justified. Religious ideology, culture and tradition could be the sources of such a conviction. But, however self-righteously a person develops the belief that it is right to inflict harm on others, it is a pre-requisite that he or she should also be in a position to overpower the other. The relative weakness of the other reassures the perpetrator that he can commit the atrocity. If this equation is broken, the atrocity cannot materialize. Atrocities are thus enabled by the prevailing judicial process–the perpetrators operate on the assumption that, by virtue of their caste standing, the police investigation and the trial in court will be weighted in their favour–the crime may indeed not even be deemed cognizable as an offence (ibid, 2010).

Thorat (2015) discuses the aspect though the formulation of theories of psycho-social and economic point of view. For which he cited the argument put forward by Baker (1950). According to Baker, people discriminate because they have taste for discrimination from which they derive utility and satisfaction. The taste for discrimination emanates from prejudices that a group holds against other group, in Baker's case the other groups were black and women (Baker, 1993). The other approach, known as belief based theory, postulates that people discriminate, not because of tastes for discrimination, but because they perceive that others, on average, have low skills. Due to imperfect information, the employers make hiring and wage decisions based on the averages productivity of the individual from a particular group, which may not be the case and thus may result in discriminatory outcome. In belief perspective, the discrimination is based on a set of belief about others (Arrow, 1973).

Recently Akerlof and Kratnon (2010) have argued that while discrimination still persists, the taste and belief based theories cannot help the understanding of many patterns. They bring the influence of social context into economic decision by the individuals. The social categories and their norms constitute the identity. Individual pecuniary and non-pecuniary motivation, test and preferences are influenced by social contexts and norms. In so far as Identity theory brings the social contexts in economic decisions made by individuals, this has changed the economist old presumption that tastes and preferences are individual characteristics independent of social context. The identity theory maintained that, the social categories, and their norms would decide how someone in those social categories would behave.

According to the Authors this "socially framed conception of individual decision making should help economists working at various levels to construct sturdier accounts of the economy (Akerlof and Kranton, 2010; pp. 13–20). In its application to race and poverty, identity theory explains the racial discrimination in terms of what authors call "oppositional Identity". The behavior of white towards blacks is determined by different codes or norms which perpetuate a distinction between "us" and "them". Thus white Americans think of black Americans as "them" rather than include them in 'us all' (p. 100). This division of 'us' and 'them' based on the norms is what the authors call 'oppositional identity' with an expression of opposition and differences result into discrimination that explains the high poverty of blacks.

The Decline of the Dalit Movement and Political Weakness

During Colonialism Ambedkar has built the dalit movements with a lot of efforts. He had academically and administratively argued with the British Government for the rights of Dalits. With mass mobilization of dalits an atmosphere for emancipation of Dalits was created. However, Post-Ambedkar dalit leaders proved incapable of a dialectical handling of the contradictions in his legacy and soon fell apart, catching at one or the other strand of his ideology in support of narrow self-interest. The Republican Party of India fell down for pursuing the petty concerns of Dalit leaders. The dalit polity and politicians became subsumed as adjuncts of the ruling class parties for which symbols and identities mattered more than the material interests of the people. Though, the leadership of Bhaurao Gaikwad

(Nasik) demonstrated its potential strength when, in 1964, he launched a country-wide struggle demanding land for the landless. Today, the movement is characterized by all-round weakening through hopeless fragmentation in every sphere. Dalit Panther a radical youth movement, formed in 1972 has also proved to be a flash in the pan and soon went the way of the RPI. Both the RPI and the Dalit Panthers still exist today but in innumerable factions, most of them engaged in a competitive pursuit of favours from the ruling class. Around the same time, in 1973, under the leadership of Kanshi Ram (1934-2006) the dalits formed Backward and Minority Employees Federation, or BAMCEF. This later changed into the Dalit Shoshit Samaj Sangharsh Samiti (DS4), the Dalit Oppressed Classes' Resistance Committee, for agitational politics, which then launched itself as a full-fledged political entity, the Bahujan Samaj Party (BSP; the word bahujan means 'those in the majority'). The BSP came to power in the state on its own strength in 2007, riding a cross-caste/class sarvajan (everyman) plank. Emerging as India's third largest political party, its establishment as a ruling contender should have been assured, and its grand state assembly victory did indeed briefly dazzle. But the shine appears quickly to have worn off, if its sub-par performance in the 2009 parliamentary election is any indicator. In any case, the BSP in setting dalits to chase after a mirage of political power which has effectively decimated the movement in the pockets of its influence. One more phenomenon has, somewhat paradoxically, also contributed to the weakening of the dalit movement. Over the years, dalit movement has centered. Around the reservation issues, however more than 80 percent dalits live in villages and urban slums and these have now remained a part of Dalit Movements. They have been excluded in practically every conceivable way from any possibility of progress. Conscious of their human rights but bereft of either organizational backing or material wherewithal, this mass of dalits has become increasingly vulnerable to upper caste attack (Teltumbde, 2010). The weakening of the dalit movement has resulted in a new phenomenon of caste atrocities. Atrocities are essentially human rights violations with the added association of unbridled cruelty, brutality and inhumanness. There may be a combination of factors and aberrations that leads to such behaviour, but the foremost is the conviction that what one is doing is right.

5. CONCLUSION

Atrocities on the dalits in Post-colonial period are increasing though there is strong law to prevent the atrocities in the country. The assertions against the traditional Hindu practices of religion are the main reason of atrocities against dalits. Violence against dalits is the act of power by upper caste dalits. The social boycott against dalits is increasing against dalits in places, where, there is small number of population in the village. However, Government has failed to take steps against such a social boycott. During the period of social boycott the government should support the victims and immediately take steps to rehabilitate them in safe areas particularly, in nearby cities or where there are sizable numbers of dalit population situated.

REFERENCES

Bayly, Susan (1999). Caste Society and Politics in India, Cambridge University Press; Cambridge, United Kingdom.

Human Rights Watch (HRW) (1999). "Broken People: Caste Violence against Untouchables", New York: HRW.

Jodhka, Surinder S. (2012). Caste, Oxford University Press, New Delhi.

Navsarjan, Trust (2009). "Legally Immune from of Discrimination: Report on Socio-economic Boycotts of Dalits in Gujarat", Ahmedabad, India.

Pai, S. (2014). Dalit Assertion, Oxford University Press, New Delhi.

Ramaiah, A. (1998). The Plight of Dalits: A challenges to the social work profession. *Indian Journal of Social Work*, 59(1 part 1): 124–146, Tata Institute of Social Work.

Rao, Anupama (2010). The Caste Question, Permanent Black, Ranikhet.

Teltumbade, Anand (2010). The Persistence of the Castes-the Khairlanji Murders and India's Apartheid, Zed Books, New York.

The Scheduled Castes and Scheduled Tribes (Prevention of Atrocities) Act (1989). "Act No. 33, dated 11 September 1989". Ministry of Social Welfare and Empowerment, Government of India, t & w Delhi, Also available at: *http://www.socialjustice.nic.in/ pronearea.php*.

Thorat, S. and Negi, P. (2007). Maharastratil Samajik Bhedbhav, Nagari Hakkabhang Aani Atyachar (Exclusion and discrimination–Civil Rights Violation and Atrocities in Maharashtra), Sugava Prakashan, Pune.

Thorat, Sukhdeo (2015). Why Caste Atrocities Still Persist and How to Prevent Uiem? Keynote Address at the 'National Conference on Exclusion and Atrocities on Dalits in India', 29-30 June 2015, Tata Institute of Social Sciences, Tuljapur Campus.

Dr. Ramesh Jare, Master in Social Work from Tata Institute of Social Sciences, He has done Ph.D. In Social Work from YCMOU, Nasik. At Present he is Associate Professor at Tata Institute of Social Sciences, Tuljapur Campus. He is the Convener of Academic Programme at TISS, Tuljapur Campus. He has earlier worked on the Monitoring and Evaluation of Rehabilitation and Rehabilitation of Sardar Sarovar Project. He has also worked on as a team member of Community Participation Consultant for Govt. of Maharashtra the for the project on Monitoring of Rehabilitation and resettlement of Earthquake affected people in Latur and Osmanabad district in Maharashtra. He is expert in Participatory Rural Appraisal (PRA) and Participatory Methodologies and conducts training programmes on PRA for academicians, NGO Workers and Government officals. His research areas are Local Self Governance, Human Rights, Social Marginalization Exclusion etc.

Chapter 3

Changing Nature of Caste and Caste Based Atrocities Against Dalits: A Case Study of Kharda, Ahmednagar Dist, Maharashtra

SAMPAT KALE[1]

INTRODUCTION

The aim of the present paper is to understand the issues involved in violation of civil rights in the era of modern and modernity in our country and to examine and analyze causes and its aftermath. The author has selected a recent case for the analysis based on primary and secondary data collected and has understood statewide magnitude of the atrocities against the dalit youths.

Maharashtra being a progressive state, has a history of Rajarshi Shahu Mahatma Phule and Dr. Babasaheb Ambedkar's thought but it seems that it has not percolated to a large share of citizen of our country. Caste/Class, Gender, Region, and Minority based discrimination, humiliation, exclusion, inequality and injustice is

[1] Tata Institute of Social Sciences, Tuljapur Campus, Taluka Tuljapur, Dist. Osmanabad, Maharashtra, E-mail: samkale@tiss.edu

still prevalent in society of India. There have been violations of civil and human rights irrespective, of strong legislations and affirmative measures in India and Maharashtra. Why has this been increasing in modern society? Why are the dalit youths targeted and brutally killed on the issues of caste? This shows that Government has failed in protecting the rights of marginalized sections of the society.

There have been a number of cases registered as violation of human rights, protection of civil and political rights of the citizens. If one looks at the case of Khairlanji and Kharda there are a lot of similarities in organized killings and attacks on dalits. This grim picture is quite prevalent in rural Maharashtra. The incidents of attacks during festivals and celebrations have triggered conflicts between dalits and non-dalits. There have been five to six such incidents in Marathwada region and several cases have occurred in the year 2014–15.

The incidents of atrocities are categorized under civil rights violations, which are very fundamental in nature; even Constitution of India guarantees these rights to all citizens irrespective of caste, creed and sex. Therefore, this paper discusses the causes and forms of violations and its aftermath on society at large.

Khairlanji and Kharda is a manifestation of caste based discrimination and new from of casteism in modern era. The villagers shared the view that there are no incidents of atrocities in the region.

The National Crime Records Bureau, Ministry of Home Affairs, Government of India reveals the truth that about 33655 crimes against SCs have taken place all over the country during 2012 whereas incidents of crime against Scheduled Caste in Maharashtra reported in 2010 were 1132. As many as 1091 cases of crime committed against SCs have been reported by the State Government in 2012. A large scale human right violation, crime and atrocities are perpetuated against dalits in rural Maharashtra. Dalit atrocities are quite rampant in Maharashtra on the basis of socio-economic, cultural and political issues.

THEORETICAL FRAMEWORK OF SOCIETY AND CASTE

In Hindu social system Varna and Jati system has been discussed by several sociologists. Varna is only a reference category and it is not a functioning unit of social structure. The Brahmin, Kshatriya and Vaishya were known as twice born. The Shudra fourth level includes a multiplicity of artisans and occupationally specialised Jatis who pursue cleaning that is all non-polluting occupations.

One of the important uniqueness of the Indian Society is Caste. Here the binary approach can be applied and discussed that pre-colonial and post-colonial. In the pre-colonial castes were known as Jatis and after the entry of Portuguese to India it became Caste. Jati is known as endogamous community with more or less defined ritual status and some occupational traditionally linked to it. Jatis are sub-divisions of the three upper Varnas. Later it became Jatis and with the advent of colonialism constructed caste as hereditary and hierarchy in the society. Members of the Jati shares their common culture and rituals. Even they have had intra-village and inter village mechanisms of social control and conflict resolutions mechanisms. Now, the village sites have become the caste oppression and reproduction of caste-based hierarchy and inequality and more marginalisation of dalits or scheduled caste and scheduled tribes' communities. The higher caste and so called lower caste have rules about the maintenance of purity and pollution in the society. Though the Constitution of India has repealed the caste based discrimination and untouchability and recognised equality of the Scheduled Caste in theory. There is no much hierarchy in other religions on the basis of Varna or Jat. There is only hierarchy seen is that of the high-caste or low caste.

As we are aware about Indian society is a very much complex and diverse society. It will be very difficult to say that this is one of the forms of society. It has its different attributions and uniqueness. The way it has gone through different phases and historical journey it has resulted into a very diverse and complex society. However, the Indian society is the product of long and complex historical processes. As T.K. Oommen described that there are seven major events that contributed to the formation of this process at the Aryan advent, the emergence of Indian protest religions-Jainism, Buddhism, and Sikhism, the entry of the non-Indic religions into the sub-continent as immigrants' religions, the Muslim conquests, western colonialism, the anti-colonial freedom struggle and the partition of the Indian sub-continents in 1947. The above-mentioned seven phases is our in-one society.

Like all societies, Indian society too is stratified based on age, gender, rural-urban differences, and caste-based differences and classifications of castes. The Indian society is marked by considerable cultural heterogeneity, and we have large scale of languages and communities as a part of the Indian society. There are more than 680 tribal communities there and they have different languages and dialects and different ways of life. Indian society has several religions and there are of non-Indic origins. Therefore, the caste-based hierarchy is legitimised through the Hindu doctrine of Karma and reincarnation.

As Surinder Jodhka discussed in his recent book on 'Caste' focused on Varna and Caste. We have a long history of Varna and caste system in the Indian society. The Varna system was only useful to the extent of being a model, a framework of hierarchy. Unlike the Varna system which was presumably a pan-Indian system but Jati had a regional character. The term caste is an English translation of the Spanish word casta first used in the Indian context by Portuguese seafarers. Similarly, Nicholas Dirks argues that caste was widely recognised by the colonial regime as a local form of Civil Society which was responsible for India's political weakness and symptom of the over development of its religious preoccupations.

Louis Dumont: Caste is set of relationships of economic, political and kinship systems, sustained by certain values which are mostly religious in nature. According to Dumont caste divides the whole Indian society into a larger number of hereditary groups distinguished from one another and connected together by following characteristics. Separation on the basis of rules of the caste in matters of marriage and contact whether direct or indirect (food). Interdependent of work or division of labour each group having in theory or by tradition, a profession from which their members can depart only within certain limits Gradation of status or hierarchy which ranks the groups as relatively superior or inferior to one another.

G.S. Ghurye: G.S. Ghurye described six core features of the Hindu caste system: Segmental division of society: membership based on birth not by choice. Hierarchy: each group occupied a social status in overall framework of hierarchy. Restriction on social intercourse: Hindu society had its rules about social relations like what to eat and not to eat and drink. Civil and religious disabilities and privileges: segregation of individual castes or groups of castes in the village the most obvious mark of civil privileges and disabilities. Restricted choice of occupation: Each case considered a particular occupation as its legitimate occupation. Restrictions on marriage: caste groups observed strict endogamy. Members of caste group married only within their castes.

Max Weber: Max Weber viewed the Indian caste system as an extreme of what he described as Status Groups. In a way Weber accepted orientalist's view about the rigidity and unchanging nature of caste. In Celestin Bougie's thinking caste was indeed a system of inequality and though in its purest form it developed among Hindus and it was not peculiar to India. He identified three core elements that make caste: hereditary specialisation, hierarchy, and repulsion.

The structural basis of Hindu society is caste, and it is not possible to understand Sanskritisation without reference to the structural framework in which it occurs. The caste occupying the top positions in the hierarchy are more Sanskritised than castes in the lower and middle regions of the hierarchy and this has been responsible for the Sanskritisation of the lower castes as well as the outlying tribes.

M.N. Srinivas: A cultural and social aspect of Caste, Sanskritisation "Lower caste people imitate the style of life, rituals and practices of the upper castes with a view to improve their status for positional changes" Positional change is horizontal but structural change is a vertical arrangement of the social order.

The Non-brahmanical: Castes adopt not only Brahmanical ritual, but also certain Brahmanical institutions and values. This can be applicable to the institutions of marriage-kinship and family. In Indian society the idea of hierarchy is omnipresent in the caste system not only do the various castes form a hierarchy, but the occupation practised by them, the various items of their diet, and the customs they observe, all form separate hierarchies. The practicing of an occupation like butchery, tanning, handling toddy, puts a caste in a low position, eating pork or beef is more degrading than eating fish or mutton.

Castes which offer blood-sacrifices to deities are lower than castes making only offerings of fruits and flowers. The entire way of life of the top castes seeps down the hierarchy. It is not a question of traditional society of modern society it is happening in many village sites and urban sites in our country. Purity and pollution is still being practiced in many states. The lesser human treatment is meted out to so called out caste peoples. Of course, there is consciousness and people are changing their way of life and following upper caste people's styles and giving up eating non-veg and drinking liquor. These are the examples which help in understanding knowledge and practices in society.

SOCIAL AND GEOGRAPHICAL BACKGROUND OF THE CASE

Tata Institute of Social Sciences, Tuljapur strongly condemns the inhuman and brutal killing of 17 years dalit educated boy on 28th April 2014 in village Kharda, Taluka-Jamkhed, District-Ahmednagar. A team of the faculty, social workers and NGO representative has visited Nitin Aage's (victim) parents and relatives on 6th May 2014 and discussed about the incident and expressed their deep condolence. In this matter Jamkhed Police had arrested three persons. They have also arrested seven other persons who were part of the assault on Nitin Aage.

Caste, Class, Gender, Region, and Minority based discrimination, humiliation, inequality and injustice is still prevalent in the society of India. This shows that Government has failed to protect the rights of marginalized sections of the society. There have been a number of cases registered as violation of human rights, protection of civil and political rights of the citizens. If one looks at the cases of Khairlanji and Kharda there are a lot of similarities in organized killings and attacks on dalits. This grim picture is quite prevalent in rural Maharashtra. The incidents of attacks during festivals and celebrations have triggered conflicts between dalits and non-dalits. There have been five to six such incidents in Marathwada region and several cases have occurred in the month of April and May, 2014.

Khairlanji and Kharda incidents are manifestations of caste based discriminations and new forms of casteism in modern era. Technological developments and the dream of superpower country will not be achieved unless and until we establish and secure and safe life without fear for the marginalized and disempowered people of the country. Growth, development is the new mantra of globalization but it is meaningless when it comes to caste based discrimination happening at grassroots level. The villagers were sharing that there are no indications of atrocities in the region.

The National Crime Records Bureau, Ministry of Home Affairs, Government of India reveals the truth that about 33655 crimes against SCs have taken place all over the country during 2012 where as incidents of crime against Scheduled Caste in Maharashtra reported in 2010 were 1132. As many as 1091 cases of crimes committed against SCs have been reported by the State Government in 2012. A large scale human rights, violations, crimes and atrocities are perpetuated against dalits in rural Maharashtra. Dalit atrocities are quite rampant in Maharashtra on the basis of socio-economic, cultural and political issues. These incidents are resulting in social, economic and cultural boycott in rural India.

Nitin was brutally beaten and killed by people belonging to the dominant Maratha caste for having friendship with an upper caste girl from his school. He was picked up from his school by girl's brother, uncle and their accomplices. The Principal and teachers neither informed Aage's parents nor the police. He was tortured and assaulted by the girl's brother, uncle and their accomplices for 9 hours behind a brick kiln and Kanhoba hill on 28th April 2014. The torture continued for more than nine hours but not a single person intervened and tried to inform victim's parents, police or any social institutions.

"Our village does not believe in any casteism, we jointly celebrate Shiv Jayanti and Ambedkar Jayanti" is what the villagers say today. But why do they not allow having friendship, fraternity, and marriages outside the Caste? Kharda is calm and still after the murder of Nitin Aage by upper caste people, the privileged and resource rich people of the village. Here it is important to understand the dynamics of this incident and complexities of caste based honored crimes in Indian society. Our team has interacted with Raju Aage (father), Rekha Aage (mother), his sister, relatives, villagers and political party workers.

Kharda is about 127 km from Tuljapur and 100 kms from the district headquarter Ahmednagar. The population of Kharda is about 10,000. There are twenty dalit families but Aage's family lives far and seems isolated from the main village. They have close association with their previous residence in Gitewadi. The Aage family is totally dependent on their wage employment on a stone crusher for their livelihood. They have a BPL (below poverty line) card and avail PDS food grains regularly. Raju Aage has three daughters of which two are married. Nitin was studying in 12th Class of English School, Kharda and the concerned girl was studying in 10th standard. The school is about one kilometre from Nitin's house.

On 28th April 2014, Sachin Golekar (brother of the girl) saw Nitin and his sister talking in a garden behind the school at 07:30 am. After this, Sachin Golekar, his uncle and his friends came into school carrying a hammer (Hatoda) and started beating up Nitin. Seeing this, the school teacher told them not to create a ruckus on the school premises and that they can take him away where ever they wanted. They dragged Nitin from school to brick kiln industry which is about one km from the school. They tortured him from morning 7.30 to 4.30 pm. They strangled him to death and hanged his body from a tree.

It was observed that the victim's family members were in deep stress, sorrow and were disturbed. They were not in a position to speak with so many visitors. It was shared by a lady that there is lot of insecurity in spite of deploying security by the Government of Maharashtra. Some people shared that if the criminals got bail then there will be more fear and threat to the dalit families of Kharda. We observed that there is complete silence after this incident in the surrounding area in a radius of 15 kilometres.

Hence this paper argues that the dream of anti-caste movement or Casteless society is a myth or reality? Technological developments and the dream of being a superpower country will not be achieved unless and until we establish and secure and safe life without fear for the marginalized and disempowered people of the country. Growth, development is the new mantra of globalization but it is meaningless when it comes to caste based discrimination happening at grassroots level.

Now, all the key leaders of different political parties have visited and have promised Nitin Raju Aage's family that they will provide economic assistance and ensure proper inquiry into the incident and strong action against the culprits immediately. Eventually, promises have been broken and hopelessness has increased among the oppressed people of the State.

SUMMING UP

The government should provide best legal assistance to the victim's family including the appointment of a special public prosecutor. The

Government should provide police protection to the Aage Family and other dalits of the village. There should be a stringent action against assaulters of Nitin Aage under the SC/ST (Prevention of Atrocity) Act and Protection of Civil Rights Act. There should be an in-depth inquiry against those school teachers who have handed over Nitin to girl's brother, uncle and their associates. This case should be taken into a fast track court and the government must set up new courts in caste sensitive areas of rural Maharashtra. Police must document and record the account of key witnesses and ensure protection to minors. The concerned girl must receive emotional support and counseling. She is a key witness so her safety must be ensured. The home department must ensure that this matter be presented in fast track special courts and ensure justice to the victim's family. There is an urgent need for creating a cadre of trained Human Rights defenders under the State Human Rights Commission. The responsibility should be shouldered by CSOs, government and private institutions and universities. Government, Non-government and Community Based Organizations must start awareness and sensitization campaign about caste*based issues including atrocities all over the State. State must ensure reasonable relief and rehabilitation of Aage's family. Eventually, our country should be taking care of all the marginalised sections of the society then only people would be free from any kind of injustice happening at individual or institutional levels.

REFERENCES

Atal, Yogesh (1993). 'Understanding Indian Society: Festschrift in Honour of Professor S.C. Dube'. New Delhi: Har-Anand Publications.

Bottomore, T.B. (1986). 'Sociology: A Guide to Problems and Literature'. New Delhi: Blackie and Sons (India) Ltd.

Dahiwale, S.M. (2006). 'Understanding Indian Society: The Non-brahmanic Perspective', New Delhi: Rawat Publications.

Dube, S.C. (1990). 'Indian Society'. New Delhi: National Book Trust.

Jodhka, Surinder S. (2013).'Village Society'. New Delhi: Orient Blackswan.

Jodhka, Surinder S. (2012). 'Caste'. New Delhi: Oxford University Press.

Maciver, R.M. and Page, C.H. (1977). 'Society-an Introductory Analysis'. New Delhi: Macmillan India Ltd.

Rodrigues, Edward A. (2013). Reading Material for the Participants of 36th Refresher Course in Sociology'. New Delhi: ASC, JNU.

Dr. Sampat Kale is with School of Rural Development, Tata Institute of Social Sciences (TISS) as a Senior Assistant Professor. He is the Programme Convener, MA/M.Sc in Sustainable Livelihoods and Natural Resources Governance. He is the in charge of the Social Protection Office of the Tuljapur campus. He has done M.A. and Ph.D. in Sociology at the Department of Sociology from the University of Pune in 2008 and cleared UGC NET in 1999. He is a Life Member of the Indian Sociological Society and the Marathi Samajshastra Parishad. Prior to this, he has worked with National Centre for Advocacy Studies (NCAS), Pune, which is a development organization working on issues related to people centred advocacy. He has written more than two dozens of articles, several books and some papers in national and international journals. He has presented his work at various conferences and seminars at national level. He has visited Karachi-Pakistan, Stockholm-Sweden and presented papers as well.

Areas of Interest: Sociology of Development and Change, Sociology of Marginal groups, Rural Development, Voluntary Organization - NGOs, Social Movements, People-centred Advocacy, Human rights and social justice, Local Self-Governance, Good Governance, Transparency and Accountability, Livelihood and Marginalized, Natural Resources-Land, Water, Forest & Work, Food Security, Displacement & Development. Right to Water and worked toward water security in Maharashtra.

Specialization:

A. Teaching, Training and Capacity building in local self governance, rural livelihoods and decentralization

B. Policy advocacy on livelihoods and natural resources

C. Studies on issues of land rights, water rights, forest and drought

D. Studies on development of tribes and nomadic tribes and food security

E. Studies of NGOs and Social Movements

Chapter 4

Atrocities and Discrimination Against Dalits: A Critical Examination of the Response of the Law

SAUMYA UMA[1]

A large proportion of the Indian population lives highly precarious life, shunned, segregated and deprived of access to public services as 'untouchables', reinforced by the caste system. Justice Chinnappa Reddy aptly referred to the caste system as a system, of "layer upon layer of gradation and degradation".[1] Dr. Ambedkar an architect of the constitution of India and the first Minister of Law of the Republic of India was convinced of the potential of law as a weapon to end the practice of untouchability, discrimination and atrocities against the marginalized Indians, especially Dalits.[2] The 'weapon' consists of a

[1] KC. Vasanth Kumar and Another *vs.* State of Karnataka AIR 1985 SC 1495

[2] This paper uses the term 'Dalits' which encompasses not only Dalit Hindus, Buddhists and Sikhs, but also Dalit Muslims and Christians. It also uses the administrative/ legal term 'Scheduled Castes' that excludes Dalit Muslims and Christians vide The Constitution (Scheduled Castes) Order (also called the Presidential Order) 1950, and includes people from only those castes listed in the Schedule.

1 Centre for the Study of Social Exclusion and Inclusive Policy (CSSEIP), National Law School of India, Bangalore, E-mail: saumyauma@gmail.com

Constitutional framework complemented by special legislations to address the phenomenon of atrocities and discrimination against Dalits. This paper examines the adequacy and effectiveness of the response of the law *vis-a-vis* the lived realities of Dalits in India.

The paper is divided into five parts. The first part briefly outlines the socio-legal status of Dalits in India. The second part evaluates the provisions pertaining to the Protection of Civil Rights Act 1955 and its impact on the eradication of untouchability and discrimination against Dalits. The third part critically examines the provisions of The Scheduled Castes and Scheduled Tribes (Prevention of Atrocities) Act 1989, and its attempt to address violence against Dalits. The fourth part discusses the amendments to the 1989 Act, which were passed by both the Houses of Parliament in 2015. The final part of the paper discusses a possible agenda for the future.

A. SOCIO-LEGAL STATUS OF DALITS IN INDIA

According to the 2011 Census, the Scheduled Castes form 16.2% of the total Indian population more than 200 million/20 crore people. The actual number of Dalits is likely to be much higher if the Christian and Muslim Dalits are included.

A constantly widening gap exists between the ground reality of Dalits and the Constitutional guarantees made in their favour. The Indian Constitution guarantees the right to equality and prohibition of discrimination on grounds including caste (Art. 14 and 15). A provision was made for abolition of untouchability in the Fundamental Rights chapter of the Indian Constitution in 1950 (Art. 17), as a right that is available against state and non-state actors.[3]

The Constitution has notionally abolished untouchability but not the caste system. As a manifestation of the caste system, to this day, Dalits are unable to own the land which they till despite the existence of land distribution laws, leading to a vicious cycle of debt and an

[3] People's Union for Democratic Rights *vs.* Union of India AIR 1982 SC 1473

exploitative economic arrangement. Affirmative action in the form of reservation in educational institutions and public sector jobs has been guaranteed in the Constitution [Art. 15(4) and 16(4A)], to enable Dalits to participate in socio-economic and political processes, and for the empowerment of the community; yet these provisions have not been implemented fully.

Despite a guarantee of rights of all people to life with dignity (Article 21), the exploitation of Dalits continues as they are made to take on degrading work such as manual scavenging, notwithstanding the provisions of Prohibition of Employment as Manual Scavengers and Their Rehabilitation Act 2013. Additionally, laws designed to address and eradicate exploitative work arrangements, such as The Minimum Wages Act 1948, Equal Remuneration Act 1976 and The Bonded Labour System (Abolition) Act 1976 are routinely flouted and rarely implemented.

In the last few decades, an awareness of rights and an awakening of the exploitation have led to resistance from the Dalit community. However, as the resistance of the Dalits has grown, so the frequency and brutal ferocity of atrocities have grown pace.[4] It is reported that crimes against Dalits have increased by 245% in the last decade.[5] Dalit women are doubly vulnerable due to the inter-sectionality of caste and gender, and are targeted for varied forms of atrocities including sexual and gender-based violence. The National Crime Records Bureau indicates a total of 2233 registered cases of rape of Scheduled Castes women in 2014 - an increase from 2073 in 2013, 1576 in 2012 and 1557 in 2011. This amounts to an average of 6.1 rapes per day.[6] In short, despite legal safeguards, Dalits are

[4] P S Krishnan (2009), 'Atrocities Against Dalits: Retrospect and Prospect', Combat Law, 20 December

[5] 'Crimes Against Dalits Rise 245% in Last Decade', The Times of India, 9th August 2014

[6] National Crime Records Bureau (2015), Crime in India 2014, New Delhi: Ministry of Home Affairs, Government of India at p. 108. See also Thenmozhi Soundararajan, India's caste culture is rape culture', June 9, 2014, available at *http:/ /www.thedailvbeast.com* accessed on 7 June 2015

stripped of the right to a life with dignity - one of the most sacrosanct fundamental rights under the Indian Constitution.

B. ADDRESSING UNTOUCHABILITY AND DISCRIMINATION: THE PROTECTION OF CIVIL RIGHTS ACT 1955

The Untouchability (Offences) Act was enacted in 1955 with the object of awarding punishment for offences amounting to the practice of untouchability and enforcement of social disabilities with regard to entrance and worship at temples, access to shops, places of work, common water resources, and other offences Dissatisfied with the lack of effectiveness of the law in curbing the practice of untouchability, in 1965, the Indian government established the Elayaperumal Committee.[7] The Committee submitted its report in 1969, on the basis of which the provisions of the law were expanded UP0rf in 1976 to include removal of certain disabilities, provision for stringent punishment, rechristening of the law as the Protection of Civil Rights Act (PCRA).

From 1955 to 1976, a total of 22,470 cases were registered under the law. Out of a prosecution in 19,893 cases, convictions were secured only in 6178 cases (31% of the total cases registered).[8] In 2013, only 62 cases were registered nationwide under the PCRA despite the rampant practice of untouchability and imposition of disabilities on Dalits.[9] This increased to 101 cases being registered in 2014.

The Centre for the Study of Social Exclusion and Inclusive Policy, based in National Law School of India, Bangalore, carried out a study in 2005-06 aimed at evaluating the impact of the PCRA and its

[7] The Government of India appointed the Committee on Untouchability, Educational and Economic Development of Scheduled Castes, with L. Elaya Perumal as its chairperson, in April 1965 to examine the practice of untouchability *vis-a-vis* the implementation of the Untouchability (Offences) Act and to make suitable recommendations.

[8] Vichitra Meena *vs*. Union of India and Others AIR 1982 Raj 297 at para 27

[9] National Crime Records Bureau (2014), supra n. 6 at p. 111

effectiveness in the eradication of untouchability. It involved a survey of 24 villages across 12 districts in six states - Andhra Pradesh, Karnataka, Madhya Pradesh, Rajasthan, Uttar Pradesh and West Bengal. Approximately 648 people were interviewed across six states on issues of religious disabilities, social disabilities, political disabilities and other offences arising out of untouchability that are spelt out in the PCRA. The findings of the study include the following:[10]

a) There has been some progress on the issue of religious disabilities in many states, all untouchables were allowed temple entry. However, there are many notable instances which assert the fact that the caste-based discrimination continues to exist in the religious sphere, pointing to the need for a better implementation of the PCRA; (p. 72)

b) Social disabilities continue to be imposed on the community; segregation has continued in practice and restriction of access to basic human resources was rampant, both in the public domain such as marriage processions and common water resources, as well as in the manner of invitation to one's own household; (p. 90)

c) Discriminatory practices still exist on the issue of access to public services such as public schools and hospitals; women often face discrimination in the context of their appearance and clothing; (p. 96)

d) Largely, access to hotels, public eating places etc. exist for the untouchables; however there were disturbing instances with some persons not being able to touch goods in a shop. Further, a large percentage of untouchables were found to be apprehensive about selling their goods in the village shop; (p. 106)

---

[10] Centre for the Study of Social Exclusion and Inclusive Policy, National Law School of India, Bangalore (2006), 'Evaluation of the Protection of Civil Rights Act 1955 and its Impact on the Eradication of Untouchability', on file with the author.

e) Dalits continue to render forced services such as drum beating, grave digging, removal of carcasses and manual scavenging, discrimination in payment of wages, discrimination at the workplace and in irrigation facilities; (pp. 106-116)

In critiquing the provisions of the PCRA, the study arrived at the following conclusions:

a) The alteration of the title of the Act in 1976 indicates that the amended law was not intended only to punish the offence of untouchability, but to address myriad forms of caste-based discrimination that exists in society. However, the contents of the law do not reflect clearly the responsibility of the State to make a concerted effort to address, not only the manifestations, but the root cause of the problem;

b) Although the Statement of Object and Reasons of the PCRA states that the law is not confined in its application only to Hindus, it is persistently associated with the Scheduled Castes, thereby excluding Muslims and Christians who suffer similar kinds of discrimination as the Hindu untouchables; FIRs are not registered and remedies under the PCRA are routinely denied on grounds that the affected person does not belong to a community that is notified as a Scheduled Caste for the particular state;

c) There is a very close co-relation between PCRA and POA Act - while the PCRA aims at removing disabilities (religious, social and those imposed on the exercise of rights under the law) and awards punishment for milder offences related to the practice of untouchability, the POA addresses aggravated offences (named as 'atrocities'). However, in practice, the POA is being used as a substitute for PCRA and results in acquittal, in those instances in which there could have potentially been a conviction under PCRA.

d) Witnesses turning hostile are a principal cause for the large number of acquittals under the PCRA; hence incorporating provisions for witness protection into the PCRA is of prime importance; and

e) Institutional reform is also required - the investigation of crimes is not given importance by the police; the Special Courts established under the Act do not deal exclusively with caste-based violence and disabilities; Vigilance and Monitoring Committees under the Act have not been established.

In short, the study found that while the PCRA targets the manifestations of untouchability, such as social disabilities and restrictions on civil rights, it is unable to address the root cause of the practice-caste-based discrimination and oppression that are embedded and deep-rooted, founded upon caste hierarchy.

C. RESPONDING TO ATROCITIES AGAINST DALITS: THE SCHEDULED CASTES AND SCHEDULED TRIBES (PREVENTION OF ATROCITIES) ACT 1989

With an increase in incidence of heinous forms of violence against Dalits, it was found that a new and stringent Act was warranted for addressing the growing atrocities against Dalits. The Scheduled Castes and Scheduled Tribes (Prevention of Atrocities) (POA) Act 1989 was enacted for the prevention of offences, prosecution of the offenders and relief and rehabilitation of the victims.[11]

The preamble to the Act states that the law intends to "prevent the commission of offences of atrocities against the Scheduled Castes and the Scheduled Tribes, to provide for Special Courts for the trial of such offence and for the relief and rehabilitation of the victim of such offences and for matters connected therewith of incidental thereto.

The POA Act contains many salient features. The term 'atrocities' was coined for the first time to accurately reflect the gravity of the

[11] The preamble to the Act states that the law intends to "prevent the commission of offences of atrocities against the members of the Scheduled Castes and the Scheduled Tribes, to provide for Special Courts for the trial of such offences and for the relief and rehabilitation of the victims of such offences and for matters connected therewith or incidental thereto."

offences perpetrated on Scheduled Castes and Scheduled Tribes. The Act provides for special public prosecutors and special courts, preventive action by officials[12] and punishment for officials who are found to be negligent in discharging their official duties;[13] punishments under this Act include imposition of punitive and collective fines;[14] it provides for compensation to the victim from the State[15] and for procedural guarantees, such as the requirement of investigation to be conducted by an officer of the rank of Deputy Superintendent of Police (DSP) and above.

Studies indicate that despite these path breaking provisions, a large proportion of the atrocities remains unreported, and poor and biased investigations have led to at least 25% of the registered cases being disposed of at the investigation stage itself, on the ground of 'mistake of fact'.[16] Pendency of cases is massive (over 80% in 2013), and conviction rates under the POA dismal (22.8% in 2013) according to official data.[17] Studies also highlight various contributory factors for a denial of justice under the Act. These include an utterly negligent police investigation, a hostile role played by public prosecutors, a lack of awareness of rights and the law, complicity of the state in arresting and charging Dalit rights activists with offences under national security legislations, and the state's lack of political will

[12] Sections 9, 10 and 17

[13] Section 4

[14] Section 16

[15] Section 12(7); Rule 12(4) and Rule 14 of POA Rules

[16] National Coalition for Strengthening POA Act (2011), People's Report on Implementation of SCs and STs (POA) Act 1989 and Rules 1995, available at processes of justice, and suppression of spontaneous and peaceful protests against the violence on Dalit women by state governments.

[17] Minister of State for Social Justice and Empowerment, in a reply to a question raised in the Lok Sabha in February 2015, provided this data and stated that the conviction rate had reduced between 2011 and 2013, while the pendency rate of cases increased during the same period. Available at http://www.dailyexcelsior.com/conviction- rate-in-cases-under-scst-declined-between-2011-13/, accessed on 8 June 2015. See also Suhas Chakma, 'Combating Caste Violence', Tehelka, 26 April 2012

and commitment to implement the POA Act.[18] Reports also highlight pattern of impunity in attacks against Dalit women, the utter failure of the criminal justice system to provide justice to them, police complicity with the accused in scuttling processes of justice, and suppression of spontaneous and peaceful protests against the violence on Dalit women by state governments.[19]

Against this backdrop, a study was conducted by the Centre for the Study of Social Exclusion and Inclusive Policy (CSSEIP) with specific reference to two existing challenges to justice and accountability - a high rate of acquittals and a delay in disposal of cases. The study aimed at achieving this objective through an analysis of the functioning and performance of the Exclusive Special Courts established under the POA Act. For this purpose, 24811 case entries from the Trial Registers, and 245 case files from 55 Special Courts from the six states of Andhra Pradesh, Bihar, Chhattisgarh, Gujarat, Karnataka and Uttar Pradesh were examined. The major findings are summarized below:[20]

Delay in Disposal of Cases

The right to speedy trial is an inalienable and fundamental right under Art. 21 of the Constitution.[21] However, the study indicated

[18] See Human Rights Watch (2007), Hidden Apartheid: Caste Discrimination Against India's "Untouchables", New York: Human Rights Watch; Smita Narula (1999), Broken People: Caste Violence Against India's "Untouchables", New York: Human Rights Watch; see also the findings of the study conducted by Vajibhai Patel, Secretary – Council for Social Justice – published in Communalism Combat, March 2005

[19] Smita Narula (1999), ibid; National Campaign on Dalit Human Rights (2014), Report: National Tribunal Violence Against Dalit Women in India, 30th September-1st October 2013, New Delhi, available at http://www.ncdhr.org.in/others/Report-on-National-Tribuna-%28Final%29.pdf, accessed on 9th June 2015

[20] Summarized from Centre for the Study of Social Exclusion and Inclusive Policy (CSSEIP), National Law School of India, Bangalore (2014-15), Functioning and Performance of Exclusive Special Courts Under the Scheduled Castes and Scheduled Tribes (Prevention of Atrocities) Act 1989: A Study in the States of Andhra Pradesh, Bihar, Chhattisgarh, Gujarat, Karnataka and Uttar Pradesh, on file with the author

[21] Sheela Barse and Others *vs.* Union of India and Others AIR 1986 SC 1773

that there are delays in the disposal of cases under the POA Act, both at the pre-trial and trial stages. A national average of the six states studied indicated that about 40% of the cases examined were disposed of within one year, about 28% in 1-2 years, and another 20% in 2-3 years. Approximately 12% of the cases take more than 3 years for final disposal. In short, in about 32% or 1/3 of the cases examined, the time taken from the stage of registration of FIR to disposal of the case is more than 2 years. Additionally there are state-wise variations in the time taken for disposal of the cases, both at the pre-trial and trial stages. For example, in Andhra Pradesh, there was a delay of 6.86 years at the trial stage, while in Bihar, approximately 3.31 years were spent at the pre-trial stage itself. Further, time taken also depends on the nature of cases, and the number of witnesses summoned and available for testimony.

Factors Leading to Delay in Disposal of Cases

- Although at least 166 Exclusive Special Courts (ESCs) have been established in the country under the POA Act, only 13 out of the 55 ESCs examined function if exclusively as Special Courts under the POA Act; in all other instances, these courts adjudicate on matters other than POA Act, based on the field investigators' observations.
- Inability of courts to record the deposition of important witnesses on time due to serious scheduling mistakes - such as when multiple witnesses are called on the same day;
- Frequent adjournments and adjournments on frivolous grounds, including non-appearance of witnesses and non-production of accused persons; and
- Tremendous pre-trial delays exist, from the stage of registration of FIR to committal from Magistrate's court to the Special Court. This is because the Special Courts presently do not have the power to take cognizance of an offence, and hence this has to be undertaken by the magistrate's court, before committing the case to the Special Court for trial.

Low Conviction

The study confirmed the low rate of conviction in prosecutions under the POA Act. An analysis of 14,255 judgments across the six states showed that the average conviction rate was approximately 13.9%. In some of the states examined, the acquittal rate was alarmingly high -97.3% in Andhra Pradesh, 96.7% in Karnataka and 88.3% in Uttar Pradesh.

Factors Leading to a Low Conviction

- Dismissal of cases for lack of mens rea (such as failure to prove caste-based knowledge/intention);
- Dismissal of cases on hyper-technical grounds (such as inability to produce caste certificate, investigation by an officer lower than rank of Dy SP);
- Compromise between the victim and the accused (facilitated by Presiding Judge/police in some instances, although the offences are non-compoundable);
- Judges' reluctance to convict due to a strong belief and conviction that the law is being misused by the Scheduled Castes with malice, to lodge false complaints and extract a monetary compensation from the court and the accused persons. This was reflected in the personal interactions with Special Court judges;
- Prejudice of Public Prosecutors and Scheduled Castes/ Scheduled Tribes Welfare Authorities - similar misconception as shared by the judges, explained above;
- Rampant application of S. 3(i)(x) of the POA Act[22] - a non-serious offence with a meager punishment. The study found that in 60–95% of the cases, this section was mechanically

[22] S.3(i)(x) of the POA Act is a general section about intentional insult to or intimidation with intent to humiliate a member of SC / ST in any place within public view, punishable with a maximum of six months imprisonment and fine.

and routinely used by the police, without any co-relation with the gravity of the offences alleged to have been committed.

Other Findings

- *Lack of infrastructure:* In some places, such as Chandoli (UP), a part of a government school is used as the sessions court, with proceedings being conducted on the porch, and one room serving as a record room. In other places, such as in Shrawasti (UP), a Special Court functions from a rented house. In some places, half the court hall is used as a record room, such as in Patna (Bihar). The lack of infrastructure often leads to poor coordination between concerned court and record room, and case files are retained in court after disposal (Patna). Unorganized and unmarked files related to the POA Act also contribute to the delay in court processes. This is a very sad and bad state of affairs as the temple of justice has been located at dirty corners and ugly dungeons.
- *'Compromise' by victims and their families*: A time delay in disposal of cases and a high pendency of cases in the Special Courts leads to the victims' distrust in the system. Coupled with a low bargaining power, many opt for out of court compromise/settlement, the terms of which are not necessarily fair, just or equitable from the victims' perspective;
- *Hostile witnesses*: The phenomenon of witnesses turning hostile is predominant, and is directly linked to an absence of a witness protection programme, forcing the witnesses to prioritize issues of survival over that of justice. Interactions with judges of Special Courts confirmed this phenomenon; The witnesses turn their backs to truth and justice as they find themselves insecure and unsafe on account of the hostile circumstances around.
- *Financial Hardships*: Witnesses also face financial hardships in travelling to and from court, as many are employed as daily wage labourers and incur a loss of wages; despite a provision for travel allowance, this is not always paid promptly to the

concerned witnesses. Witnesses need to be given protection and prompt and sumptuous payment for their assistance in the cause of justice.

In short, the study found that the POA Act has not had the desired deterrent effect of either preventing the commission of atrocities, prosecution of offences or provision of relief and rehabilitation to the victims.[23] Justice Krishna Iyer's words, that the POA Act "has proved to be impotent and ineffectual in practice" is an apt summary of the Act.[24]

D. AMENDMENTS TO THE POA ACT

The above sections of this paper have critiqued the ramifications of two special legislations -PCRA and POA Act, and highlighted the status of and challenges to their effective implementation. Justice K Ramaswamy reiterated the importance of the PCRA when he said:[25]

The Act is not a penal law simpliciter but bears behind it monstrous untouchability relentlessly practised for centuries dehumanising the Dalits, constitution's animation to have it eradicated and to assimilate I/5th of Nation's population in the main stream of national life.

As a logical corollary, improving the use and implementation of PCRA is of prime importance, to address various forms of disabilities associated with untouchability, experienced by Dalits,

Particularly in rural India. Mass awareness programmes for laypersons, as well as inclusion of the PCRA in the syllabus for police

[23] See Committee for the Welfare of Scheduled Castes and Scheduled Tribes (2005), Fourteenth Lok Sabha - Fourth Report: Atrocities on Scheduled Castes and Scheduled Tribes and Pattern of Social Crimes Towards Them (SCTC No. 658), available at http://l 64.100.24.208/Is/committee R/SCTC/4threp.pdf, accessed on 5th June 2015

[24] 'Forward by Justice Krishna Iyer to P.L. Mimroth (2000), Dalit Utpidan Aur Vidhik Upchar, New Delhi

[25] State of Karnataka *vs.* Appa Balu Ingale AIR 1993 SC 1126 at para 11

training and administrative training programmes, could be potentially helpful.

Comprehensive amendments to the POA Act, to improve its implementation, have been carried out recently. The Amendment Bill was passed unanimously in the Rajya Sabha in December 2015, while the Lok Sabha passed the same in August 2015. A nationwide effort of civil society groups had been made in this regard over the past several years.[26]

Salient features of the amended law are as follows:

a) *Offences*: The law amends certain existing categories and adds new categories of actions to be treated as offences. These include:

   - Forcing an SC or ST individual to vote or not to vote for a particular candidate in a manner that is against the law;
   - Impeding certain activities related to voting, and wrongfully occupying land belonging to SCs or STs. (The amended law defines 'wrongful' in this context, which was not done previously);
   - Garlanding with footwear;
   - Compelling to dispose of, to carry human or animal carcasses, or do manual scavenging;
   - Abusing SCs or STs by caste name in public;
   - Attempting to promote feelings of ill-will against SCs or STs or disrespecting any deceased person held in high esteem;
   - Imposing or threatening a social or an economic boycott;
   - Preventing SCs or STs from undertaking the following activities will be considered an offence under the amended

[26] See for example, Brief Report of the National Consultation on 20 Years of SC and ST Prevention of Atrocities Act 1989, 11 Aug 2009, available at http://www.ncdhr.org.in/others/11_Aug_Consultation_Report.pdf, accessed on 9 June 2015

law: (a) using common property resources, (b) entering any place of worship that is open to the public, and (c) entering an educational health care institution.

b) *Expansion of provisions related to sexual violence against SC / ST women*: Due to the increased incidence of sexual offences against SC and ST women, provisions related to the same have been elaborated upon and strengthened. Assaulting or sexual exploiting an SC or ST woman was an offence under the original law. The amended law adds that: (a) intentionally touching an SC or ST woman in a sexual manner without her consent, or (b) using words, acts or gestures of a sexual nature, or (c) dedicating an SC or ST women as a devadasi to a temple, or any similar practice will also be considered an offence. Consent has now been defined - as 'a voluntary agreement through verbal or non-verbal communication'. In addition, a proviso [Proviso 1 to S. 3 (l)(w)] states that a woman belonging to a Scheduled Caste or a Scheduled Tribe who does not offer physical resistance to any act of a sexual nature is not by reason only of that fact, is to be regarded as consenting to the sexual activity. This is due to the power dynamics that exist between the perpetrator and the victim, as a result of which the victim may be unable to offer physical resistance to the sexual violence inflicted on her. A second proviso further states that a woman's sexual history, including with the offender shall not imply consent or mitigate the offence. This is in line with a similar amendment brought about, some years ago, to the Indian Evidence Act in relation to the rape law.

c) *Presumption as to knowledge of caste of the victim*: S. 8 (c) has been inserted through the Amendment Act, which states as follows: "if the accused was having personal knowledge of the victim or his family, the Court shall presume that the accused was aware of the caste or tribal identity of the victim, unless the contrary is proved." The presumption of knowledge is intended to make it slightly easier for the prosecution to secure a conviction in cases tried under this law.

d) *Role of public servants*: The amended Act specifies that a non SC or ST public servant who neglects his duties relating to SCs or STs shall be punishable with imprisonment for a term of six months to one year. The provision regarding penal consequence for dereliction of duty is an important one. The amended law specifies these duties in S. 4(2), including:

- to read out to an informant the information given orally, and reduced to writing by the officer in charge of the police station, before taking the signature of the informant;
- to register a complaint or a First Information Report under this Act and other relevant provisions and to register it under appropriate sections of this Act;
- to furnish a copy of the information so recorded forthwith to the informant;
- to record the statement of the victims or witnesses;
- to conduct the investigation and file charge sheet in the Special Court or the Exclusive Special Court within a period of sixty days, and to explain the delay if any, in writing;
- to correctly prepare, frame and translate any document or electronic record;
- to perform any other duty specified in this Act or the rules made thereunder:

e) *Role of courts*: Under the original law, a Session Court at the district level is deemed to be Special Court to provide speedy trials for these offences related with atrocities on the Dalits. A Special Public Prosecutor is appointed to conduct cases in this court. There were many designated courts which were conducting trials under this law, along with handling cases on other issues. This led to delay in disposal of cases, as well as to a very poor rate of conviction. To remedy this, the amended law specifies that an Exclusive Special Court must be established at the district level to try offences under the Act. In districts with fewer cases, a Special Court may be established to try offences. An adequate number of courts must be established to ensure that cases are disposed of within two months. Appeals of these courts shall lie with the high court, and must be disposed of within three months. A Public Prosecutor and Exclusive Public Prosecutor shall be appointed for every Special Court and Exclusive Special Court respectively.

f) *Rights of victims and witnesses*: The amended law adds a chapter (Chapter IV A) on the rights of victims and witnesses. In S. 15 A, it emphasizes on the duty of the State to protect the rights of victims and witnesses, and lists out various facets of such a protection. The provisions read as follows:

(1) It shall be the duty and responsibility of the State to make arrangements for the protection of victims, their dependents, and witnesses against any kind of intimidation or coercion or inducement or violence or threats of violence.

(2) A victim shall be treated with fairness, respect and dignity and with due regard to any special need that arises because of the victim's age or gender or educational disadvantage or poverty.

(3) A victim or his dependent shall have the right to reasonable, accurate, and timely notice of any Court proceeding including any bail proceeding and the Special Public Prosecutor or the State Government shall inform the victim about any proceedings under this Act.

(4) A victim or his dependent shall have the right to apply to the Special Court or the Exclusive Special Court, as the case may be, to summon parties for production of any documents or material, witnesses or examine the persons present.

(5) A victim or his dependent shall be entitled to be heard at any proceeding under this Act in respect of bail, discharge, release, parole, conviction or sentence of an accused or

any connected proceedings or arguments and file written submission on conviction, acquittal or sentencing.

(6) Notwithstanding anything contained in the Code of Criminal Procedure, 1973, the Special Court or the Exclusive Special Court trying a case under this Act shall provide to a victim, his dependent, informant or witnesses—

(a) the complete protection to secure the ends of justice;

(b) the travelling and maintenance expenses during investigation, inquiry and trial;

(c) the social-economic rehabilitation during investigation, inquiry and trial; and

(d) relocation.

The courts are empowered to take measures for protecting the rights of victims and witnesses, such as:

a. concealing the names and addresses of the witnesses in its orders or judgments or in any records of the case accessible to the public;
b. issuing directions for non-disclosure of the identity and addresses of the witnesses;
c. take immediate action in respect of any complaint relating to harassment of a victim, informant or witness and on the same day, if necessary, pass appropriate orders for protection.

Agenda for the Future

Through a long and arduous process spanning over several years, the civil society groups, lawyers, academics, activists and others have been able to advocate for amendments to the Atrocities Act, in order to address the gaps that existed between the law and the harsh ground reality. The government took a serious cognizance of these advocacy efforts, which ultimately fructified into the passing of the Amendment Act in December 2015. However, the duty of the State and civil society does neither stop nor end with this. In order to ensure that the amendments lead to the desired outcome, the government and civil society groups must work together towards the following short term agenda:

- create awareness among members of SC and ST communities about the provisions of the POA Act - including substantive, procedural and evidentiary provisions;
- build the perspectives of various stakeholders in the criminal justice system in order to make them fully understand the need for and context in which the amendments came to be effected, and the particular vulnerability faced by members of SC and ST communities;
- dispel the myth of misuse of the POA Act by the victims, which has seeped into the minds of all stakeholders of the criminal justice system, particularly the Public Prosecutors and the Judges;
- ensure a proper system of true transparency and just accountability in the administration of justice; and
- the government should provide for infrastructural facilities and adequate budgetary allocation to ensure that the amended law can be effectively and efficiently implemented.

Additionally, the establishment of an Equal Opportunity Commission has the potential for research and data gathering, monitoring and audit of the impact of laws and policies, policy intervention, grievance redress, developing, gathering and publishing evidence of all forms unfair discrimination, including those that are caste-based. The EOC was recommended by the Sachar Committee, and has been given shape to through a draft Bill by a group of experts under the chairpersonship of Dr. Madhava Menon in 2008.[27] A salient feature of the Bill was that it was applicable not only to the

[27] Equal Opportunity Commission: What, Why and How? Report by the Expert Group to Examine and Determine the Structure and Functions of an Equal Opportunity Commission set up by the Ministry of Minority Affairs, Government of India, February 2008, available at https://www.nls.ac.in/csseip/Files/Additional/EOC.pdf, accessed on 9th June 2015.

State and its entities but also to private enterprises and institutions. This is of significance in addressing the discrimination faced by Dalits at the hands of state and non-state actors. Since the EOC's mandate extends to all marginalized communities, discrimination and deprivation of equality based on the inter-sectionality of caste with gender, religion, class and other markers can potentially be addressed in a holistic manner. The EOC approved by the UPA government in February 2014 is a much-diluted version of the Bill and has been rightly criticized.[28] However, a robust, autonomous and independent EOC with effective powers and resources has the potential to be an important instrument to ensure equality for and non-discrimination of Dalits.

Additionally, the advocacy initiative for a comprehensive anti-discrimination law in India holds promise in contributing to the promotion of equality, particularly in entry into and treatment in educational institutions and workplaces (in the organized and unorganized sectors). It also has the potential to address discrimination in and deprivation of access to public services and infrastructure, including water, food, sanitation, housing, health and legal services. As in the case of the EOC, an anti-discrimination law would extend to all forms of discrimination including those that are caste-based.

In conclusion, atrocities and discrimination against Dalits could be addressed through a combination of legal strategies aimed specifically at the Dalit community, as well as those that extend to all marginalized communities, A complex issue such as the practice of untouchability, perpetration of caste-based atrocities and unjust and unfair discrimination requires a solution that addresses not only the manifestations but the root causes of it-the deep-rooted prejudices that have been transformed into entrenched and discriminatory social norms and practices through the caste system. A rights-based approach could be complemented by development-oriented policy

[28] See Irfan Engineer (2014), 'Cabinet Decision to Constitute Equal Opportunity Commission: Two Steps Backwards', Secular Perspective, 4 March

interventions. Needless to say, the rights-based approach through the law forms a limited yet significant part of a comprehensive, holistic, multi-pronged strategy that combines legal with social, economic and political approaches, towards restoring human rights and citizenship rights to Dalits in India.

The author is grateful to Prof S. Japhet - Director of Centre for the Study of Social Exclusion and Inclusive Policy (CSSEIP), National Law School of India, Bangalore and the CSSEIP for making the reports of studies undertaken by it available for this paper.

Ms. Saumya Uma, presently works as an Assistant Professor (Law) in Maharashtra National Law University (MNLU) Mumbai. Her areas of specialization are Constitutional law, family law, clinical legal education, human rights, and women and the law. She has previously worked as Assistant Professor in National Law School of India University (NLSIU) - Bangalore, and as Assistant Director of Centre for Study of Social Exclusion and Inclusive Policy at NLSIU. She has 22 years of work experience as a lawyer, law researcher, writer, campaigner, trainer and activist on gender, law and human rights. Her endeavour has been to facilitate access to justice for the poor and the marginalized, and to incorporate a rights-based perspective and a clinical approach into legal pedagogy.

Chapter 5

Contemporary Caste Conflict and Violence in Maharashtra

KAMBLE SANJAYKUMAR[1]

INTRODUCTION

Modern Maharashtrian society with its multi-dimensional character and multi-layered structure attracted the attention of many social scientists. Alongwith the intense social reform movements and Ambedkarite ideology, Maharashtrian society has been equally known for the caste conflicts especially for their intensity and political ramifications. There have been scores of social scientists who worked extensively on the caste issue, paid attention only to understand the character of caste per se; certainly not to unfold the dynamics of caste especially when it is in conflict with other caste. Caste conflict is something that social scientists cannot remain indifferent to. Similarly, it is not merely an offshoot of the mismanaged administrative issue or a law-order problem. Therefore a full-length study is required to comprehensively unearth the entire dynamics of caste conflict. Above all, it is necessary and pertinent for social scientists to seek a comprehensive framework for conflict resolution for caste confrontations. Therefore a full-length study combining both

[1] Krantijyoti Savitribai Phule Women's Studies Centre, Savitribai Phule Pune University, Pune - 7, E-mail: Kamble.sanjaykumar@gmail.com

the character of caste conflicts and conflict resolution are relevant and important. The present study seeks to analyse the character of caste conflict, intensity of the conflict, intervals of recurrence and conflict resolution. The analysis of violence is an important part of sociology. While it has sometimes been pushed to the margins of sociology, nevertheless, violence emerges repeatedly in the analysis of both everyday life and momentous social change; interpersonal relations and crime; governance and resistance; relations between states, north and south; and multiple varieties of modernity. New ways of making violence visible unsettle old notions of the nature and direction of violence; challenging assumptions that the disadvantaged are more violent than the powerful; and that modernity is increasingly less violent. Two features have marked the sociological analysis of violence: (a) disparate clusters of research on various forms of violence that have been the object of urgent social concern, and relatedly, (b) an overwhelming focus on forms of violence that are socially deviant and motivated by willful malice. The resulting literature is balkanized and disjointed, and yet narrowly focused. The systematic understanding of violence as a broad genus of social behavior has suffered accordingly. That discussion highlights the widely varying forms of violence in social life, including many instances that are neither driven by malicious intent nor socially repudiated. I consider the diverse motives that drive violent actions and the variant social acceptance or repudiation that they meet. I propose a generic definition of violence, freed of ad hoc restrictions, that encompasses the full population of violent social actions. This directs us to more systematic questions about violence in social life.

Since the decade 1960–70, sociological scholars and researchers are working on topics like caste system, pride and politics, as well as struggle between upper castes and Dalits. Similarly, in the field of women's studies, while dealing with issues of domestic violence, abuse of human rights, feminist movements, problems of Dalit women, there is also a deep study of the relation between caste, class, and gender.

In the past decade, India has suffered religious violence as well as caste conflicts. In fact, the nature of caste conflict is more deeply rooted and dates long before religious conflict. However as historian Dilip Menon says, caste conflict has not been theorized unlike religious conflict. Menon rightly points out that the attention received by issues of caste conflict has been limited to newspaper reports. In Anupama Rao's book on Dalits, the Caste Question: Dalits and the Politics of Modem India', it has been argued that there has been an unprecedented increase in the violence against Dalits after independence rather than in the pre-independence era. Against this background as well, there has not been much success in the theorization of caste conflict. The ultimate objective of the mutually beneficial financial relations among casteist forces, besides providing support and encouragement to the capitalism of underdeveloped traders, is also to postpone the decline of the power of the caste system. Therefore, it is also necessary to discuss religious conflict and caste politics in the light of the strengthening of the caste system.

If we think on the following opinions of Maratha Seva Sangh, Dalit Panther, Bhaiyalal Bhotmange-Khairlanji, and Prime Minister of India we can get the their views and stance on the caste atrocity. "The Government is also being blackmailed by threats of atrocities. They are not even allowed to work as per the rules. So please withdraw this law. Our campaign vouches for the provision of reservations to the poor from all castes and religions on a financial basis. Apart from Shiv Sena and BJP, no political party can talk against atrocities. We are getting a huge response from the rural areas, and we are confident that we will get entry into Lok Sabha". Shalinitai Patil, Lokmat, Aurangabad, Thurs. 16 April, 09 p. 8 'The Independence has brought nothing but injustice to the Dalits. Elections became a game but Dalit–workers, landless–labourers are still victims of slavery. All political parties are profiteers, the problems of the Dalit menial workers cannot be solved within the framework of race and religion. We want a total revolution. Partial development is impossible. Parliamentary petitions, requests, demands for concessions, elections, satyagrahas will not change the social situation."–(From the Dalit Panther Manifesto)" It is necessary that the governments of all states pay serious attention to the strict implementation of the Atrocities Act for crimes against the Dalits, and ensure proper justice for them. Because, of all the crimes that are filed under this Act, less than 30% receive a hearing from the court. These statistics are shocking, and the government of each State must give priority to accelerating the process of such cases."-Prime Minister, Dr. Manmohan Singh (Prabhat (Pune) Roopgandha, Sunday, 15th August, 2010, p. 2)" I don't want a job, I don't want money, I don't want a house, I just want justice. I want to live only to witness severe punishment meted out to those who ruthlessly murdered the dignity of not only my family but of all the Dalits." - Bhaiyalal Bhotmange (Khairlanji)

As we take note of the history of violence in the history of the human race, we realize that violence for the purpose of entertainment, human sacrifice due to blind superstition, slavery to avoid work, resorting to fratricide for the usurpation of property, torture and physical torment in the name of punishment, killing as punishment for disagreement, killing for power politics, rape as a celebration of victory, massacres to vent out depression, bloodshed as a solution to problems, have been accepted as an inevitable part of numerous eras of human civilization. But the situation has certainly changed today. It has almost been eradicated in the Western world. In other regions, its scope has remarkably decreased. If such events occur, they are concealed, if they come into the open, they are severely condemned. It is not easy to note and calculate the degree of violence in the past. It is like a tree withering away and dying quietly in the forest without the outer world having the least inkling of it. Even in the recent past, statistics about violence are rarely found. It is not easy to reach any conclusion about the prolonged struggle from the extreme cases of bloodshed in the intermediate period.

The major change seen today is in our readiness to actually act upon our violent instinct. According to the social scientist Norbert Elias, western modernization has accelerated a sense of civilization through self-control, long-term planning and sensitivity towards others' emotions and thoughts. Only the government would reserve the right to use violence and that too in an unbiased manner, only for the purpose of punishing wrong-doers. This would end the tension in the atmosphere and restrain instinctive violence for self-protection.

Whether violent behaviour, especially towards one's own species, is a part of man's intrinsic nature or a result of changing social reality is a matter of heated debate among scholars. (Kasbe and Raosaheb, p. 155) Dr. Raosaheb Kasabe says, man's basic nature is not violent. There are a number of myths about the ancient man in the mind of today's modern man. He believes that if today's civilized man is so violent, ancient man must certainly be much more violent. However, the reality is just the reverse. He was in fact the most peace-loving. As he began to bring about the development of his civilization, he began to become violent. If violence had been man's basic nature, an intrinsic part of him, the reality would have been the other way. That man was essentially peaceful and loving can be shown through the works of other human evolutionary researchers too (Kasabe and Raosaheb, p. 156).

In the current situation, the public has to face violence daily. Millions of people are dying of hunger and starvation. They succumb to minor diseases in the absence of proper medical aid. In the villages, half of the profiteering leaders have to resort to force to control the affairs. With the exception of grand industries, in the other factories and industries, goons maintained by the management and police torment the workers. Our women are constantly subject to injustice in our male-dominated society. Dowry killings, desertions are the proofs of this increasing violence. There are constant instances of Dalits being insulted, verbally abused, and occasionally beaten up by upper castes. As if all this were not enough, the public is always in fear of the Mafia that has proved inevitable to Hindu Fascists and political parties.

Even though we say that India is a peace-loving nation, five to six types, of violent take place in our country. The first of these is violence on religious grounds, usually called communal riots. Of this first type of violence, we see instances like Hindu-Muslim riots and the violence against Christians in the recent times, or 20 years ago the issue of Khalistan and Hindu-Sikh riots in Punjab after Indira

Gandhi's assassination, constantly coming up in Indian politics. The second type of violence, where the caste system is still prevalent in the economic set-up, a few people have the power and the means in their hands, chiefly they own land and all the others must be bonded labourers, working on the fields as per the master's orders, on wages decided by the master, and his wife and children are also the master's slaves. We claim that there is no slavery in India, but in areas like Bihar, land owners still hire private armies and control the public by force; bonded labour is a kind of slavery. The exploitation that this system leads to is the second type of violence seen in India. The third type is violence due to social causes. In this, we find violence against the Dalits under the pretext of reservations, and it may be in groups or by an individual. But we see a great deal of violent sentiment against Dalits. The source of the fourth type of violence is the governing mechanism itself, which we call State Sponsored Violence. That means, in order to control the movements that take place in a democratically sanctioned manner, gunshots are fired after a certain limit or lathi-charge is used. State Sponsored Violence can be understood in the context of a movement, rail roko, or rasta roko when the mob becomes violent and attacks the police. The fifth type includes the bomb blasts, accidents or eccentric firing, brought about discreetly by terrorist groups in the last 20 years. We cannot ignore terrorism saying that such instances are world-wide.

We do not realise that these forms of violence are not a part of political philosophy, nor are they a part of political mechanism. The Naxalites, for whom violence is a central part of political philosophy and political mechanism, constitute the sixth form of violence. However, the groups who accept violence as a mode of thinking never gain sympathy from the public.

Ambedkar rejected violence not as a philosophical value (unlike Gandhiji) but because he realized that violence is not effective as the chief form of revenge. Ambedkar's philosophy was an intellectual one; it may be described "as the philosophy of social liberation. It was necessary to accept the caste system was a reality. In this regard, Ambedkar stands out from the Marxists. The Marxists saw the bourgeoisie as a revolutionary class. They ignored cultural and social aspects. The tendency of the Congress to turn a blind eye to the tradition of exploitation and suppression in India was also evident. Briefly, the capacity to kill someone, even for the upkeep of 'values', is demeaning to humanity. Even if it is convenient to philosophize it, this is not in the interest of the society. Those who take to arms against the system are seen to give birth to a parallel system of terror. Violence obstructs democracy.

It is commonly believed that sociology is related to caste struggle while power struggle is more important in politics. The power struggle is between the public at large and the nobility. In this form of power struggle, contradictory factions related to issues like right to power, prestige, and development start forming. There is a great contention between public associations and the mutual relations, pride and power politics of the ruling classes.

In the edition of November-December 2011, the Journal for the Eradication of Superstition has published the views of various scholars following a debate on the topic of 'Caste groupism, caste conflict and end of casteism'. In the article 'Caste makes waste', Rajan Khan says that India is on the tip of an extremely perilous and destructive volcano. Every Indian harbours a sentiment of extreme hatred, rage, disdain, envy and fury towards other castes. Because it is possible to practice groupism in the name of democracy, each one nurtures immense pride about his caste. But in the mind of each one, the mention of another caste is an insult, a disgusting word. (Khan Rajan, 2011; p. 89)

After India won its independence, the people took some time to understand the meaning of 'democracy' and as they gradually began to understand it, instead of becoming wise, national citizens, they started taking greater pride in their own caste and religious identity. To put it frankly, they interpreted democracy according to their personal convenience and individual profit Man is used to living in groups since the ancient times. This instinctive tendency of groupism came up in democracy, and realizing that abusing democracy was not the task of one man, and that it would be easier to exploit it systematically as a group, people started abusing democracy at their will. Caste and religions were already there to provide the grounds for such groups. It was very easy to found their groups on this basis. These groups then gained rapidly in strength and within 20-25 years of independence, they started clamouring for their rights and expressing dissatisfaction with the system (Khan Rajan, 2011; p. 89).

Today, even if caste system is not in total control of the contemporary society, it is still highly influential in the social organization of independent India. Due to the influence of caste, class and male dominance, no note is taken of the daily suppression of the dignity of Dalits, tribals and women folk. These events should be considered as a part of oppressive male dominance. It is difficult to find adequate details, statistics, or academic information about these issues due to the silence and apathy with regard to laws for the prevention exploitation, social ostracism and the individualization of such crimes. In this article, detailed notice will be taken of the important caste conflicts in India and the related literature. Often, higher castes claim that the Dalits themselves are responsible for the crimes against them, the news are falsified and that the cases are purposely filed. Therefore, it is also important to understand basic issues like 'What is abuse?', 'How is it related to caste?', 'What role does gender play in this?' and others. We must also realize that in the influence of caste and male dominance, the issues of Dalits. Tribals and women folk subtly affect every aspect of their lives. That is why it is essential to understand this crucial question in its historical context and then think of it in the contemporary social setting. For this, it is also necessary to see how the nature of injustice and abuse against the Dalits is changing in the modem globalized world, and how the social system is undergoing a change child's maintaining its basic nature.

For this article, a detailed study has been undertaken regarding the issue of the renaming of the Marathwada University in Maharashtra taking account of the stance of the Dalit Panther against violence during the 1970s, the conflict between upper castes and Dalits, Khairlanji and other instances of violence against the Dalits. While studying the nature of injustice against the Dalits in the contemporary social setting the issue of 'honour killing' will be taken into account. Also, efforts will be made to understand structural violence and community violence in the light of the Ranveer Sena of the upper classes and the violent struggle of landless Naxalite Dalits in Bihar. This will help realize that 'there is no resistance without organization, no protection without resistance and no self-confidence without protection'.

In the Indian Brahmin male dominated society, the idea that women must accept the injustice meted out to her by the male member without the least protest, is widespread. That is why, the history as well as the present of such an oppressive social order is equally oppressed. As we take an account of the injustice and violence against Dalit women in India, we realize that its scope is extremely large. The caste conflict is expressed through the male dominated social order and hence the women fall prey to oppression. This study makes an effort to understand the consequences of the injustice towards women. Violence is used as an 'oppressive weapon' to preserve the established social order. However, while describing the nature of injustice against Dalit women, the criterion of 'caste' is seen to be largely neglected. Since the influence of Brahmin male dominance is prevalent on women as well, upper caste women with such a mindset also give backing to the oppression of Dalit women. The criterion of 'woman' is certainly not homogenous, but the rift among them is increasing. Those who are influenced by the Brahmin upper caste ideals unjustly respond to the demand of rights for Dalit women. It may or may not be in the form of physical assault which gets noted in the government's statistics of caste oppression, but certainly proves harmful to the well-being of Dalit women. This has also been taken into account.

INDIAN SOCIETY: THE BACKING OF PATRIARCHY TO A SEMI-CAPITALIST AND SEMI-FEUDAL CASTE ORDER

The focus and tradition of today's middle and upper class is still

Brahmin dominated. That is why, even if today's middle class and upper class is composed of various castes, its cultural character is still majorly Brahminist. Although the nature of caste system has changed today and it is no longer the pillar of social order, it is still one of the important influences of social control in independent India. Similarly, as long as the vestiges of the regime of the casteist forces of Brahminists and capitalists who have enjoyed great power through the times are not completely eradicated, we cannot say that India has been freed from the caste system. Otherwise the constitution and legal policies based on caste and gender will have to continue. Because even though we claim to be modem, the core of Indian society is a half capitalist and half socialist community, strongly rooted in male dominance. This system has to be called Welfare State because the class that wields the power, namely great industrial societies, higher administrative staff, and the politicians running the Central and State Governments hails from specific Supremist castes, and they are still rooted in Brahminist and Ernpirist relations. And it is called a system close to the capitalist because the old system did not come to an end, but was given a new coating by the development of capitalism. Against this background, the current parliamentary system seems like a coating of democracy on a semi-capitalist administration. Indian citizens are faced with the challenge of converting this into a meaningful democracy.

Caste system is still functioning as an oppressive system. Yet, it is not as though every member of the upper caste is casteist. Some people accept the modern way of thinking and their behaviour is not affected by caste differences. This outook must be positively welcomed. This social order has been created carefully for proper management. When we say it is exploitative, it is controlling the social affairs through various factors, by means of oppression.

The documentation of the injustice against tribals is done in the form of reports or articles, police force, periodicals, newspapers, academic research and revolutionary movements. In the articulation of these incidents, various instances of injustice against Dalits and tribals were recounted one after the other, or detailed information was given about a single incident. Holding the caste system responsible for all this, it was met sometimes with fury, sometimes with sympathy.

ANALYSIS OF CASTE ATROCITY AGAINST DALITS POST 1970

Due to the influence of law, modem social life, the spread of some modem views, the scenario of extreme untouchability was pushed back into the past. Besides, through steps like reservation, scholarships, and different programs, the government made efforts for the progress of the Dalits. At the same time, with Ambedkar's struggle, political awareness and spread of education, the miserable, supplicant Dalit became proud and courageous. Untouchability was banned. The government carried out various programs for the progress of the Dalits and they became confident. Many higher castes started feeling insecure because of these three developments. Some socio-political parties also supported this sentiment of the higher castes. This created a false sense of touchiness towards their traditional socio-cultural position in the society. The higher castes failed to see the distinction between poverty and racial injustice. Many upper castes wrongly started perceiving the white-collared Dalit, the Dalit labourer on a tiny piece of land, the Dalit cowherd as their competitors. In the 60 years of independence, the relations between the Dalits and the upper castes were strained and suspicious because the upper castes did not believe that the Dalits have the right to progress. Believing that concessions to Dalits would hinder their own progress, the upper castes nurtured resentment against the Dalits.

The Hindu doctrines and philosophy that justify caste and class system have become outdated and void. Some reformist Hindus and Dalits started feeling that this philosophy was responsible for creating rifts among humans. Dalits were discontented by the social misery imposed on them by Hinduism. They felt the need to redefine their existence and pride. The awakened Dalit society started clamouring for a new social culture. They tried to define their social position. For this, they upheld cultural nihilism. Such a cultural struggle was a major reason for the rise of Dalit Panther.

In the book 'Dalit Panther Movement', Dr. Lata Murugkar says, "The Dalit youths were in great unrest because of the increasing injustice in different forms. The struggle was on for freedom from the exploitation and suppression by higher castes. They wanted the leaders to take a strong, firm and revolutionary step against it. However the inert leadership was unable to relieve their misery. Similarly the government also failed to prevent the abuse. The Leftist party was also not successful. As mentioned in the booklet 'The graph of the bravery of the youth in Mumbai', the chief reason for the rise of Dalit Panther is the increasing injustice against the Dalits! At that time, there was not a single day in Maharashtra when there were no attacks on the Dalits. In fact, a rise in these incidents has been noted in the report of the Perumal Committee in 1971.

The newspapers did not take proper note of the report of the Perumal Committee that was published in 1971. The Perumal Committee had diagnosed backwardness and carelessness as the main reasons for the laxity in the execution of the Act for Eradication of Untouchability. The Maratha Sugar Barons and the higher caste members in the state actively participated in the injustice against the Dalits.' Caste' had become an important criterion in the rural elections.

Due to the increasing racism among the upper castes who had newly obtained political and financial power and whose social superiority was uninterrupted, and increasing awareness of Fundamental Rights among Dalits led to constant overt and covert conflicts between the two (Murugkar and Lata, 1995; p. 47-48). According to the information provided by the Home Minister Mirdha in the Parliament on 19th August 1970, between 1967 and 1969, 63 Dalits were murdered in Maharashtra, 332 in UP, 76 in Punjab and 34 in Gujarat. (Appendix, p. 48)

In the 1980s, the orthodox Hindus who were irritated by the demand for equal human rights by the Dalits in every sphere of activity resorted to opposition impose the traditional lower status upon them. While their Dalits were being attacked in the 1980s, they would pounce upon the Dalits during their processions, in their houses and on their community while shouting the slogan of "Hail Bhavani Hail Shivaji". They believed that they could achieve a great feat (?) in the name of Chhatrapati Shivaji. In this period, high caste youths started blaming their unemployment on the concessions given to the Dalits. It seems everyone objected to the threefold program of the religious conversion of the Dalits, the modernization and civilization of society and providing concessions to Dalits in the process of modernization. In this period, the blame for the attacks in the rural areas was pushed onto the profane language of the Dalits. However, when Dalits were being murdered, their limbs cut off, eyes pulled out, their sisters were being raped, and they were being paraded naked in the village, in such a situation it was but natural for the oppressed to react in profane language.

Sulabha Brahme in her 1979 book 'Dalit-Caste Hindu Tension: A Radical Analysis' has given detailed information about the atrocities on the Dalits. In 1991, Kumar Shiralkar in the booklet 'Social Injustice and the Labour Class' analyzed the reason for this and the direction for protest, and expounded that the Labour bond of the menial working classes could truly play a crucial role against social injustice and atrocity.

The Committee against Injustice made a detailed analysis on the events in Belchi, Agra, Pantnagar, Marathwada, Bajitpur and other places in the special article 'The Marathwada Riots: A Report'. 'The Committee against Injustice' had been established to analyze the role of the caste system, inter–class tension and caste based organizations in the atrocities against the Dalits. This Committee studied the injustice against the Dalits in Marathwada (Nanded, Parbhani, Aurangabad) and Maharashtra, and determining the pattern of the abuse, wrote articles promoting unity among the Dalits, poor farmers and farm hands in order to restrain this oppression. (EPW - Vol -14, No-19; 12 May 1979. p. 845–52)

In the initial article of 'Satyashodhak Marxist' (March 1982), through the article 'Riots in Marathwada: Going beyond Thought' pointed out the limits of one-sided caste conflict which was the reason for the inertness of the Leftist organizations towards Dalit injustice, and propagated the multi-faceted historical argument for the establishment of a new approach based on caste struggle.

Following the renaming of the Marathwada University after Dr. Babasaheb Ambedkar, Prof. Gopal Guru wrote an article analyzing the reasons for the atrocities inflicted upon the Dalits by the upper caste Hindus, 'Understanding Violence against Dalits in Marathwada', on 26th February 1994 in the 'Economic and Political Weekly'. In this article, while raising some important issues, Prof. Gopal Guru made a comparison of the five riots that took place in Marathwada in 1978. He said that the riots in 1978 were of extremely high intensity that destroyed the lives, property and dignity of the Dalits. He pointed out that it was necessary to think about the violence against the Dalits in Marathwada in the context of the level of social and financial progress and their ownership of land. While determining which castes were subjected to violence and in which regions, he also stated that not only were the Dalit women attacked by upper classes, but the huts of the handicapped too were cruelly burned down. Besides physical injury, the important and useful goods of the Dalits were stolen and the food and grains were also destroyed.

These rioters had also attacked the supporters of the then Chief Minister Sharad Pawar. In this period, the higher castes not only attacked the Dalits but even the Muslims. Besides they also attacked Government property such as Government hospitals, railway stations, offices of Grampanchayat, State Transport buses, schools of Zilla Parishad, telephone system and government godowns. The rioters brought about the destruction of property especially in the areas affected by the riots.

In this article, Prof. Gopal Guru had proved that the Marathas were responsible for the violence against the Dalits and the destruction of Dalits' property as well as public property. It was shown that the violence of the upper classes was not a result of the actions of the Dalits but rather founded in the protests of the Dalits. Development Studies Centre, Mumbai prepared a number of research reports related to the issue of violence against the Dalits and published them. This Centre published the research report of the Committee for Preservation of Democratic Rights, Mumbai, 'Violence against Dalits in Marathwada -The Caste Cauldron of Maharashtra' in 'Politics, Power and Poverty in South Asia' (Vol-XI/ No; 2 & 3 - 2003). At that time the events against the Dalits were extremely complicated, that is why they tried to analyse its subtle and novel reasons. This report was then translated into Marathi and was published by Sugava Publication.

According to Mukherjee, generally caste riots are due to the character of the castes. That is why, in Bihar, Maharashtra, Tamil Nadu and other states where financial backwardness is linked to caste, there are constant conflicts between castes. According to Vagishwari, between 1950 and 1970 the financial status of the subcastes among the Harijans and other castes has improved.

According to Sinha, atrocities against the Dalits, rape of their women, their insult and murder are a caste was against the Dalits. According to another study in the EPW, due to the emergence of rich farmers in Bihar, many labourers came into being from various castes and for their relations; class struggles were seen taking place. Thus we see castes being divided by the class struggle. But on the other hand, the Chambhars or the Harijan labourer does not mingle with the Brahmins and Bhumihars who are one with their class position. In independent India, the farmers of the backward classes are the highest on the scale of the caste system and are seen fighting for their social and political position. In Bihar, during the period of public government, the backward classes had been encouraged to fight against the upper castes. The general feeling at this time was that the higher castes are higher classes and lower castes, lower classes.

The backward classes are on a mean position in the caste hierarchy. The public government in Bihar brought about a change in this order through various programs. The political influence of Brahmins was destroyed in this. A study done in Andhra Pradesh clearly shows that Settibalija and Harijan castes are socially considered economically deprived while Kapu Brahmins, Devanga are influential.

According to the Belchi, Agra, Pantnager, Marathwada Committees against violence and the injustice against scheduled castes in Bajitpur and other regions, such instances are a result of the caste system which includes class system. In a detailed analysis of the issue the Committee noted some important points showing the relation of the caste system to the system of production:

Caste system is an effective mechanism of economic exploitation. Due to their higher caste, they acquire prestige and political power and their position in the caste hierarchy is strengthened. Also, caste hierarchy is dependent on land ownership and financial status. Means of production are determined by caste (especially in rural areas). Riots are a symbol of economic relations. The transactions of individuals and groups are controlled and regulated in the framework of caste. B.R. Ambedkar's rightly observed that caste is not only division of society but also Division of Labour. Caste is a division and also a way of thinking. Caste and religion are used to preserve the class organization. Caste is a part of feudal thinking.

This report of the Committee will aid our discussion of constancy and change related to caste and class. Caste is an important part of Indian social reality. It is an exploitative mechanism related to production. In a report of a village in Punjab presented by Singh, the farm worker and the rich farmer in that region were Jat Sikhs and the chief demand in that village was for a hike in wages. That is why the higher and medium farmers there came together against the farm workers. Here we see caste and class having come together. In North India, the following important factors are seen as responsible in accelerating caste and class violence. This includes non–observation of the Minimum Wages Act created by the administration for the rural labourers, lack of good employment opportunities, rigid caste based social organization, abuse of lower caste women, lack of industrialization and other programs, usurpation of public fields by landlords, lack of irrigation facilities in rural areas and especially in the fields of lower caste farmers, denial of political rights to the rural poor, alliance between landlords and the police, fight for political superiority and caste and class violence in rural areas. (Hindwan Sudhir, 'Caste Violence in India,' Global Vision Publishing House, New Delhi-2 Page No. 12)

Violence/abuse – Inherent Aspect of Caste: Major Points

Dalits are oppressed all over India. Even the so called modern state of Maharashtra is not an exception to this. The oppressors are higher caste, rich people. Their policy is to maintain the Dalits in their downtrodden state. They cannot tolerate Dalits speaking up for justice. They are so supercilious in their pride or their caste that a protesting Dalit is usually not kept alive. When attacking Dalits, they do not take into account whether they are men/women/children. All of them are cruelly attacked. In the attacks, their sense of superiority is evident and mob attacks are prevalent. Any trivial reason is enough to trigger violence. The caste-related instincts in the mind only need an excuse to come out in the form of violence. The higher caste does not want any reasoning for the crimes committed by Dalits or enquiry into the action. In their eyes, Dalits are criminals for having committed the crimes. The established upper castes have political asylum, and hence they do not fear the law or administration. The attacks on the Dalits are sometimes planned and sometimes spontaneous. For centuries, the system deprived Dalits of their legal rights and inflicted injustice upon them which is shameful for humanity. Seeing that this prevails even in the 21st century, we must say that caste system gives birth to inhuman violence, as the above points exemplify.

Caste is determined by birth and whilst national law outlaws discrimination against people of low castes, in reality there is still widespread oppression and violence against the Dalit people. Dalit means 'broken' or 'ground down'. Many people still use the word 'untouchable' which indicates the extreme discrimination which affects Dalit people. Even today, most higher caste people would not marry a Dalit person, invite them into their house or share food with them. Recent statistics indicate that every week in Dalit communities across India there are: • 13 murders • 5 Dalit homes burnt • 6 Dalit people kidnapped or abducted • 21 Dalit women raped Atrocities against Dalit people are a daily occurrence. The Scheduled Castes and Scheduled Tribes (Prevention of Atrocities) Act 1989 in India defines the type of abuses; which are illegal, including: • forcing Dalit people to eat obnoxious substances • assaulting a Dalit woman with intent to dishonour and outrage her modesty • using a position of dominance to sexually exploit a Dalit woman • corrupting or fouling a Dalit water source. By listing these and other offences, the law reveals the awareness of the many-ways in which Dalit and Tribal people are subjected to indignity, violence and abuse. It is estimated that a crime is committed against a Dalit person every 18 minutes. The problem for many is not the law but the lack of political will, at local and national levels, to apply to it. In 2006, the official conviction rate for Dalit atrocity cases was just 5.3%. The statistics are horrifying: • In rural areas, 37.8% of government run schools make Dalit children sit separately from other children. In 27.6% of rural villages, Dalit are prevented from entering police stations • in 33% of rural villages, public health workers refuse to enter Dalit homes • 48.4% of Dalit villages are denied access to water sources • in 70% of rural villages, Dalit and non-Dalit people cannot eat together. Dalit women experience triple discrimination based on their caste, their economic situation and their gender. In rural India, 70% of Dalit women are illiterate. In the Southern States, thousands of girls are forced into prostitution before they reach puberty. Temple prostitutes or Joghinis (literally 'female servants of God') are usually Dalits Once dedicated, the girl is unable to marry, is forced to become a prostitute for upper caste members and eventually auctioned off to an urban brothel. The International Dalit Solidarity Network states: *"Violence, including sexual assault, is used by dominant castes as a social mechanism for humiliating entire Dalit communities."*

(http://www.overcomingviolence.org/fileadmin/dov/images/women_campain/Dalit%252 eet.pdf)

According to Merton and Nisbet, all the factors that are essential for a great revolution in society are seen in the Indian society. These are as follows:

In the course of modernization after Independence, the social condition of the upper castes increased very rapidly as compared to the scheduled castes. Due to special concessions, more than a change in the living conditions and social situations of the scheduled caste, their ambitions and desires soared higher.

The gap between the Dalit and upper caste groups increased. As the educated Dalit youths became aware of their exploitation and deprivation, the offensive and rebellious Dalit Panther came into being.

(Murugkar Lata, Dalit Panther Movement, 1995, Sugava Publication, Pune-30)

Attacks on Dalits in Villages

It was said that renaming riots would be restricted to cities and not villages. However riots reached the villages in no time. The nature of riots was the same everywhere. Initially disregard towards Dr. Babasaheb Ambedkar or Mahatma Buddha's photo or idol, ill-talk flowed by destruction. 200-300 people should attack Dalit localities and destroy. How can a group of 30-40 oppose 300-400? Who would come to their rescue? There were horrible incidents in some villages. Pochiram Kamble of Tembhurni was beaten by 100-150 people and later burnt alive because he was the President of Dr. Babasaheb Ambedkar Birthday Celebrations Committee. He was therefore uprooted and Dalit locality was burned down. The riot at Eklara was similarly shameful. It was openly announced in the town that houses of Dalits were to be burned down and houses of neo-Buddhists were burnt accordingly. Even Maang houses were burnt. Crops from fields of Dalits were fed to cattle. Women of Sugaon can still be seen with marks of axe-attacks. While hitting them, the attackers were shouting, “Where are your Ambedkar and Buddha? Will you give their slogans now? Will you join rallies?” Such stem people cannot be called human. How can such inhuman acts occur openly in a democratic state?

All acts of violence in villages were backed by the prestigious people in the village. However people did not support such acts in some villages. There was opposition and so some villages remained safe. However such good people had to face the agony of the village (Padma Lohgaonkar, ‘Razakar in Marathwada’, Bayja, Year 3, Volume 2, March-April 1979).

Political System, Unique Identity and Violence

In a society where there are plural identities, if the political system recognizes only one identity, it is bound to create problems. This is because other identities are thus denied political space. Complications in affairs related to politics increase. Democracy is person–centric but logic of politics based on elections depends on the principles of majority party. Due to identity of the majority all other minority identities are thrown out of the perimeter and become foreign. The dalit slaughtering in Ramabai Ambedkar Nagar in Mumbai on 11th July 1997 is historical in several aspects.

50 rounds of firing in Ramabai Ambedkar Nagar in Ghatkopar, Mumbai on 11th July 1997 took toll of 10 and injured 26. People saw that the statue of Dr. Ambedkar in the locality was abused. People expressed their objection in silence near the statue. Shivsena-BJP government sent Inspector Manohar Kadam of State Reserve Force to the place of event. Standing several metres away from the statue they fired the pedestrians. Then they entered the lanes in locality near Gunny Art and fired. Manohar Kadam was arrested after fifteen years but he was roaming around freely till then and those that were injured and the activists were tirelessly pleading for justice. Comrade Vilas Ghogare was deeply moved by all this and he committed suicide. Anand Patwardhan prepared a documentary on it named ‘Jai Bhim Comrade’. Ranvir Sena of upper class brutally massacred 58 Dalits

to support the upper class government in Laxmanpur Bathe of Johanabad in Bihar on 1 December 1997. Mostly women and children were killed in this incident.

Rulers of all castes are organizing people into anti-revolutionary groups and using them against public conflict. This is a favourite pastime of political systems. State and police force openly allow communal and casteist organizations and parties that they should target a particular community in a particular period and openly resort to dacoit, rape, burning, massacre and so on. After all the destructive violence is over, political system steps ahead as 'protectors of peace and good-will'. The oppressed are further tortured in the name of law and order. Political leaders that commit crimes and security forces are never punished. Bal Thakare who designed the 1992 riot, Lalkrishna Adwani who was the architect of Babri Masjid demolition, Narendra Modi who championed the massacre in Gujarat, Manohar Kadam who fired in Ramabai Ambedkar Nagar, Buddhadev Bhattacharya who caused Nandigram event, Raj Thakare who threatened foreign elements, Congress leaders who slaughtered the Sikhs are all roaming free with respect. Those who experience government violence either accept it or express their sensitivities against it. The increasing violence and insecurity today is prompting people to take shelter in caste-system largely. People feel secure within their caste.

The massacre in Mumbai was the biggest such event so far. Muslims were purposefully targeted after the demolition of Babri Masjid. Dalits were next. Abuses of Dr. Ambedkar's statue followed by massacre in Ambedkar Nagar were all steps of a fascist programme. (Reference: 'Report on massacre in Ramabai Ambedkar Nagar 1997', published by Ramabai Ambedkar Nagar Massacre Objection and Justice Support Committee, Mumbai, page 5)

Dr. Babasaheb Ambedkar's statue in Ramabai Ambedkar Nagar had been abused. Upper classes feel the need of abusing Dr. Babasaheb's statue in order to act against the Dalits. They are seen to make comments full of hatred, against the Dalits. Balasaheb had written objectionably against Babasaheb's statue in Shivesena's journal Saamna. He had drawn attention to April 1996's 'Saamna' issue talking about 'Statues are increasing and how should they be removed' (As mentioned above page 40). Arun Shoure and Durga Bhagwat go to the extent of calling Babasaheb a traitor. They write in this way to shape their readers' mentality and on this background Manohar Joshi, the then Chief Minister ordered to find out the person who abused the statue in July 1997 and declared the 'Maharashtra Statue Abuse By-law 1997' (As mentioned above, page 40). By this law, erecting statues was banned and protection of statues was entrusted to the erection committee. However the original problem has been side-tracked and thought has been given to only moving away statues.

Statues of Phule and Ambedkar are not just sculptures but have become identities of Dalits. These statues are not useful even for paying tributes. No rituals for eradicating sins can be done before these statues. They are useful to keep their self-respect throbbing. Hindu community gives credit of their emancipation to crores of lifeless deities. Similarly, Dalits will worship their emancipator. Hindu community can tolerate smearing their idols with milk but if Ambedkar's statue is abused in any way, Dalits get enraged and embrace death. Violence on Dalits, either cruel, animal-like or minor is an indispensable part of their lives. When feminist activists brought violence on women to the forefront, dowry-deaths were on the top as compared to other oppression. So their work basically revolves around dowry-death and caste-violence is comparatively not that important. Violence on Dalits in India is due to capitalism and patriarchy. If oppression is complete and effective in daily life then even the victim is not aware of the oppression.

The Issue of Communal Identity of Castes

All castes in India express themselves in their shells. Within the broad identities of Dalit tribals, there are their own identities hidden but these sub-castes accept their dalit identity during the period of social strife. They realize that they have been enslaved and suppressed and so Dalit tribals stand up with their 'original' identity.

Therefore the fight of Dalit tribals addresses the idealism of transformation overtly. As against this, the question of OBC communal identity is graver. These castes comprise 52% of Indian population and they are not aware of oppression and suppression. Some of the castes that want to assert their identity are not even aware that they are backward. OBC constitute the multitude of our population but they are putting their casteist relations on political agenda. In such a situation it is difficult that the extensive OBC groups get a communal identity.

Caste hatred is no more a topic of fiery lectures and writings. Even reports of lectures given by casteists and communals, without any fear of the government are shocking. Communals have gone even beyond that. Criminalization of politics is accompanied by making the society criminal. Gangsters, leaders of any and all parties plan riots and massacres. Police support these things. Such riots suppress the voice of farmers, workers and women.

Dalit population through experience of oppression and torture is ready for defence from inheritance from Ambedkar. M.N. Srinivas exemplifies how inter-caste competition murders Indian politics. Farmers of Kamma caste in Andhra Pradesh support communism. Reddys who are in opposition to this caste support Congress. When Congress was ruling in near-by Mysore, Lingayat and Wokkaling castes were fighting to get Congress in their pockets. Maharashtra and Madras were witnessing Brahmin *versus* anti-Brahmin conflict. Bihar was witnessing internal strife between Congress amongst landowner Bhumihars and Rajputs. Neighbouring Uttar Pradesh has lower castes united. A conflict may start there between Rajputs and Chambhar for political power (Guha Ramchandra, page 702). Srinivas adds, "Caste is becoming powerful these days even in the north these days. One has to see if caste-conflict in north becomes as grave as in south" (As mentioned above, page 702).

Awakening of self-respect in Dalits is parallel to communal conflicts. There were violent riots in the decade of 1990 in rural areas. Dalit community suffered the maximum in these riots. But the reason of these conflicts was physical. It is a fact that upper classes and OBC communities own lands. It is also a fact that Dalits cultivate these lands. However the conflict was expressed in the form of theoretical roles. Upper classes could not tolerate that Dalit community demanded increased wages and humane treatment and they wanted to curb it by cruel action.

One stage of this conflict was an extreme southern district of Tamilnadu. The conflict here was between Thivar and Dalits. Thivar is a group of middle-class landowners that is newly getting shaped. Dalits were landless. Any reason was enough to strike a riot among them. Demand for increase in wages could be a reason. These castes doing low jobs till now were aspiring for higher bureaucrat *i.e.*, jobs now and this also could become a reason. Dalits had become more courageous and refused to accept tea in separate cups in hotels. When Thivars erected a statue of their ear Muthuram, Dalits erected a statue of Dr. Babasaheb Ambedkar. Some bloody riots were due to their destruction of statues erected by opposing groups. These conflicts were not only physical but also theoretical. They were repetitive and destructive. That one decade saw the death of nearly hundred people in Tamilnadu.

Oppressing Dalits was not a prerogative of just the upper caste Hindus. Landowner Jat Sikhs also could not tolerate the confidence of working class. Dalit Sikhs were striving for lands and entry into Gurudwaras, right from the beginning of twentieth century. Both of these were controlled by Jat Sikhs. Some Dalit Sikhs tried to establish their own sect 'Aridharam" to escape this. The recent green revolution opened new avenues for the lower castes. They started going to cities and factories for livelihood. They also set up their own business. Many Sikhs also started settling abroad. They sent money to their relatives from there.

Another conflict is representative. It started over the ownership of Gurudwara at Talhan. This town is on the boundaries of Jalandar. This Gurudwara was built in memory of saint Baba Nihal Singh. The Gurudwara construction committee was prominently dominated by Jats. All the decisions were therefore taken by Jats. Dalit Sikhs sought representation on the committee for a long time but they always were refused. Finally they decided to approach the court. During the trial of the case in January 2003, Jats decided to socially ostracize Dalits. Dalits went on a strike to show their objection. Six months later, there was a terrible war in the two groups in the town-fair. As a result of government interference, two Dalit Sikhs got representation on the committee. However they had to keep a beard and hair as per the tradition.

Information procured regarding crimes in a period of 11 years from 1999 to 2009. The number of cases of oppression under SC/ST oppression regulation by-law 1989, between the periods from 1999 to 2009 was 11,591 and 2723 respectively that is 14,314 in total. Of these scheduled castes were 426 and scheduled tribes were 527 in which the concerned were convicted whereas in 9111 Sc and 2764 ST cases, crime could not be proved. So the concerned were released as innocent. Court gives justice according to police-records and hearings. These instances prove how particular police-records were regarding complaints made under this law.

Pending cases of oppression against Scheduled Castes and Tribes at the end of 2009 are 71,767. These cases remain pending in the courts for years together. Criminals are free and so can seek ways of escaping. Evidences are destroyed and complainants are threatened to compromise. Those that were convicted as guilty in this period through documents submitted by police were only 527. Those that escaped are relatively many.

In the past few years, there was a series of oppression on Dalits, massacre etc. There were storming discussions on this in the Vidhan Sabha and the then Chief Minister Sushil Kumar Shinde has offered to resign (Teltumbde Anand and others, 2003, Atrocities on Dalits in Marathwada: Report by Caste-Conflict Research Committee in Maharashtra, Sugava Publication, Pune, page 3). This is a reaction of a Dalit who was chosen to be chief-minister for the first time. This was what people felt. Some felt that this was a political move in the light of forthcoming elections. Some analyzed that this was an obvious result of weakening of Dalits due to their broken unity. At that time, Shivsena had proposed to unite Bhimshakti and Shivshakti. The slogan given was, Bhimshakti, Shivshakti, Deshbhakti. All this was linked to the incidents.

A unique specialty of these events was that the oppressed belonged to the Matang caste. Matangs are not politically aware and assertive like the Ambedkar-oriented Buddists. Buddhists severely oppose the acts of inequality of the upper castes. 'Human Rights Watch', a representative American Committee had toured India in 1998 and had surveyed the atrocities on Dalits in Gujarat, Maharashtra, Tamilnadu, Kerala, Karnataka, Andhra Pradesh, Bihar and Orissa states. A 291 pages report of their survey has been published. According to the report, even today Dalits do not have entry into temples in many areas of Gujarat, they cannot take water from wells belonging to the upper castes. In Tamilnadu, women of Dalit Sikkaliers caste are exploited by upper caste Thiravs. Dalits are socially ostracized in some or other area of India. The news of upper castes shooting 61 Dalits in Johanabad in Bihar is not old. Dalit houses are burnt down due to casteist hatred. Indian caste-hatred was thus brought in front of the world.

Person or society that follows caste distinction is narrow-minded. Such people or society follow age-old rituals and traditions. They are not prepared to accept modern values or they donot have the mental prowess to do so. We can see several well-educated people still following traditions blindly. A person believing in caste distinction tries to influence others. Many times, one such person instigates the emotions of the society and inspires everyone to collectively oppress Dalits. Such incidents have occurred.

Increasing atrocities against Scheduled Castes

There is a 17 per cent increase in registered cases of atrocities against members of the Scheduled Castes in 2013 as compared to the figures in 2012 and the conviction rate is around 23 per cent (Minister for Social Justice and Empowerment Thawar Chand Gehlot).

The government had made some amendments to strengthen the Prevention of Atrocities Act and he appealed to the states to implement the law so that quick action could be taken in cases and the aggrieved parties could get compensation. The Central government had many welfare schemes for the Scheduled Castes but the states were not utilizing the funds allocated in the sub plans while some states were under utilizing it, he said. The Centre allotted funds for specific programmes and states should ensure that they were utilized only for that purpose. Funds could also not be released on time since states had not submitted their utilization certificates on time.

In 2011, there were 39,401 cases registered under the Atrocities Act. The number increased to 39,512 in 2012 and jumped to 46,114 in 2013, according to the National Crime Records Bureau (NCRB). Ten states accounted for over 90 per cent of the cases and Rajasthan has the maximum with 8,126 cases in 2013;

Uttar Pradesh follows with 7,103; Bihar with 6,812 cases; Madhya Pradesh with 4,241 cases and Orissa with 3,382 cases. There were 3076 cases registered in Karnataka; 2,064 in Maharashtra; 1,867 in Tamil Nadu and 1,414 in Gujarat. The percentage of pendency of cases has increased from 79.9 per cent in 2011 to 84.1 per cent in 2013. Low rate of disposal of cases were observed in Bihar at 12.1 per cent; Maharashtra with 10 per cent; Kerala 11.7 per cent; Gujarat 10.2 per cent; Himachal Pradesh 17.6 per cent; and Karnataka 21.8 per cent. Bihar has 11 courts to deal exclusively with crimes under the Atrocities Act, while Kerala has two and Karnataka eight. Gujarat has 25 such courts while Maharashtra and Himachal Pradesh have none. Madhya Pradesh is the first state in the country to have police stations dedicated to crimes under the Atrocities Act in all its districts with a deputy superintendent of police deputed to investigate the cases. Forty five special courts have also been set up in the state. While the conviction rate for cognizable crimes under the Indian Penal Code is 40.2 per cent in 2013, for the Atrocities Act it is 22.8 in 2013, down from 30 per cent in 2011. Only three states — Harayana, Maharashtra and Tripura — have set up sub-division level committees for review of implementation of the Atrocities Act and relief and rehabilitation of victims (Meena Menon, The Hindu, New Delhi, August 23, 2014).

Oppression against Matangs in Marathwada Region

In the last few years, Marathwada region has experienced atrocities on Dalits, killing them and a series of such brutalities. The uniqueness of this event was that all the oppressed belonged to the Matang caste. Many a times, Buddhists fighting against casteism right from the period of Babasaheb Ambedkar experience such atrocities. Buddhists strongly oppose the acts of inequality of the upper castes. Other castes however have not associated themselves with this struggle.

The upper castes were completely against the Buddhists during the naming propaganda because the Buddhists are aggressive and politically united. As a result, at least in Maharashtra, oppression on Dalits meant oppression on Buddhists. However, in recent times the upper castes had attacked the Matangs deliberately. This had occurred for the first time. There is a huge number of Matang population in Marathwada. Apparently the Matangs hadnot tied up with the Buddhists and hence it was unexplained why they had invited the wrath of the upper castes.

SATEGAON ISSUE: SEVERE CASTEISM STILL EXPERIENCED IN MARATHWADA

Entire Maharashtra was shaken by news on 9th January 2008. A love affair gone sour, girl's relatives catch couple, who eloped, gorge out youth's eyes. The eyes of the lover were removed by knives...and such news filled the newspapers. The oppressed youth in this incident, Chandrakant Datta Gaikwad was of Matang caste and the girl was a Maratha. A tender emotion like love met a brutal fate bringing the role of rampaging casteism to the forefront. Several contradictory news-reports regarding the incident were being published. It was necessary to bring out the truth underlying the incidents and bring it before the public and so 'Development Studies Centre' and 'Dalit Intellectual Collective' appointed a committee to look into it. This committee brought out certain findings and solutions which brought some important facts to limelight.

Chandrakant Gaikwad (Matang-SC) and Premala Jadhav (Maratha) knew each other for five years. Their families and the whole town were aware of this friendship. This was evident from the letters that Premala had written to Chandrakant. However both were unaware of the grave social consequences of their love affair. Buddhist and Matang students in Sategaon get along well together and so Chandrakant and Premala took along their Buddhist friend Milind Jondhale with them and both Milind and Chandrakant are bearing the fearful result of the act. Chandrakant wanted to finish his education and then marry but due to tremendous insistence from Premala, they decided to leave the town and get married.

Chhawa union had first accused the two of rape after beating them up in order to camouflage the act of inhumanly beating up two Dalit youths (Report of Sategaon Satyashodhak Committee page 21). Everyone kept telling the committee that Sategaon police and Sarpanch as well as other officials were not present in the town when the two were being brutally beaten. The committee guessed that all this was being prompted by someone from Kuntur. It was being told that even Dalits had participated in beating. However this was wrong. They wanted to subdue the case by projecting it to be strife amongst the Matangs and Buddhists. Maratha population is highest in this town. A handful of powerful people empowered by caste, political hold or wealth were trampling the rights given to ladies and scheduled castes by the constitution. Initially it appeared as if the Kuntur police station was functioning efficiently but due to pressure from 'unknown power', both the oppressed and the oppressors were convicted similarly. A criminal group in Sategaon continuously waters cattiest differences. A few of these had warned Chandrakant against marrying Premoar two months before the incident. The committee had proposed that the state government and social influences striving to maintain social harmony should take this issue seriously.

Chandrakant has completely lost one of his eyes and vision of his second eye has become extremely poor. Milind can also see very faintly by one eye. Their power of vision has been disabled. Satyashodhak committee had given several suggestions regarding this issue. It was also suggested that rather than forming a 'Mahatma Gandhi No Strife Committee', 'No Violence Committee' needs to be formed and it should be given complete powers to stop all types of violence. If she wishes so, Premala Jadhav should marry Chandrakant and the government of Maharashtra should provide all types of financial assistance. (Ref. Sategaon) (Report generated in February 2008; of the Committee appointed by Dalit Intellectual Collective and Development Studies Centre, Mumbai to look into the removal of eyes of a Dalit youth in Taluka Naigaon, District Nanded).

The incidents that occurred were highly complicated. Several incidents have taken place over the use of public hand-pump. Hand-pump is the only source of water for everyone in the famine-struck Marathwada region. It is important to study where these pumps were located and how they were used. The entire process of development in the state needs to be questioned due to such incidents. Nobody had paid attention to this matter. Political parties started exploiting such incidents for their selfish interests. Congress party led by Sonia Gandhi had presented their report which called this incident 'a strife between two anti-social principles'. Dalits had naturally opposed these findings and expressed their anguish. Maratha Mahasangh openly claimed that such notorious incidents had never occurred and that the 'Anti-oppression Law' should be cancelled. The Dalits gave a thought to the victims. They tried to bring it to the forefront but they couldnot create a havoc due to internal rivalry. None can however deny that their real interest was political selfish advantage.

Many times, low social status as compared to higher castes is the main reason of conflict. Dalits cannot utilize their rights properly.

They are not able to take cognizance of legal equality and if they try to do so they have to bear dire consequences. Had the Dalits opposed the violence they were exposed to actively, they would never have had to face it. Upper castes would not have dared to torture the Dalits as in the recent case in Marathwada. All these incidents can be linked to divisive Dalit parties. This nurtured favourable atmosphere for casteism and racism in Marathwada.

In the report 'Oppression on Dalits in Marathwada'. Dr. Anand Teltumbde and others say that political incidents revolve around election and take shape due to it. Those political parties that participate in elections purposefully employ violence to force worship for political empowerment. Violent incidents clearly reflect that alliances are made just for their selfish benefits. They do not care a damn for the Dalit parties. If there is a lacuna is the upper-class parties, they instigate violence amongst Dalits. Even if they get all upper class votes and Dalit votes are not important for them, they still benefit from violence against Dalits. It can be said that victory in elections is based on such strategies, their follow-up and spreading of casteist violence amongst the Dalits. So the strategy of any party is always in accordance with this principle. (Teltumbde Anand, 2003; p. 33)

The second point is that these incidents are caused by the internal conflict between traditional prejudice between the upper castes and the metropolitan sensitivity of the Dalits. Dalits want to eradicate casteist identity and encourage the awareness of democracy whereas the upper castes want to nurture the traditional power-play. Increasing globalization is subjecting primarily the upper classes to a sense of insecurity. Besides, conflict is rural areas is increasing. Instances of oppression on Dalits are increasing. The police-attack on Pardhis in Rajulwadi, Ravi-Pardhi murder, Dhoki slaughter, killing of school children under pretext of theft in Yamgarwadi, Osmanabad....seeing several such instances, it may be said that attacks on nomadic tribes are on a high these days.

The third point is that our education system has failed in instilling modernity and human values. An educated person had performed the crime of inhumanly pouring kerosene and burning a Dalit in Bhutegaon in Jalna district. This act can be routed in his traditional caste-position and contemporary political patronage.

The fourth print states that through the right 'connections', such events are suppressed by the parties concerned. This incident was mellowed down in spite of pressure from political parties and media. In short, Dalits are being oppressed everywhere in India. Superiority complex about one's caste keeps on oppressing the Dalits. Dalits are not oppressed just in rural areas but also in towns and cities. Such incidents occur even in modern places. Dalits bear the insulting treatment of upper class officers. Its quality and percentage differs from place to place.

Nearly all political parties look at oppression on Dalits as a political opportunity. Political parties exploit such a situation to fulfill their interests. Government reports are seen to analyze such incidents as 'internal conflict between two anti-social principles'. In such a scenario, Dalits cannot implement their rights properly. They cannot assert their legal equality because if they do so they have to pay for it.

Today Dalits are kept away from political power, judiciary, police force and bureaucracy. How are we going to curb exploitation and atrocities in such a situation? How can acquire our rights, justice and emancipation? This is an important issue that we need to address in the present. On the other hand millions of prosecution cases involving oppression on Dalits are still pending.

'Vidrohi' journal dedicated the issue of July-August 2010 to 'Where is the atrocity act? Oppression has not reduced.' The issue shows how Dalits are being exploited even today. The editorial of this issue addresses the topic, 'abolishing casteist terrorism'. The principle propounded therein is 'No resistance without organization, no protection without resistance and no confidence without protection'. Shahir Chandar Kamble has been quoted, 'oppression will not stop without retaliation' in order to instigate a 'firm resistance' to casteist slaughtering.

Violent Culture and Celebration of Valour - Insane Ideas of Valour

Violence has cast its shadow on our social activities and mutual relations. The age-old caste-system has hidden suggestions of violence. It becomes evident at times. Lower classes believed in the theory of caste due to creed and so accepted the violence as their fate. Even women considered that being born as women was their ill fate due to past sin. Overt and hidden violence therefore continued without resistance for ages and ages. Violence is being glorified these days. Few may indulge in actual violence but there are many that engage in threatening, warning and spreading terror. These people are not just accepted but respected in society. They are automatically becoming leaders. Surprisingly the number of people supporting violence is on an increase.

Those who commit violence are often talked about. They are punished or even victimized at times. But the power hidden behind this violence is ignored. Corrupt capitalism is directly or indirectly giving a shelter to violence. This social and economic state nurtures neo-fascism. It prepares a situation for spread of such ideology. It gets followers. Educated middle class is gradually accepting violence. Thoughts that glorify violence challenge the existence of women. Male-prowess is glorified. This ideology is based on the inequality between men and women. A man should be 'violent' and 'aggressive' and women are also expected to follow suit. Atmosphere is created in a way that feminity is looked down upon. Those men that refuse to be violent are taunted as being womanly. They are instigated to take up violence.

Due to age-old patriarchy brothers too are aggressive right from childhood. Festivals like Rakhi Pournima and Bhaidey entrust the responsibility of protecting sisters to brothers and so if anyone dares to look at their sister, men feel responsible and resort to violent measures, at times slaughtering even the one they are supposed to protect. Our history and our films have many such incidents described in detail and these inspire today's youth. Men are zapped by insane ideas of bravery. So they take weapons and start fighting. These days violence is not just for retaliation but also for sadistic pleasure. This feeling of mastery that is kindled the minds of boys is a product of our patriarchal system. Violence is on the increase but this does not mean that all our social behaviour is based on violence. Our culture, our mentality, our point of view are all under the influence of violence. We have started believing in violence. We have started supporting violence. Middle class that is responsible for nourishing values is also under the influence of violence and this lifestyle is influencing the entire society. This violent culture is destroying the roots of our society.

Extremely Methodical and Fundamental Nature of Atrocities and Violence

22 Dalits were killed as a result of few elements Tsundur in Andhra Pradesh. The incidents that occurred here are related to the changes in political economics and tension in education and agricultural field. New public systems were challenging the power enjoyed by upper castes. This was the background of terrible violence. Vasanta and Kalpana Kannabiran have written a very effective and guiding essay that will provide reference to this discussion:

In Kannabiran's 'Caste and Gender: Understanding Dynamics of Power and Violence', it is explained how caste and gender cross each other and prompt the upper class to be violent towards Dalits. A Dalit boy unknowingly touched a Reddy boy with his foot and this culminated into the slaughtering of 22 Dalits. Reddy girls complained of Dalit boy purposely touching them and Reddus took this up to kill the suspected youth. In another case it was claimed that a Dalit boy eve-teased girls on the road (The boy was killed for this). After killing 22, upper class women came on the roads to advocate the slaughter by saying that they had been insulted. Dalit women are not supposed to have freedom and respect and so upper castes can manhandle them and manipulate justice as per their whims. For e.g., Mothama, a Golla Dalit woman was paraded naked because she supported a Reddy girl to elope with a Golla boy. Nobody could intervene into this. Golla men could not this abuse and so closed their eyes, whereupon upper class men called them unmanly. Kannabiran says that this is a two-fold insult; establishing power over a Dalit woman's body and by doing this ridiculing the lower caste men to be impotent (Kannabiran Vasant and Kalpana, Economic and Political Weekly, September, 199 p. 2130-2133).

Violence that Dalit men and women are exposed to is covered up by fellow caste members and especially in Hindi belt; women are suppressed under the word 'prestige'. 'Prestige' is a broad term because even an upper class woman cannot define 'prestige' outside the definitions provided by men in her family and community. It was seen at Rupaasur that women can just instigate action, 'prestige', 'honour' or 'respect' may be used in quotes but it is very difficult to use them as a pro-Dalit woman. Whenever we use these words they come along with their connotations in the field of male discussion. Violence is justified to protect this 'prestige' but the prestige of those who bear that violence is deliberately covered up. Uma Chakravarti in her book 'Caste: Through Gender Lens' says that when those who directly rob honour in such a manner, are punished, these acts are to keep intact the social power relationships. This is a part of the complex structure to control land, status and women's sexuality. Therefore social power is centrally situated on physical power or class, status-based power or class and power over women or male domination (they work together). Caste dominance or influence is often seen as being impartial to gender biases, but in reality are brought into practice from gender-biased and patriarchal rules. Yet when caste and class are seen as precipitators of social power, patriarchal power is not seen in that manner. We have to accept this fact to see the influence it has on the class system in India.

Caste atrocities are not of ordinary nature. They have obtained justification by caste-influenced thought processes and culture. The culprits who commit such crimes are filled with feelings of self-righteousness. When a man from lower caste marries a higher caste woman or elopes with her, he has to face the communal wrath of the higher caste. This is because even today a woman's sexuality is transferred from her father to her husband, besides this marriage is considered to be inverse marriage and these killings are directly approved of. At such times, not only the lower caste man is killed, but the woman (who has lost her status by her transgressive behaviour) also has to die, because she has violated rules related to marriage system. People who commit such brutal acts are seen to be favoring private judicial systems. They are seen to assert that irrespective of whatever laws say about such relationships, such misled couples should be punished severely. It is clear from this how closely caste and patriarchy are related, from which relation between love and marriage is totally eliminated. Caste-based atrocities indicate this relationship. Feminist thought schools assume that by lowering the status of a woman, exploiting her sexually, imprisoning and using her sexuality in whichever form they want, creating myths about her sexuality, entertaining imaginary series of thoughts, are all done to gain an upper hand over the process of knowledge production in a patriarchal society. In such circumstances, an ideal picture is created where a woman is the happiest within the institution of marriage.

A while ago, Maharashtra was rocked by a very cruel and inhuman incident that occurred in Satara district. A person named Shankar Shinde killed his own daughter Asha while she was asleep because she wanted to marry a man belonging to another caste. Asha, who worked as a counselor in the KEM Hospital in Pune after completing her course in social studies, could not even convince her father of the idea of marrying outside caste. Shankar was so obsessed with the thought of losing his family's honour if she married outside the caste, that he took her life and surrendered himself to the police. Even today, he has no remorse over the horrible crime he committed with his own hands. There is a huge dominance of customs and traditions in our society. There are societal pressures. There is abundance arising from wealth. Therefore in Maharashtra, casteist cudgels are frequently raised within the Maratha community. Brutal beating of the mother of a boy, who married outside his caste in Mulgaon (dist. Patan) before Asha's murder, is symbolic of this attitude. Similarly honour killing is strongly suspected behind the slaying of Arushi Talwar.

Sangli town in Maharashtra was brought into limelight twice in the year 1998. In the first incident, a girl named Amruta was murdered on the streets. In the second, a higher caste girl was kidnapped by a Dalit man for marriage and in retaliation the girl's community attacked the Dalit settlement and set fire to it. Both these incidents have references to the male-female relationship. The convicts in both these incidents are young. Also the 'emotion of love' in both incidents are similar. Following only one incident, after a lot of discussions about cinema, crimes, sexual attraction and revenge, the society kept quiet even though the killing was done in broad daylight. There were no murders committed in the second incident, but the society seemingly woke up from a deep slumber after a higher-caste girl was lured into eloping. Nor did they just wake up, but their collective rousing was encompassed with feelings of revenge and they marched on the Dalit settlement with lit torches in hands with the sole intention of burning it down. Law was taken in hands and used as desired, and they did not calm down even when some people were victimized due to this outbreak of violence. They kept clenching their fists and kept repeating - 'these bastards have become very arrogant!' (Pawar and Sanjay; p. 146-7)

Many have conquered India till date but they could not conquer the caste system; clearly the caste system conquered them. Dr. Babasaheb Ambedkar says that due to the graded inequality, there was no revolution against the Brahmin community. (Ambedkar, 1916) Brahmin class is leading the religion and philosophy of the entire caste system, economic rulers are the Baniya capitalist class, and the political leaders are dominantly farmers' class, the revivers of caste system, the supposedly kshatriya or warrior caste Rajputs who fiercely practice 'beti vyavhar within the caste' and the big farmers' class. A few years ago, the Rajput community tried to impose boycott on the Maharaja of Jaipur because the princess married a youth from the same clan. What was this community doing when Rajput kings gave away their daughters to the Muslim Emperors?

Even now couples who wed within gotra or outside caste are brought before the Khap Panchayats and killed, before their parent's eyes, and mostly with their consent! On 10 February, 2003, Jaat landlords from Kaithal District in Haryana ousted 275 Dalit villagers from the village. These Dalit farm workers were only demanding their minimum wages. A Valmiki labourer was slaughtered by crushing under a tractor. A Dalit woman from Kajarkara, Rohtak District was gang raped. Jaat and Gujar landlords in Julana, Panipat District beat up several Dalits for entering a temple. Several such incidents have happened. Not one but hundreds of such blood curdling incidents keep happening all across the country every year. The Dalit population keeps falling prey to various atrocities such as violence, arson, eve-teasing, rapes, burning down of farms and homes and other forms of atrocities. There is no need to describe them all.

According to a report by All India Agricultural Workers, there is existence of bonded labour tradition on a large scale in Punjab and Haryana. According to this institute's report, this system is practised in the districts of Fatehabad, Sirsa, Kaithal, Jind, Karnal, Panipat and Rohtak. These bonded labourers are Dalits. The ownership of lands is largely held by the Jaat landlords who pay the Dalit farm workers in advance and make them bonded labourers. These farm workers are not paid any minimum wages. These Dalit farm workers do not have any other alternate means of livelihood and hence they are trapped in this bond. The higher caste communities have now become more aggressive to reorganize their caste and to empower themselves. This has led to increased atrocities on the Dalits. Economic policies adopted under the garb of new economic reforms which only favour prosperous higher caste communities and politics for appeasement of higher classes by all parliamentary political parties have appeared in the country at the very same time. In this manner in India, new economic policies, caste system, patriarchy and violence are seen co-existing hand in hand.

In the conflict between the Landlords versus class of farm workers, will the process of uniting by overcoming influential caste consciousness between the intermediate caste (OBC) farmer caste farm labourers and Dalit form labourers for their common vested interests, be achieved by such class struggles? For that, should not there be an awakening and people's fight for ending the caste system? The caste system will not be ended even by establishing power without resorting to the parliamentary and voting methods and by reallocating lands. The middle classes are the ones who commit major atrocities on the Dalits.

Feminist Researchers and Theoretical Presentation of Violence against Women

Feminist researchers have presented various theories about the atrocities on women. Majority of these feminists agree that these atrocities are of very methodical and organized nature. When thinking about these feminist thought schools, it is seen that the environmentalist feminists have determined the roots of this violence in the Western Science, Technology, and influence of international imperialism; whereas Dalit Feminists have theorized this violence arising from the contradiction between the gender biases and caste with reference to the male domination. They feel that unless attention is given to the inequality and dissimilarity between castes and within a caste, solutions cannot be found for violence against women in various castes and tribes. Dalit feminists have also theorized the meaning of the active participation of women that is seen in acts of violence against women. Although there are different theories with reference to such violence, there are mainly two facets to the acts of violence against women. The open acts of atrocities on women in society as well as domestic abuses carried against women behind closed doors and walls of homes need to be mentioned here. Intention of such violence is to demoralize a woman by insulting her and to maintain control over her. There is longstanding misuse of power and strength in such acts of violence. Violent behavior is the manifestation of the upbringing by the family and the society. During the period after 1970s, we see rising of a sharp analytical thought process only when the feminist movements took up the agenda of violence related to dowries. From discussions about dowries questions were raised inevitably about the nature of marriages and the assumptions about the foundation on which they are based.

Earlier, violence against Dalits was perpetrated mainly against isolated individuals. However, recently instances of mass frenzy against Dalit groups have become more common. For example, 5 Dalits were killed in the presence of police at Jhajjar in Haryana. Even in a small village like Bhutegaon in Marathwada, a Dalit was burned to death by sawama-hindu crowd. Violence committed on Bhootmange family at Khairlanji depicted extremely brutal face of violence. Horrific incident parading a mother and daughter naked in front of the villagers, murdering them and throwing their bodies in a gutter would send shivers down anybody's spine.

In Marathwada a man was killed by cutting into pieces, 32 people were murdered and huts of Pardhi community were burned to ashes. But, the news about this incident was not allowed to leak to the outside world. Khairlanji residents 'celebrated' the release of culprits. The administration suppressed the case of the culprit 'effectively', thus giving a message of amnesty to criminals.

The interest of upper castes and exploitative classes are being protected under the banner of 'Hinduism'. Even, the interest of capitalist feudalism is being supported. Inequality, exploitation, torture and harassment are receiving strong backing. Therefore the masterminds behind such violence, its propagators and supporters should be isolated from working classes. Their crooked intentions should be exposed, their tactics and manoeuvres to establish hegemony, thwarted by educating men and women from labour class. In the atrocities against Dalits, human rights are basically trampled upon but they have not found a place in the deliberations on Human Rights. Hence, the issue cannot be viewed only in the context of the globalization process. This Dalit problem has many facets and layers.

Exploitation and impediments are increasing and there is deprivation and denial on all fronts. Natural and man-made resources are being denied. The intensity of injustice and atrocity is rising. Tendency to commit atrocities targeting Dalit women is seen to be growing. Dalits are being reduced to the status of 'marginal man' and made perpetually dependent on others. Their cultural values are under attack. Their self-respect is being eroded and they are being made pliant and submissive by showing them pity. Crooked efforts are being made to drive them out of their lands. In cities, houses and huts of Dalits and other poor are demolished under the pretext of development. All these indicate that a collective effort is underway to displace and enslave Dalits. If people concerned do not take early cognizance of these burning problems, survival of Dalits itself will be threatened.

However, the Government and the civil society are turning a blind eye to these issues. There is an insensitive class of higher castes claiming that the caste menace has been eradicated from our society and hence opposing time and again, the Act of 'Prevention of Atrocities against Dalits-1989'. On the other hand, they try to appease Dalits by raising slogans like 'Let us forget castes...' and bring them under the influence of Brahmin culture to maintain caste system and prevent them from uniting. In short, hegemony or egoism of higher castes is leading to promotion of mobocracy/groupism (Zundshahi), and in turn it leads support caste system that protects 'Hindutwa'. Therefore, it is immensely necessary for the follower and disciples of Buddha, Phule and Ambedkar and believers in democracy to be ever watchful to avoid creation of indiscreet society with caste-system.

Difference between Fighting Spirit and Violence

There is a difference between these two. In violent agitations people become aggressive and attack their attackers to take revenge; in such circumstances violence becomes the ultimate purpose. Social transformation, in fact, should be the goal of achieving such agitations. If it becomes necessary, blocking traffic, stopping railways, striking work are also available as a method of agitation in democracy. Until people are able to gain something on the might of their own strengths, they cannot retain what they gain by violent agitations. It will only breed further violence or terrorism. There, agitations should have the purpose of releasing the energy of people. “Make a slave conscious and slavery and he will rise in against it” said Babasaheb. They get strength to get their own rights in future in this manner. Violence - non violence are not rigid values but a way of life; hence, one should choose the way using discretion, you cannot stop or avoid this part. A “democratic” view is taken support, also say that if “people themselves favour violence” or they consider it an inevitable choice, why should anyone deny it to them. However, the aspect not considering other avenues for agitation and “not ending in a statement or reading a point of no return” being the end result a violence is ignored in such an argument the consequence what gets ignored is the consequences of ignoring other avenues. Agitation, as also the end result of violence generally being a statement or reaching of a point of no return.

Stringent Punishment for Atrocities on SC, ST under New Act

An Act which provides for stringent action against those committing atrocities against SC and ST communities or indulging in actions which are derogatory to their dignity, including social or economic boycott, will come into effect from 26 January 2016. As per the Scheduled Castes and the Scheduled Tribes (Prevention of Atrocities) Amendment Act, 2015, actions like tonsuring of head, moustache, or similar acts which are derogatory to the dignity of members of SCs and STs will now be treated as offences of atrocities. The offences include denying access to irrigation facilities of forest rights, “garlanding with chappals”, compelling them to dispose or carry human or animal carcasses, or to dig graves, using or permitting manual scavenging, dedicating a SC or ST women as devadasi and abusing in caste name. Imposing social or economic boycott, hurting a SC or ST woman by removing her garments, forcing a member of SC/ST to leave house, village or residence, acts or gestures of a sexual nature against members of SCs and STs. Impeding certain activities related to voting especially vote or not vote for a particular candidate will also be considered an offence. “Certain criminal (IPC) offences like hurt, grievous hurt, intimidation, kidnapping etc, attracting less than ten years of imprisonment, committed against members of SC/ ST, will be treated as offences punishable under the PoA Act.

"Presently, only those offences listed in IPC as attracting punishment of 10 years or more and committed on members of Scheduled Caste/Scheduled Tribe are accepted as offences falling under the PoA Act," said a statement issued by the Ministry of Social Justice and Empowerment. Under the Act, Exclusive Special Courts will be established and Exclusive Special Public Prosecutors will be appointed to try the offences under the PoA Act to enable speedy and expeditious disposal of cases. Special Courts and Exclusive Special Courts will have the power to take direct cognizance of offence and as far as possible and complete trial of the case within two months, from the date of filing of the charge sheet, it said (Published On: Sen Times-Online Newspaper for Bureaucrats, Mon, Jan 25th, 2016).

Why are Indian Laws Unsuccessful to Prevent Caste Violence?

There is no thought given to the capacity of the depressed and deprived people to pursue their struggle in a democratic manner and to achieve end result. One can understand the possibility of not being discrete while taking decisions in a war situation. However, while finalizing value based action plan, the long term reformist will need to go beyond thinking only the short term influence or consequences of violence and peace and devote attention to the frame work of human values.

Blockages in the process of registering complaint against crime. If Dalits and Adivasis suffer violence in a village, they have to go through severe ordeals for seeking redress against the violence. The information about crime, every effort made to see that the information is not leaked out or does not cross boundaries of the village. It is a commonly experienced difficulty in getting the police, registering the complaint if attempted to register under the Atrocity Act. Then a cross complaint against the plaintiff is obtained to nullify the effect of the original complaint. Eventually if the compliant is registered by the police, there is no surety what so ever that they will register it under appropriate clauses, investigate it properly and submit chargesheet in the court.

In the meanwhile the town tortures him economically and mentally and government does not help him or provide him proper help. Consequently the Dalit distressed by atrocity experiences further harassment. Many times the information is given to the opposite party beforehand. It adds tension to the situation. This is how the police system works in this country and if the crime is registered not under IPC, rather than atrocity clause depriving the plaintiff of the assistance of the government lawyer; the crime is also not taken to Dy. SP level and no compensation and benefits are given to them.

The atrocity cases are twice the numbers not registered under the act. We are discussing about atrocity that we otherwise discussed so much. "Mahatma Gandhi crimeless town", changes in criminal code and violent town, the three schemes mainly will benefit Dalits, tribals and women. It will be decided only by the future. In the context of Dalit violence, the scheme became controversial and changes in the criminal code will need to be understood further. Villages which continuously lead against violence and atrocity better be named as violence-less town. On 15th August 2007, Maharashtra Government launched "the scheme of Mahatma Gandhi crimeless town" to resolve conflicts in village itself. It is said that in this context the government is trying to get self rid of its responsibilities by transferring them to the villager. The basis on which these committees will resolve the conflicts is yet unexplained. If the control still remains in the hands of perpetrators of crime, how are the Dalits and poor going to get justice? This is a big question. The scheme in "Mahatma Gandhi violence-less town" is to keep them away from the clutches of law and the society is freed from violence. "Quarrel free scheme" does not affect the frame work of traditional feudalistic scheme. It only provides upper caste an escape route. Even if such laws are enacted by public demand or bureaucracy, the entire administrative system is in full control of Brahminism. A small group of Dalits has entered in the system through reservation in the era of privatization and globalization. Dalit labour is prevented from entering bureaucracy. For implementing the laws of reservations, we have to depend on the supporters of Brahminism.

Ruling authority, judicial system, police force and bureaucracy are closed for Dalit and tribals in such a situation. How are we then going to stop exploitation in justice and violence? How are we going to get our rights, justice and freedom? Today this is the key-question faced by Dalit Adivasis. Brahminist characteristic philosophy, parables, language and culture are reinforcing the caste system in the society. The reasons for the Dalit labour's agony and violence are basically more materialistic than feeling psychological in nature. How can we then free the Dalit labour of the pain and injustice of Brahministic system based on inequality by following meditation and vipashyana? Proximate reason behind the violation and suppression of Dalits is the casteist philosophy. Caste based social system and its thinking pattern has become the strong pillar supporting the feudal exploitation and atrocity. Even if the parliament, democracy, constitution, judiciary do exist; caste system is the main social reality.

Bloody violence, cruel massacres of Dalits, brutal rapes on women are inevitable consequences of this caste system. Caste based hatred, ego, and inequality in human cruelty, declivity, massacre, boycott, exploitation, terrorism are the supports of this system. The Maharashtra police force is behaving like a ruffian or rowdy. Politicians are engrossed in power. The downtrodden have a support only organization. To prevent violence on Dalits, an action plan to fight jointly against the caste and creed based system in right earnest.

In view of the cruel history of the caste system and the recent post independence inhuman violence against Dalits, it will not be a surprise, if such instances happen again and again. In addition to that many other reasons for increasing cruelty against the waning influence of Dalit politics and the silent acceptance of violence by the middle class are the main reasons.

An editor has mentioned in an editorial that Brahminism based social system, legislative assemblies with majority of "Manuvad (philosophy)" based on democracy, the central and state government, bureaucracy are the main sources of energy for injustice against Dalits. Therefore, the committees of injustice and violence are being empowered. Forget about the development of Dalits, their life, property, honour are not safe. Because they have to seek justice from these committees, the main question of Dalits is to find methods to stop these sources of energy. Supporting injustice is a serious crime itself. This seems to be a big question that needs to be answered satisfactorily.

SUMMARY

The contribution of social and political parties, organizations and intellectuals are valuable in strengthening and in becoming the main contributors to strengthen democracy in our country. However, these entities seem to be operating in a limited field. Some of them are operating in a wider field but their work cannot be considered as liberating or revolutionary. Their work suffers from the limitations of caste, creed, language, gender, way of thinking regionalism. Individualistic thought processes are further contributors so that not only there is the injustice and violence against Dalits tribals, women; but an aggression or modernization progressive thought continues. Their feelings others cannot experience. This is a sad state of the existing situation. The legal system, resistance, redistribution of resources, awakening of caste creed and patriarchal system are considered as remedies for ending the violence against Dalit Adivasis. Not searching for various remedies after the violence, it is essential to take preventive measures beforehand; there is a need to take serious cognizance of this aspect. However, various movements seem to be giving priority to some aspects only and ignoring others. There seems to be an agreement about eradication of violation against Dalits and tribals. There are differences in the views about the methods to be followed.

The existing network of NGO's does not present a complete analysis of a problem, so as to hold the entire system answerable. Their analysis is restricted to particular verdict policy an individual. They do not raise questions that can challenge the basics of existing system. They do not raise points that will facilitate political educational needs of people. On the contrary, their nature is such that it drives the people away from politics. Therefore the NGO's have to take action on the issues of violence against Dalits. Dalits do not seem to act on the issue of caste, creed or slavery of women. Indian government and bureaucracy depict a Brahministic and Feudalistic character on the issue of injustice and violence against Dalits. However NGO's and other condemning parading of Dalit women or other violence end in calling them as a blot on humanity and take a stance that it is the government's responsibilities to solve these problems. Therefore how the members of Dalits and other exploited communities can leave with self esteem is a ticklish problem in India.

The doors of political power judiciary, police and bureaucracy are closed to Dalit and Adivasis. How are we going to stop exploitation, violation in such a situation? How can Dalit and Adivasis get their rights, justice, freedom? This is the problematic question today.

Even in this adverse situation, we will have to raise lawyers to fight the court battles and also a fleet of trained social workers. We will have to keep our efforts on public education and struggle to end caste system without increasing the hatred amongst castes. For this, we will have to generate public opinion on a large scale. Globalization has made the differences to fade away. In this phase of globalization the fading at the caste and culture has taken place. There are economically strong elements in every caste, we will have to unite them on equal footing very urgently. If the progressive public organization and bureaucracy respond positively to the relevant laws, the possibilities will increase. However the real limiting factor is that occasional transformation takes place in fear of position of laws. The sole remedy for this is to eradicate the blocks or impediments of liberty, equality, brotherhood and justice. How much we as an Indian society will succeed only the future will decide it?

REFERENCES

Atyachar Virodhi Samiti (1979). 'The Marathwada Riots: A Report', *Economic and Political Weekly*.

Dahiwale, S.M. (2009). 'Khairlanji: Insensitivity of Mahar Officers, *Economic and Political Weekly,* Vol- XLIV No. 31, pp. 29–33.

Gaikwad Sharad (*ed.*), 'Atrocity Kaydyacha 20 Varshe; Yash Apayashachi Karma-Mimansa va Jaatianthachi Antachi Disha', publisher - Republican Panthers Jaativyavastha Chalwal, Maharashtra Murugkar Lata, Dalit Panther Chalwal, 1995, Sugava Prakashan, Pune 30.

Gaikwad Sharad and others (*ed.*), 'Atrocity Act Che Kay Jhale? Atyachar kami Jhalech Nay, 'Vidrohi', Year 8, Issue 4.

Guru Gopal (1994). 'Understanding Violence against Dalits in Marathwada,' *Economic and Political Weekly.*

Hindwan Sudhir, 'Caste Violence in India,' Global Vision Publishing House, New Delhi-2 age'M). 12)

Palshikar Suhas (1997). 'Putalyachi Vitambana Vicharanche Vidamban: Ambedkar vadya Pudhalvan', Bayja, Deepawali issue.

Rajput Jairaj (1992). 'Kumherche Dalit Hatyakand', Purogami Satyashodhak, Year 17, Issue 3, (*ed.*), Baba Adhav, Pune.

Shaikh Shamshad (1978). 'Marathwada Danglicha Shodh va Bodh', 'Muslim Satyashodhak Patrika', Editor Munir Sayyad, Year 6, Issue 26-26.

Teltumbde Anand (2007). 'Khairlanji': Atyachar ani Udrek acha Anvay artha', Sakal, Year 8, Issue 220.

Teltumbde Anand (2008). Khairlanji: A Strange and Bitter Crop Navyana Publications.

Thorat Subhash (2006). 'Khairlanjicha Dhada', 'Parivartanacha Vatsaru' (*ed.*), Abhay Kanta, Pune.

Thorat Sukhdeo (2009). 'Dalits in India: Search for a Common Destiny, Sage Publications, India Private Limited, New Delhi-44.

Thorat, C.P. (*ed.*) (2010). 'Editorial', 'Anvekshan', Year 1, Pune 1.

Vikas Adhyayan Kendra produced and published Dalit Bulletin, A Bulletin of Dalit Resource Centre, Mumbai-64. (*http://www.overcomingviolence.org/fileadmin/dov/images/women_campain/Dalit%2520Fact %2520sheet.pdf*)

National Seminar on

Exclusion and Atrocities on Dalits in India

29th June-30th June, 2015

Organised by

School of Rural Development, TISS, Tuljapur

Development Under the Threat of Caste Atrocities in Post-Colonialism

(Study of Caste Atrocities on Dalits and Their impact on Their Participation in Public Sphere)

Submitted by

Pradeep Jare, MASW, BASW (TISS.)

Assistant Professor of Social Work

Centre for Studies in Rural Development

Institute of Social Work and Research, Ahmednagar,

Maharashtra, India.

Email: pradeep.tiss@gmail.com

Contact No.: +91-8956981380

Sanjaykumar Kamble is assistant professor at Krantijyoti Savitribai Phule women's studies Centre, Savitribai Phule Pune University, Pune. Under the supervision of Dr. Sharmila Rege he had worked on the topic "conflicting perspectives of Dr. B.R. Ambedkar and Dr. G.S. Ghurye regarding caste. "Currently he is pursuing Ph.D in sociology on" Thoughts on caste, class and gender in Maharashtra since 1970s with reference to comrade Sharad Patil, Gail Omvedt and Raosaheb Kasabe. His specialization is in caste, class and gender, Dalit studies, Globalization. He had written a book on "caste and census-critique of Sociology" Along with that he had published several articles in various journals and books.

Chapter 6

Development Under the Threat of Caste Atrocities in Post-Colonialism (Study of Caste Atrocities on Dalits and their Impact on Their Participation in Public Sphere)

PRADEEP JARE[1]

"Caste has killed public spirit.
Caste has destroyed the sense of public charity."

Dr. B R Ambedkar

1. INTRODUCTION

Caste violence in India has become horribly vibrant and terribly violent in post-colonial period. India being the largest democratic country in the world has always witnessed the brutal realty in terms of caste violence and atrocities. With the passing of time the atrocities on Dalits are becoming more and more frequent in some of the pockets of the country. "The roots of these caste-based violent incidents can

[1] Centre for Studies in rural Development, Institute of Social Work and Research, Ahmednagar, Maharashtra. E-mail: pradeep.tiss@gmail.com

be traced into the history of Indian society. Dalits known as "untouchables" before independence were always treated as impure sections of the society as they were involved into "dirty" jobs. The segmental division of the society was based on the occupation of the each caste community. This distribution of occupation was based on the theory of varna. The Brahmins, Kshatriya, Vaishya and Shudra were four major varnas in society whose duties were preaching, security, business and cultivation respectively. There was another section which was out of this varna system called Ati-shudra, which was mainly involved into the serving the above four varnas. Their main job was to clean the places, remove all dirty things and carrying out dead cattle from the villages. The outcome of their involvement into this job led to inhuman unfair unjust violent and brutal practices by the above four varnas. The practices involved un-touchability, un-seeability, prohibition on entering into the temples, public, places, houses of the, upper caste communities and public offices. These practices had a tremendous negative impact on the socio-economic and political development of the Dalits in India. The practice of discrimination based on the caste of the person restricted them from availing of all the public services and the common facilities. Dalits are not only excluded from the public sphere but they have been also given humiliating treatment by the upper caste communities.

During colonial period Dalits were oppressed by both the insiders and the outsiders. This double discrimination from both the sides had its depressing impact on their assertions of basic human rights. Their fight was to avail the status of a human being as they were trying to create their identity as a human being. During this period the violence on Dalits was considered to be a routine regular practice. However, the antagonistic approaches by Mt. Phule, Dr. Ambedkar, Periyar, began to challenge the existing orthodox system to bring out the changes in the lives of the Dalits. For them this struggle was more against what Mao termed as "primary contradiption".

The movement assertion of basic human rights of Dalit Comunity was started by Dr. Babasaheb Ambedkar during colonial period only, Post colonial reforms brought out major changes in terms of constitutional provisions to abolish the caste based discriminations and practice of untouchability based on the caste of the person Dr. Babasaheb B.R. Ambedkar emphasized on the need and spread of education to change the existing social system. He as the Architect of the constitution of India included many provisions of reservations into the constitution to bring parity in the social status of dalits and non-dalits. However caste based humiliations and atrocities have taken multi-dimentional forms in terms of caste-based atrocities in the contemporary times.

The rise in awareness level and the enhancement in educational status among Dalits have challenged the orthodox nature of caste system with the support of protective measures which are incorporated in the Constitution of India. Hence, the tension and social interaction between Dalits and non Dalits has become more complicated as Dalits have started asserting their rights. These complications lead to harmful activities by upper caste communities to save their prestige in the society. It can be understood by the increase in number of atrocities on Dalits for various reasons and even some tribal reasons. Increase in number of atrocities on Dalits is due to the sickness of caste Hindus which is increasing day by day.

In recent years Maharashtra has become very vibrant in terms of caste based atrocities and violence. Some incidents of violence such as Khairlanji in 2006, Sonai village incidents in 2012, Kharda village in 2013, Limpangoan in 2012, and many more incident which are on and off the records have made Maharashtra in famous for such caste atrocities. The increase in such incidents is a gross violation of basic human rights as well as Constitutional provisions. Empirical studies show that there is tremendous impact of such brutal atrocities on other Dalit members' in-terms of their socio-economic development, their social interactions with other "upper caste" communities and their participation in public spheres.

This paper attempts to explore the impact of atrocities on the development of Dalits in rural Maharashtra. The series of atrocities in the form of killing has become a threat potential threat to the Indian democracy in a progressive state like Maharashtra. The atrocities not only affect the victim but the whole Dalit community in particular in villages. Hence, in this paper the author has made an attempt to explore the impact of these atrocities on all the members of Dalit community. It will also focus on the issues related to the social interactive patterns among Dalits and Non-Dalits in post-colonial and neo-liberal era and its impact on availing of their basic human rights.

2. NATURE OF ATROCITIES AND VIOLENCE AGAINST DALITS

Dalits broadly means the poor and downtrodden sections of the society however it is mainly connoting the Scheduled Caste population in India. As per 2011 census of Government of India, Dalit constitutes 16% population of total population. Untouchability practices against Dalits which still persist in India excluded them from the socio-economic and political development. The post-independence reforms as mentioned earlier brought the changes in their condition. Affirmative action in employment, education and politics could lead to their socio-economic development.

A report published by the National Human Rights Commission explores the bitter reality of "Shining India". According to this report, a Dalit is the victim of a crime for every 18 minutes, every day 3 Dalit women are raped, 2 Dalits are murdered and 2 Dalit houses are burnt in India, and 11 Dalits are beaten. Every week 13 Dalits are murdered, 5 Dalits homes are burnt and 6 Dalits are abducted. This data explores the facts which are registered in the police stations. It is observed from the field that there are many more cases which are un-noticed and managed at the local level by "Dalit leaders". By looking at these figures we need to analyse the history of some of the brutal incident which have shaken the nation.

Maharashtra which is considered a 'progressive' state in India has become the hub of caste based violence. The brutal killings of four members of Bhotmange family from Bhandara district was the unimaginable massacre which took place in 2006. Following this,

Ahmednagar, the "developed" district of Maharashtra came into focus on account of the caste based atrocities there. The incidents of Sonai and Kharda villages in 2012 and 2013 respectively have shaken the whole country. These incidents in consecutive years and many more atrocities in various parts of the state have proved the existence of caste discriminations for those who claim of "no caste" in India.

The brutal killings are duly considered to be acts of atrocity but it is a true that tendency exists to neglect the other forms of atrocities which are taking place in a large number in day to day life. These forms could be use of slangs while talking to Dalits which denotes their caste, humiliating treatment at the public places such as PDS shops, Gramsabhas in rural areas and government offices.

The Objectives of the study are:

1. To study the nature of caste violence in contemporary time.
2. To explore the impact of caste violence o Dalit community.
3. To understand the communication pattern among Dalits and Non Dalits in respect of research methodology the descriptive research design and method is used in this study. This study is a qualitative study in which "the researcher has used focus group discussions and case studies of victims to seek the quality data. The formats were developed for both FGDs and Case studies. Primary data was collected from the 12 villages of 6 blocks of Ahmednagar district. These villages have been declared as most sensitive villages by the district social welfare department. The secondary data was taken from the books, journals, newspaper clippings and earlier studies on this issue.

3. ANALYSIS OF FINDINGS OF THE STUDY

In order to describe the findings of this study, the researcher has conceptualized the findings and has analyzed then based on the data sought from the field.

The following section presents the analysis of the data.

4. CASTE ATROCITIES: NATURE AND CAUSES

One of the objectives of this study was to explore various kinds of violence based on the caste. Usually, when we think of violence, the first thing we visualize is physical abuse- beating, killing, physical torture, etc. Another side which is often ignored is the mental abuse, humiliating treatment at the public places, verbal abuse to Dalit communities by using the caste related words and slangs, denial of access to the government services, exclusion from development process, harassment of women in the workplace by knowing her caste, discriminatory practices at the government hospitals, schools, grampanchayat offices could be included in the various forms of violence inflicted on the dalits in the six sensitive villages in Ahmednagar District in Maharashtra.

We have found that post–colonial notion of caste based violence has taken new shape in above mentioned forms. While discussing in one of the FGDs we have found that, mental torture based on the caste affects to a very large extent. The new form of discriminations and exclusionary practices are also one of the violence as it is not been acknowledged as violence by the "mainstream" society. One of the most crucial findings regarding the nature of violence is about the denial of cremation ground for Dalit community in the villages. While discussing with respondents in FGDs, it was found that, burial ground is one of the major issues in most of the villages. It was seen that, the cremation ground for Dalits and other castes of the village are created separately. Recently, one of the studied villages had a huge crisis among the Dalits and upper caste community over the funeral of a Dalit person. The upper caste community of the village who holds the belief that the smoke spreading due to the cremation process of the Dalits' bodies pollutes them. This has caused atrocious problems to the latter. Dalit community had taken this issue seriously and fought against the upper caste when they were denied the funeral rite of one Dalit person.

Reservation in political sphere is helping in empowering the Dalit community. It is seen as a means for the Dalits to overcome the problem of utter exclusion from the public sphere (Manor, 2010). 73rd constitutional amendment has introduced the reservation for SCs, STs and women in Panchayati Raj System for seeking active participation of these groups in local politics. It was believed that reservation will bring democratic political changes to create equitable society by weakening the caste discrimination in politics. In many parts of the country, the above mentioned sections of the society have enabled these sections of the society to participate in local political process in-terms of contesting the election. There are posts reserved for Sarpanch (Village head) on rotation in village Grampanchayat. However, caste remains a key factor in the functioning of the democratic institutions of the modern Indian state especially in its local arm of governance, represented by the panchayat raj in the post- independence period (Teltumbade, 2010). The involvement in local politics has also become the reason for caste violence. It was observed from this study that, wherever we had come across Dalit members in the Grampanchayat body, their position as Sarpanch had been taken away by applying the process of passing a No-confidence motion against the Dalit Sarpanch. In one of the villages, Dalit community and upper caste community had a fight over the issue of replacing Dalit woman sarpanch especially Mahar (One of the Scheduled Caste Community) from her post without any valid reason.

The brutal killings or massacre are visible violence which is easily noticeable and action can be taken against these kinds of incident. But besides this, the aforesaid discriminatory practices which are many times remained unnoticed and have never considered as acts of violence.

The study found many reasons behind the atrocities which are taking place against Dalits in rural Maharashtra. Teltumbale in his book mentioned that, rising aspirations of the Dalits and their challenge to established structures of socio-economic, cultural and political dominance, then the violence is also an expression of resistance to these aspirations by the dominant castes (Teltumbale, 2010). It has been observed from this study that, wherever Dalits tried to establish their identity in politics and public places, they have seen made the victims of one or other form of caste atrocity. Ahmednagar district in Maharashtra relatively progressive in terms of politics and economy as there is the sugarcane lobby dominated by local politicians who invariably happen to be from the dominant caste groups. While discussing with the family members of the victims we found that their achievements in politics and economy are main reasons behind the atrocities inficited on them. A local Dalit leader from the Sonegaon village of Jamkhed block was killed by the villagers as he was continuously winning the Grampanchayat election and had also become the President of Panchayat Samati at block level. He also actively fought on the issue of gairan (common grazing land of the village for all the caste of the village). Dominant caste groups in the rural areas have authority as society had sanctioned them upper position in the ladder. According to Dahrendorf, no organization or society exists without a system of authority. The authority structure is the primary source of conflict (Abraham, 2015). The system of authority involves conflict between those who give orders and those who take them. Since, ages Dalits were receiving orders and dominant castes used to give orders. Hence, caste conflict is taking place where Dalits are trying to liberate themselves from this authoritative structure in the post-colonial period.

The rooted notion of purity and pollution in caste society leads to honour killing and brutal physical violence. It was found during field visits to Sonai and Kharda village of Ahmednagar district that dominant castes killed Dalit youths in order to save the honour of their caste. Another incident of caste atrocity took place during the study in which a Dalit woman was burnt alive as she had relation with an upper caste person in the same district. These series of atrocities of honour killing are the "gravest possible social violation" for upper castes (Waghmore, 2013).

Socio-economic development of Dalits could be one of the reasons behind atrocities. Historically Dalits were landless and had no other options to earn their livelihood. Hence they had to depend on the dominant castes to survive their families. Post-colonial era brought advancement in their economic condition by introducing land reforms, reservations in employment and in education, targeted development and welfare programmes and policies. These initiatives could help to change the economic relation between Dalits and other dominant caste communities in rural areas. The independent process of accumulation of economic resources in neo-liberal economy leads to antagonistic situation among Dalits and non-Dalits.

The social interaction among Dalits and Non-dalits has now become better as compared to the colonial period. It has been observed that, Dalits are getting entry into the temples and other religious places. The contribution for local Yatra or religious festival is also collected from Dalits. However, at the managerial level they are discriminated and are not allowed to be the part of the religious trusts of the village temple by orthodox Hindus.

Religion brings rigidity in the caste system by imposing rituals and religious values based on the philosophy of re-birth. There is a segmental division of Dalits in Maharashtra *viz.*, Mahars, Matangs, Chambars, Dhor, Bhangi, etc. There is a graded inequality based on the segmental division of these groups. Mahars are relatively empowered communities in Maharashtra. Most of Mahars have embraced Buddhism as Dr. Ambedkar did so. Hence they do not consider themselves as Hindus. The socio-economic development and political empowerment of Mahars is comparatively in better position compared with the condition of other Dalit castes. Dalit conversions are linked to their effort to liberate themselves from the very low status attached to their caste. It was observed that, Mahars had been denied of caste certificate as they wanted to change their caste status as neo-Buddhist from old identity as Hindu. Therefore it can be seen that Mahars are the most targeted communities for atrocities. However, it is found that wherever Mahars and Matangs are staying in unity and they are in large number, they live without any fear. The mobilization of Mahars and Matangs based on philosophies of Ambedkar and Annabhau Sathe could help to change the interaction pattern of Dalits and upper caste communities.

Development *viz.*, a *viz.*, Loss of Freedom

Development can be defined as a process of providing basic necessities to the individual. Basic necessities include food, clothing, shelter, education, health and security. Notable efforts have been initiated by the state for providing these basic amenities to all the citizens. However, providing these materialistic services are not only the factors which lead to development of the person. Along with this, dignity, self-respect and freedom of the person should also be taken intro consideration (Singh, 1999). Development is a process of expanding the real freedom that an individual enjoys. It consists of removal of various types of binding and lack of freedom which leave people with a very few choices and very little opportunities (Sen, 2000).

Considering these two aspects, dignity of self respect and freedom, it is observed through study that Dalits in these villages are going through the process of development on one hand and the loss of their freedom on the other hand. Gramsabha is considered as a village assembly where all the decisions regarding village development are taken in consultation with the villagers. It is found that Dalits through education and basic literacy are somehow aware about the Gramsabha but their knowledge is restricted to their physical appearance at the place. The restriction on the participation in the gramsabha is a form of violation of their liberty and freedom of speech. While discussing with them in FGDs, respondents have shared that, "we can sit in the gramsabha but we cannot speak in that sabha, if we speak they (upper caste) get angry with us and try to hold our voices back" While making case study of one of the victims, it was found that even the Dalit Sarpanch of the village had to face problems in the meetings. They listen to the Deputy Sarpanch, as this individual belongs to the upper caste community and has the practicing of handling Patilki (village affairs) since ages. It passes on from generation to generation.

According to Dr. Ambedkar, democracy must realize social and economic aspects. Social aspect in democracy should address all mutual social relations with equality. Nevertheless, caste was always a threat for Indian society and now for the largest vibrant democracy. In Indian politics, democracy was always influenced by the caste followed by gender. Caste based hegemonic culture does not allow Dalits to be part of the democratic process. Though the Constitution promotes right to freedom of expression but the field-based analysis of the data shows that, Dalits do not have an equal say in the democratic process. Representation and participation of discriminated and excluded groups in governance is a central element of inclusive policy and of building the inclusive society (Thorat, 2010). However, the situation is status-quo in reality as Dalit in rural areas are not even considered as partner of the mainstream development process. They have always been at the receiving end while upper castes are on the other side.

Another critical aspect discovered during the study is the threat of being killed or abused by the upper caste. Dalits are always in fear of brutal atrocities by upper caste dominant groups. Discussion in FGDs highlighted that, wherever atrocities have taken place, Dalits do not raise their voices against any kind of oppression as they visualize the consequences of speaking against upper castes. It is a "fear of freedom" of Dalits which leads to violation of their basic human rights as they are scared of speaking against their oppressors.

Cultural Legitimacy of Caste Violence

"We live in good environment; there are no atrocities in our village. Our relations with Dalits are good, whatever they want we give them so that they should not speak against us". This statement was given by deputy sarpanch of one of the surveyed villages who happened to be from the upper caste in front of the Dalit Sarpanch of his village. It was very surprising to note that Dalit sarpanch totally agreed with that statement and he stated that, *"though they call us by our caste, they always welcome us in a good way; they treat us equally and invite us to their functions. It is a matter of pride for us (dalits) to be part of their functions and visit their houses. We should not always target them for whatever they are doing with us; it is the*

practice from ages. If we establish relations with their lady obviously they will kill us, it is not their fault". (Field note: 2015)

Caste violence in rural India has become the hegemony. The violence against Dalits in rural areas is considered as granted in the village. The field based observations from this study show that, teasing, calling someone by his/her caste in public places, humiliating treatment, suppression of rights, verbal abuse are seen as normal practice FGR both Dalits and non Dalits. Most of the time Dalits never consider these incident as acts of caste violence. The notable thing which is found in this study was about the harassment of women at the workplace especially in the farm land. Dalit women have to support by working in the fields for survival of their families as mostly they are landless without any livelihood options. The discussion with one of the local activists explored that Patils (upper caste-dominant) of that village always have physical relations with Dalit women working in their farms. They consider them as their "property" to establish sexual relations with these women. Most of the time these practices are ignored by Dalits knowingly or unknowingly to sustain their livelihood in the village.

It has become a cultural legitimacy in which dominant caste groups with their authority justify caste violence morally.

5. SUGGESTIONS

- Government should promote or initiate programmes where all sub caste groups of Dalit community can be united
- It was found the poor role of activist and local leaders in the past atrocity cases. A small number of Dalit communities are divided in various sub-groups according to their local leader. Hence, there is lack of pressure groups which can influence this existing structure. There is a need to strengthen the advocacy groups.
- There is a need to create a platform where all Dalit sub-caste communities can pull together which can increase the strength.

- The strong implementation of Prevention of Atrocity Act should be carried out to avoid future incidences.
- Awareness about the Prevention of Atrocity act should be organized in each village for both victims and offenders.

6. CONCLUSION

In this paper efforts have been made to explore relation between caste violence and development of Dalits in rural Maharashtra. Dalits always face exclusion from dominant caste groups in public sphere. Wherever Dalits have tried to establish their identity as members of the larger civil society group they have become the victims of the caste violence. This study has revealed the impact of caste violence on the development of Dalit community. Development should be perceived as a multidimensional process, involving the reorganization and reorientation of both social and economic systems (Singh, 1999). However, the series of violence on downtrodden communities has dented the empowerment and development process of Dalits of Maharashtra in general and Ahmednagar district in particular. Dalits are scared of asserting their even basic human rights due to the caste violence. The caste violence limits the space for Dalits in public sphere. These communities have always been under the threat of becoming the victims of caste violence. Caste violence in India leads to 'culture of silence' in which these marginalized communities will be forced to be less assertive about their exploitation in public spheres.

REFERENCES

Teltumbade, A. (2010). The Persistence of Caste-The Khairlanji Murders and India's Ridden Apartheid, Navayana Publishing, New Delhi.

Sen, Amartya (2000). Development as Freedom, Oxford University Press, New Delhi.

Thorat S, (2010), Blocked by Caste-Economic Discrimination in Modern India, Oxford University Press, New Delhi.

Singh Katar (1999). Rural Development- Principles, Policies and Management, Sage Publications, New Delhi.

Waghmore, S. (2013). Civility against Caste-Dalit Politics and Citizenship in Western India, Sage Publications, New Delhi.

Abraham Francis, M. (2015). Modern Sociological Theory- An Introduction, Oxford University Press, New Delhi.

Tiwari, A. (2007). Human Rights Violations against Dalits: A Case of Failed State? *Indian Journal of Social Work*, 68(1).

Sivanna, N. (2014). Politics of Exclusion: The Case of Scheduled Castes in the Panchayats of Karnataka, *Social Change*, 44(1): 39–66

Thorat and Negi (2007). Exclusion and Discrimination- Civil Rights Violations and Atrocities in Maharashtra, Indian Institute of Dalit Studies, Working Paper Series, Volume-2

http://ncrb.gov.in/ (National Crime Record Bureau)

censusindia.gov.in, (Census 2011)

Mr. Pradeep Jare (MA-TISS), Assistant Professor, CSRD-ISWR, (Centre for Studies in Rural Development-Institute of Social Work and Research), Ahmednagar. He has presented several papers in national and international conferences on Social Exclusion and neo-liberalisam, and issues related to marginalized sections of the societies, Social Policies and local Governance.

Chapter 7

Anti-Oppressive Social Work Theory and Practice: Contextualising the Caste Debate in Indian Social Work Education

BHAT IQBALL[1] AND SUDHIR MASKE[2]

INTRODUCTION

Social work education as a stream of higher education system is more than 100 years old in the world and grew remarkably in the past few decades Mid (Bodhi, 2014) gley 2000). In India, it has already completed 75 years and has celebrated its platinum jubilee in the year 2012. The social work education and its professional practice in India is growing day by day but still professional identity and reorganization is far from wide. The status of social work education in India, especially of its knowledge base, is still debated and commented upon in published work (UGC Report, 1980) as well as in academic gatherings (seminars, conferences). Social work education as a profession is often considered as an emerging profession due to insufficient indigenous knowledge base and absence

[1] Department of Sociology and Social Work Central University of Jammu, E-mail: bhat.iqbal@gmail.com

[2] Department of Social Work, University of Delhi, E-mail: sudhir.maske@gmail.com

of indigenous orientation to knowledge component and lack of linkages between classroom learning and field realities (Howe, 1987; UGC Curriculum Development Report, 1990; Kulkarni, 1994; Singh and Srivastava, 2003: 87). Caste which is the bedrock of Indian social structure forms a pivotal role for the social analysis of Indian society. Therefore any social exploration in Indian society has to necessarily take into consideration caste as a lived reality. Caste as social context and foundation of many social problems has never been never taken into consideration to make social work practice more relevant and contextual to solve the individual, group and community problems in India. Rather what is noticed in pedagogy of social work India is the euphemism of social reformation within the oppressive social structure. This euphemism has been so elugosied and made sacrosanct as anyone critising reformers like Swami Vivekananda would be branded as unpatriptic and anti-national. The traditional social work educators have not taken serious interest in build his social work macro-practice around caste as an oppressive social structure. The traditional social work practice was so embedded in the pro-state policy that even the questions pertaining to oppressive social structures had to pass the litmus test of state policy. However we believe increasing assertion of voices of oppressed groups and communities across the western world has forced social work educators to address many social problems from the prism of anti-oppressive social work theory. Anti-oppressive social work theory has potential to address different types of oppression. Anti-oppressive social work theory would be a boon to social work practice for annihilation of the caste structure along with the inducing of social change.

Historical Trajectory of Social Work Education In India

The training for voluntary social workers started for the first time in 1930 by the Social Service League (SSL) in Mumbai. The services for industrial labouring classes conducted by the Nagpada Neighborhood House highlighted the need for trained workers around that time and this led to the commencement of full-fledged professional education in social work with the establishment of Sir

Dorabji Tata Graduate School of Social Work in 1936. This institution was later renamed as the Tata Institute of Social Sciences (TISS) (D'Souza, 1978; Narayan, 2001). The founding-director of the institute Clifford Manshardt was an American missionary and J.M. Kumarappa, a well-known Indian educator with MA.Ph.D degrees from Columbia University, was his collaborator. Thus the seed of social work profession in colonial India was sown by the American professionals (Kendall, 2000). Since then the American-tradition of social work tremendously influenced social work education and training in India (Nagpaul, 1972; Mandal, 1989; Mohan, 2008). Influence of American model on the pattern of social work education in India was further reinforced by the appointment of an American social worker as a visiting lecturer at Tata Institute, Mumbai (Pathak, 1975). Furthermore, Indians trained in professional social work in the USA returned to teach in the Indian school which led to further strengthening of this western model of social work influence. Finally, fortification of the American model was done with the appointment of a team of American social work educators under the auspices of the US Education Technical Mission 9 and the Council of Social Work of the USA (Gore and Gore, 1976) to act as consultants to some schools of social work and conduct annual seminars on social work education for the faculties of all the schools of social work in India (D'Souza, 1978). For 11 years from 1936 to 1947 TISS was the only institution for social work training in India till independence. In 1947–48 the second school was established for training in social work in Delhi. This was the first institution affiliated to the university system. Most institutions that came into existence in the 60s and 70s were established within the university system (UGC Report, 1980; Narayan, 2001).

Locating Caste in Anti-oppressive Social Work Theoretical Framework

Most of social work theories are derived from social sciences and there is disagreement as to the methods of social work intervention and relevance of the theories from which they are derived (Yelloly and Henkel, 2002). Theories for practice draw substantially on discourses drawn from other disciplines and fields of service activities. For example, anti-oppressive practice draws on ideas from sociological discourse. In the process of creating theories for practice, social workers transform ideas from service discourse for practice in specific contexts of social work practice. Theories for social work practice are usually developed within actual or intended contexts of practice. Thus, in the process of theory development, ideas from service discourses, are combined with social workers' specific purposes and experiences within particular practice contexts (Healy, 2005: 93). Elucidating the term 'theory', Prasad (2003) contends that as compared to its meaning and use in natural and physical sciences, the term is used loosely in social and behavioral sciences and in 'practice of social work profession'. According to him the use of social work theories in professional literature is rather ambiguous and sometimes the concept, frames of reference, practice model and philosophical proposition have been termed 'theory (ies).' Some social work practitioners maintain that due to the very nature of fast changing society-social relations, social institutions, culture, economy and polity, attitudes and behavioural patterns, dynamics of client practitioner relationship and very eclectic nature of the profession, theory has no value in professional practice. However, there is little appreciation of relationship between theory, knowledge and practice of social work all over. The development of social work profession in India has not taken into consideration the social reality of Indian social fabric rather it has adjusted itself to the existing social structures (Ramaih, 1996). Thus, what it led to was the continuous denial by social work educators for developing an indigenous knowledge base that could guide the practice of the profession. The educator, who is the 'key person,' is largely responsible for the growth and establishment of the profession. Fulfillment of this responsibility depends upon the role played by the educators who are involved in training the professionals and developing knowledge for the profession (Desai A., 1994; Prasad, 1997). The social work educators (SWE) impart knowledge and skills to the students to develop appropriate attitude for working with people and establishing linkages between theories and praxis wisdom within the socio-economic, political and cultural context in which they are embedded

(Shetty, 1996; Pathak, 2000). In this context, one observes that for many critical social work educators in India today, their foremost struggle seems to be positioned around the need to redeem social work education from the gripping clutch of western formulations and upper caste commonsensical charitable conceptions and practice (Bodhi, 2014).

The development of anti-oppressive social work theory has lent support to the reformulation of pedagogy of social work education not only in lndia but across the globe. The anti-oppressive social work theory as we see it would be an important theoretical framework for understanding the issue of caste and thus guiding the social work practice Indian social work curriculum. Anti-oppressive theory believes that oppression takes place when a person acts or a policy is enacted unjustly against and individual or group because of their affiliation to a specific group. This includes depriving people of a way to make a fair living, to participate in all aspects of social life or to experience basic freedoms or human rights. It also includes imposing belief systems, values, laws, and ways of life on other groups through peaceful or violent means. Oppression can be external as in the above examples or internal when groups start to believe and act as if the dominant belief system, values and life ways are the best and exclusive reality. Internal oppression often involves self-hate, self-censorship, shame and the disowning of individual and cultural realities. What is very interesting about anti-oppressive social work theory is it believes that everyday experience is shaped by multiple oppressions and social work is contested a highly political practice. Anti-oppressive social work theory argues that to politicise something or someone is to introduce the idea that everything has political elements; that is, to introduce the idea that nothing is neutral and everything involves an overt or covert struggle over power, resources and affirming identities (Donna Banies, 2011). Thus one can argue that anti-oppressive social work theory overcomes the blame of seeing social work as a historical and apolitical pedagooy. Anti-oppressive practice attempts to integrate the search and struggle for social change directly into the social work experience.This can take the form of new practices, new sources for and ways of understanding and building knowledge and practice, and new ways of building activism and opposition. Rather than a single approach, Anti-oppressive practice is an umbrella term for a number of social justice oriented approaches to social work, including feminist, Marxist, post-modernist, indigenous, post-structuralist, critical constructionist, anticolonial, anti-racist and anti-caste. Caste as a discourse within the padagogy of social work education has always remained as a passive reference.

The report of the UGC curriculum development which came out in 1989 for the first time noted the importance of caste in social work education and the same got incorporated as a component in social work curriculum under a course titled, "Issues and concerns of social work profession". As if to amplify the irony further, M.S. Gore came out with a book entitled, "Social Context of Ideology" which revolved around the ideas of Dr. B.R. Ambedkar. This movement was furthered by an interesting gathering of social workers around a theme 'Towards People Centred Development' organised by the TISS that purportedly deliberated on campaign and movements for empowerment of the marginalised. In 1997 the Declaration of Ethics of Professional Social Workcame out from the TISS published in the Indian Journal of Social Work (Bodhi, 2014). To our better understanding caste has been seen as a social problem just like many other prevalent social problems like poverty, dowry, female foeticide and so on. This understanding though quite old has still not been revised within the context of social work pedagogy India. What has been the case of the knowledge transformation processes across colonial countries by seeing domination of westernised theories, social work has never remained immune to it. Caste which still happens to be endemic to the social structure of Indian society started to be seen from the prism of either individualistic case work approach of social work method or from the much depoliticised method of community work. Therefore, what we see in India is a social work practice based on these two methods which have never considered caste system as a structural problem to be dealt from various levels of engagement. Social work education right form its initiation to the present time has been accused by many scholars as a project of glorifying the state interventions either of the colonial state or of free republic Soveriegn states. Though we do not deny this accusation at all but this is not to discredit many of those voices which tried to resist unjustified state interventions many times in various ways. However the marginality of those voices either in the academic domain of social work profession or in the practice domain of social work is a cause of concern. With the advent of time as we saw emerging of newer trends of social theories across the globe, be it a critical social theory or feminism, social work pedagogy also got shifted to the newer academic experiments. The influence of feminist studies and liberation studies along with the wave of decolonisation pushed the tide towards the development of newer form of social work pedagogy across many social work schools. Post colonial studies undoubtedly had a strong influence on many social work educators for teaching and framing the courses within the paradigm of raising soveriegn consciousness. One of the important developments in this sphere was the prominence of the Anti-oppressive social work theory. Many educators across different schools of social work started building the discourse with regard to the issues of racism along the lines of Anti-oppressive social work theory.

Post-colonial studies in India not only influenced in creation of new course content in disciplines like history and political science but also lead to the projection of the native knowledge as point of research and enquiry. The influencial writings like Orientalism from scholars like Edward Said not only boosted the post colonial project but also ignited the emergence of indigenous literature and knowledge across various communities and societies. However, what is unfortunate to mention here is that social work education in India remained silent to the growing popularity and influence of post-colonial studies. The Indian social work education continued with its legacy of western developed knowledge base, status-coist existence and also elitist Brahmanical supremacy of social work educators. In the article "Including Decolonization in Social Work Education and Practice" Tambura A. (2013) illustrate what is colonialism and why is it important to social workers. Tambura argues, colonization represented to the world as civilization, created European economic and governmental expansion throughout much of the world and as a result, Europeans attempted to control, exploit, and subjugate indigenous peoples. Social workers need to understand the history and current issues created by colonization to work effectively with people who have been colonized. He also demonstrate the decolonizing approaches to social work practice, relating post-colonial approaches to social work education and practice, these concepts provide an understanding of why and how the education and practice of Social Work can be decolonized The social work education not only realigned with the newer state programmes from the same knowledge base but also continued to evade the growing debates around the Caste oppression within the Indian social fabric. The regular and consistent argument that caste is weakening day by day in sovereign republic India is what kept the social work educators moving forward without doing the critical examination of the caste question either in their teaching methodology or in their practice base. However, it is pertinent to mention here that they are either resistant to believe or kept themselves blind to the fact that caste is changing its form of oppression rather than wearing or withering away. Though many sociological studies and independent research studies, newspaper reports regularly show how various caste atrocities are still being committed across India in a very brutal way.

In Indian scenario what would be interesting is to look at the caste debate in the social work pedgogy form the domain of anti-oppressive theory. Though much to the credit of writings across various disciplines In India like sociology, the debate of caste remains vibrant to this time. Even though the idea of reservation which unfortunately is seen as a poverty alleviation programme by many across the country is regarded as an effecitve measure to deal with caste system in India. To this has fallen prey many social work educators as well as practitioners. It is not suprising to see today that there are groups who are coming with the debate of reservation to be reviewed and categorised in monetary terms. Which in a way one could argue as seeing the caste structure through the prosm of class analysis. What is important for us to recollect that marxists in India have time and again criticized for doing the similar mistake of not signifying the caste system in India and rather overpowering the class analysis of the Indian social structure. As we see often in a hurry to Indianise rather than Indigenise social work pedagogy in India propped up what came to be known as Gandhian social work. This Gandhian social work is now strongly pushed as an in Indigenised pedagogy of social work education in India. Not to any surprise for us, the Ghandhian social work is nothing new but his mantras used during the freedom struggle movement. As all of us are aware of the fact as to how Gandhi viewed the caste structure in Indian society. Therefore Gandhian social work as a form of indigenised social work pedagogy would never go inconsonance with the anti-oppressive social work theory. Rather it sustains the oppression but gives a humane touch to it. One would always expect that in order to indigence the social work education in India something called as Ambedkarite social work could have been an appropriate idea. Ambedkar in his speech to Constituent Assembly on 26th November 1949 said, "we must begin by acknowledging the fact that there is complete absence of two things in Indian society one of these is equality. On the social plane, we have in India a society based on the principle of graded inequality which means elevation for some and degradation for others. On the economic plane, we have society in which there are some who have immense wealth as against many who live in abject poverty. On 26th of January 1950, we are going to enter into a life of contradictions. In politics we will have equality and in social and economic life, we shall, by reason of our social and economic structure, continue to deny the principle of one man one value. How long shall we continue to deny equality in our social and economic life? If we continue to deny it for long, we will do so only by putting our political democracy in peril. We must remove this contradiction at the earliest possible moment or else those who suffer from inequality will blow up the structure of political democracy which this assembly has so laboriously built up" (p. 207). Caste system can not be understood in any better way than what Ambedkar has analysed it in his work. or "The Annihilation of Caste". Therefore, what could have been interesting for social work pedagogy in India is the use of Ambedkar's scholarship for developing the social work practice with respect to the caste question. In this framework of debate about contexualising caste system within the social work profession in India, we argue that anti-oppressive social work theory would be a boon. Anti-oppressive social work theory recognises the marginality of a group through the criteria of oppression. Thus in terms of caste as structure and social reality oppression is embedded in its nature. Unless and until the anti-oppressive framework is not taken into cognisance the social work practice within the realm of caste system would be futile.

CONCLUSION

Indian society is very peculiar and unique in its own ways when it comes to the organization of the society. Caste becomes and is the marker of many social realities that one sees in Indian social structure. The social relations, political relations and even for that matter economic relations are not devoid of influence of the caste. Therefore caste becomes a prime demarcation for understanding and analysing the social fabric in Indian society. Thus Social work as a profession which is practice based and believes on the idea of change has to necessarily engage itself with the issue of caste. The social work educators inorder to remain relevant to the Indian social fabric have to necessarily develop the practice which should be informed by the anti-oppressive social work theory. The anti-oppressive social work theoretical formulation would analyse the caste structure in its very political and historical nature. Thus in a way it would mean social work practice have to be detached from the myth of neutrality. To summarise we would like to follow what Bodhi has agrued in his article titled 'The Practice of Anti-caste Social Work in India Towards a Theory of Dalit Social Work' "Currently the biggest challenge posed to social work education today is to free itself from its atheoretical and ahistorical certainties generally accentuated by the fact that traditional Indian social work does not seem to have the intellectual capability of generating new ideas or practice paradigms. Rarely showing or displaying any academic ability even of the most basic kind imperative for knowledge generation that is the courage for grounded and rigorous self-introspection, it has rarely taken any initiatives to engage in the politics of theory generation. Over the years it has done nothing more than reproduce cultural prejudice of the dominant groups (selling it as a knowledge) and strengthening the deeply stretched unequal structure of Indian society consciously, albeit unconsciously" (Bodhi, 2014).

REFERENCES

Bodhi, S.R. (2014). The practice of anti-caste social work in India towards a theory of Dalit social work. *Indian Journal of Dalit and Tribal Social Work*, (ISSN2320 2130), Vol. 2 Special.

Desai, A.S. (1985). Foundations of social work education in India and some issues. *Indian Journal of Social Work*, 46(1): 41–57.

Donna Baines, (2011). An Overview of Anti-Oppressive Practice: Roots Theory from the book chapter; Doing Anti-oppressive Practice: Social Justice Social Work (ISBN978-155266-428-5 (Bound) Published by Frenwood Publication (USA)

Gore, M.S. (1993). The Social Context of an Ideology: Ambedkar's Political and Social Thought, Published By: Sage Publications (ISBN-10: 8170363659).

Hugo, G., Roger, J. and Waghmore, S. (2016). From the Margins to the Mainstream: Instituionalizing Minorities in South Asia (ISBN978-93-515-0623-2) Sage Publication India, Pvt Ltd, New Delhi.

Malcolm, P. (2006). What is Professional Social Work; Published by Rawat Publication ISBN81-316-0165X Jaipur.

Mankar, V. (2016). Dr. B.R. Ambedkar an Intellectual Biography of Ideas, Enlightment, Life and Liberation Work (ISBN978-81-932027-1-5) Published by Blue World Series, Nagpur, India.

Nagpaul, Hans (1967). Dilemmas of social work education in India. *Indian Journal of Social Work*, 28(3): 269–84.

Nanavatty, Meher (1985). Social work education and professional development. *Indian Journal of Social Work*, 46(3): 315–325.

Pathak, S.H. (1975). A Quarter Century of Professional Social Work in India. *In*: Gokhale, S.D. (*eds.*), Social Welfare-Legand and Legacy, Bombay: Popular Prakashan. pp. 170–92.

Ramaiah, A. (1996). The Plight of Dalits: A Challenge to the Social Work Profession. *In*: Murli Desai *et al.* (*eds.*), Towards People Centered Development (Part-1), Mumbai: Tata Institute of Social Sciences.

Reisch, Michael (2002). Defining Social Justice in a Socially Unjust World. *Families in Society*, 83(4): 343–354.

Ronald, Y. and Laavanya, P.V. (2011). Dalits, social justice and social work education: Content analysis of social work syllabi. *Journal of Madras School of Social Work*, 6(1–2): 31–42 (ISSN 0975-4040).

Thomas, P.T. (1967). Problem of social work education in India. *Indian Journal of Social Work*, 28(1): 41–53.

Thorat, S. (2005). Caste, Social Exclusion and Poverty Linkages – Concept, 2005 Measurement and Empirical Evidence, paper presented in Seminar on "Marginalization and Dalits" organised by Development Alternative, Delhi.

UGC (1980). Review of Social Work Education in India – Retorspect and Prospect, Report of the Second Review Committee. New Delhi: University Grants Commission.

UGC (1995). Social Work Education in India Universities, New Delhi: University Grants commission.

UGC (1998). Review of Social Work Education in India – Retorspect and Prospect, Report of the Third Review Committee. New Delhi: 1.

UGC (2007). Review of Social Work Education in India-Retrospect and Prospect, Report of the Fourth Review Committee. New Delhi: University Grants Commission.

UGC (2013). Review of Social Work Education in India – Retrospect and Prospect, Report of the Fifth Review Committee. New Delhi: Universty Grants Commission.

Mr. Bhat Iqball is well known academician and researcher; presently he is working as Assistant Professor at the Department of Sociology and Social Work, Central University of Jammu. Mr. Iqball has done his Master in Social Work from Kashmir University, Srinagar. He has also done M.Phil from School of Sciences, Jawaharlal Nehru University, New Delhi and also pursuing Ph.D from their itself. He has very extensive international exposure with many prestigious International Universities, Like Middlesex University, and University of Edinburgh. His major interest areas are Tribal Studies (Nomadism), Social Policy and Political Economy of Health, Caste and Critical Social Work, Social Justice, Peace & Conflicts.

Mr. Sudhir Maske has done Master of Arts in Social Work from Tata Institute of Social Sciences, Mumbai in Year 2010. He has grounded field experience in Rural and Tribal Community Development field. He has worked for one year as state consultant with Tribal Development Department, Govt. of Gujarat. He has also worked as Research Fellow in Rural Transformation Programme of TISS. Since 3 years, he has been actively involved in Teaching, Training and Research activities. He has started his academic carrier with Department of Social Work, Guru Ghasidas Central University of Chattisgarh, Bilaspur. Presently, he is working as Assistant Professor at the Department of Social Work, University of Delhi. His major research and teaching areas are Social Justice and Empowerment, Caste and Social Work Education, Anti-Oppressive Social Work Practice, Management of Non-Governmental Organization & CSR, Social Policy, Planning and Advocacy.

Chapter 8

Social Hegemony and Atrocities Against Scheduled Castes of Andhra Pradesh-Human Rights Perspective

NAGARAJU VADAPALLI[1]

INTRODUCTION

The Dalits are socially, economically, politically religiously, culturally oppressed and Scheduled Castes are one among these marginalized groups. Discrimination against them is all pervading and has religious sanction. The Indian Constitution guarantees to all citizens the fundamental rights and equal protection before the law. It provides a number of safeguards to Scheduled Castes to ensure their all-round development and protection against all kinds of the discriminations in India. But most of the provisions of the Constitution have remained only on paper because their implementation has been faulty, half-hearted and inadequate. Inequality, discrimination, exclusion and stigmatization have jointly contributed to the utter marginalization in India. No doubt, Scheduled Castes were never given human rights or treated with dignity; hence those cannot be

[1] Department of Political Science, Kakatiya University, Warangal, Telangana, E-mail: nagakalpana@gmail.com

restored to them as such. Scheduled Castes are one of the marginalized and neglected sections of the Indian society[1]. Whenever they want to get human rights they continue to suffer from utter violence even today. In this context, this paper aims to discuss how Scheduled Castes have become victims of caste society despite of human rights.

SOCIAL HEGEMONY AND ATROCITIES AGAINST THE SCHEDULED CASTES

Atrocities are to be given viewed as social and physical violence committed collectively or individually by those groups, castes and communities or their members who try to have more access to the existing resources and monopolize their status-superiority over others. The targets of such atrocities are those who have traditionally been degraded and deprived and who try to find a place other than that prescribed to them in the social structure. Such efforts are likely to disturb the status-quo and intercept the unlimited chances of the privileged one. Hence, violence and atrocities take place against them[2]. The atrocities have increased during all the years because the caste Hindus here grown increasingly jealous, intolerant and vindictive even towards the little progress made by the Scheduled Castes. The Scheduled Castes are subjected to various types of atrocities due to the caste Hindu's resentment against a number of government policies in general and the provision of reservation in education and jobs in particular adopted in their favour though the immediate causes involved in the commission of atrocities might be something else. Equally important in this regard are a number of inherent social contradictions between caste Hindus and the Scheduled Castes. However, very little is said about the growing resentments and protests shown by people of the Scheduled Castes towards atrocities perpetrated on and various types of discriminations practiced against them. Such a course of action is adopted by them more in self-defense or to gain self-respect and protect their dignity than in pursuing their social and economic development through the Constitutional measures and other means.

It does not, however, mean that the Scheduled Castes are satisfied with the present level of their socio-economic development. They are in reality more interested in achieving their freedom from traditional bondage and liberation from the economic dependence on the upper castes and classes. These obviously attract the convulsing acts of the upper castes which are resented by the Scheduled Castes. Thus, the desire and action of the Scheduled Castes, reaction to that of caste Hindus and others and then counter reaction of the Scheduled Castes placed in the sequence of chain-responses are such that ultimately take the form of the 'Scheduled Castes' protest movements[3]. The Scheduled Caste leaders had to give a very tough fight against social tyranny. The British rulers were, more or less, sympathetic to the Scheduled Castes, but their main interest was in maintaining their empire in this country. The native princes were more or less indifferent towards the problems of Scheduled Castes, except the Maharaja of Kothapur, Baroda and Pithapur. The caste Hindu leaders, except a few, were busy in the struggle for Swaraj. In that adverse situation, the leaders had to struggle for their rights. The way of struggle of course, proved to be efficacious to the Scheduled Castes[4]. Even then the downtrodden sections slowly raised their voices since after independence, they slowly realized their positions. The participation in electoral process, the introduction of adult franchise, establishment of democratic institutions and decentralization of power and constitutional guarantees awakened their consciousness slowly. Once the Constitutional guarantees are ensured their participation in electoral politics, they have expanded their political participation. They have enormously improved their capabilities even then; they have improved the social status and have tried to articulate their interests[5]. All this has occurred because of consciousness among the Scheduled Castes as Dr. B.R. Ambedkar said tell the slave he is a slave and he will revolt[6]. Every incident has its own history, nature of movement, strategy, and experience

a) Karamchedu

Karamchedu village is located in Prakasham District of Andhra Pradesh. Karamchedu incident also has some history. Venkateswarlu from Chindu Caste fought against landlords in the cause of wages of agricultural labourers and was beaten by upper caste landlords. But he ran away and hid in the house of Madigapalli to protect himself. Kamma Landlords attacked Madigapalli, bul Madigas refused to surrender Venkateswarlu with the help of Mala community. Thereafter, Malas also attacked the caste prejudiced Kamma people. Thereby, Kamma people were waiting for chance to attack the Madigapalli. The Kamma youth, particularly Gotori Laxmaiah, Isaiah, Erram Venkateswarlu behaved as 'Modern Keechakas' on Scheduled Castes girls. After the emergence of TDP, Kamma people shifted to TDP but Scheduled Castes remained with Congress Party. In general election, son-in-law of NTR contested as TDP candidate and they demanded Scheduled Castes to cast their vote to Daggubati but Scheduled Castes decided to cast their vote to Congress. Scheduled Castes were attacked by upper caste TDP men but were opposed by Scheduled Castes and returned. On 16th July, 1985 Pothina Srinu, Raineedu Prasad from Kamma caste, came to Madigapalli tank with their buffaloes and they tried to pollute water. Then Katti Chandraiah, Scheduled Castes boy objected them. For that, they tried to beat that Scheduled Caste youth. Then Munnag Suvartha, Scheduled Castes woman supported Chandraiah. Then Kamma youth threw the stick at Suvartha but she escaped with the help of steel vessel. That incident was not digested by upper caste and they attacked Madigapalli with spears, axes and iron rods. Scheduled Castes women were raped and eight Scheduled Castes men were murdered, but six were identified, another two were buried by policemen[7].

b) Audatpur

On the evening of January 15th, 1986, two Scheduled Caste farm servants Ganapathi and Manik, belonging to Audatpur, Narayana Khed Mandal, Medak district were returning home after finishing their day's work (Ganapathi was a farm servant of Pandru Patel and Manik was a farm servant of Vital Rao. Both the employers were rich peasants of the village). As they were going from their masters' cattle sheds they had to, inevitably, pass through the village. When they reached Mahboob Zab's houses, which were situated in the middle of the village, they were stopped by Manohar Patel to ask them why they had entered the village in which they were forbidden entry a few days earlier. They also abused the Scheduled Castes in filthy language when the farm servants tried to defend themselves Manohar Patel took a Kamakathai (a big hook fixed at the end of a long stick used to cut the branches of the trees) from a bystander and inflicted injuries on Ganapathi's head, legs and hands. Meanwhile, Shankarappa and others around pelted stones at Manik. Having seen Ganapathi bleeding, the landlords withdrew into their houses. After sometime, Ganapathi and Manik managed? To reach the Scheduled Castes colony. Many Madiga men who had migrated to different places for work happened to return to the village on the occasion of the Sankranthi festival. Thus, they were present in the village on that day. All the Madiga men gathered round shifted the injured to manor police station and lodged a complaint against Manohar Patel and Shankarappa. The sub inspector of manor shifted Ganapathi to Narayankhed hospital and remained indifferent to the whole incident. Angered with the Madigas who went to the police station the landlords mobilized their supporters on the evening of the 16th. They decided that the Madigas should be taught a lesson. The same evening they mobilized money on a large scale to meet the court and police station expenses. This indicates that the plan to attack the Scheduled Castes was systematically thought out. In many houses grains money, clothes, vessels and goats were either burnt to ashes or were looted. There was a deliberate loot conducted by way of snatching Mangalsutras and other small gold ornaments available on the women. The looting and arson spree continued for two hours. Thus, the loot, arson and destruction of 23 houses of Audatpur Scheduled Castes were the result of a systematic plan by caste landlords with the help of Backward Castes[8].

c) Chundur

Chundur is village of Guntur District. On 7th July, 1991 Govatora Ravi an M.A. student went to the Cinema theatre to watch a film with a Chair Class ticket. The Reddy boy who went to the same class got annoyed with the fact that a Scheduled Castes was sitting in a chair. The Reddy youth picked up a quarrel on the pretext that his foot touched the upper caste boy sitting in the front seat and beat up Ravi severely. As the Cinema theatre was adjacent to the Scheduled Castes colony, Ravi went to the colony and informed other Scheduled Castes youth. The Scheduled Castes youth retaliated and this enraged the upper caste arrogance. Thereafter, Ravi was sent to Ongole by his father. Next day the upper caste hooligans went to Bhaskar Rao (father of Ravi) and dragged and threatened to extract information of Ravi. Then Bhaskar Rao told them when he would come back. The Reddys kept a watch at the railway station and chased him and beat him to the point of death. Brandy was poured down his throat and the unconscious boy was shifted to the Police Station. The next day upper caste ordered Ravi family to leave the village. At that stage other Scheduled Castes intervened and said that the Govatora family would not leave the village and the entire Scheduled Castes colony would stand by them. Though the terrified family left the village, the upper caste annoyance shifted from Govatora family to the entire Scheduled Castes colony. Reddy's began to make preparations for a bigger attack. The police posted a picket under the leadership of S.I. Srinivasa Rao who played an impartial role for some time, but he was sidelined on the day of the attack. The presence of such a large police force itself became a death trap for the Scheduled Castes. Scheduled Castes were chased with spears, axe and knives. As the Scheduled Castes were running, their legs were cut into pieces, pushed into gunny bags and thrown into the canal. While the carnage was taking place in the fields, the police were chewing pans and smoking cigarettes in the village. The Scheduled Castes were of the opinion that one police officer himself participated in the killing spree[9].

d) Thimmasamudram

Thimmasamudram was a village of Naguluppalapadu Mandal of Prakasam District. In 1984, the struggle for land began for 430 acres of Government land. 13 castes including SC, ST and BCs occupied that land under the leadership of communists but landlords stopped that with the help of the record surveyor, Batina SubbaRao by burning land records. In the course of time, land struggle made a journey in different ways in the hands of upper caste political leaders. Finally on 14th December, 1990 it was settled by Dalit MahaSabha, District Collector and Addanki Congress MLA to distribute the land in dispute through Scheduled Castes Corporation. All this gave bitterness to upper caste landlords. Thereby, upper caste people had made preparations to attack Malapalli under the leadership of Telugu Desam MLA Karanam Balaram with bombs. Scheduled Castes were aware of upper caste people's preparations for attack and they made complaint against them. Police camp was organized but on 17th January, 1991, upper caste Goondas attacked Malapalli with spears, axes and bombs. Golla Devaram and Molathoti Arjun Rao were severely wounded; Girls Swapna and Jackamma were wounded by bombs. This incident revealed the socially conflicting relationships of untouchability and land ownership in Indian villages[10].

e) Chalakurthi

Muthamma belongs to Chalakurthi village of Nalgonda District. She belongs Scheduled Caste Communities. She was paraded in that village naked on 11th August, 1991 by Upper Caste People. This incident exhibited the class and caste prejudices of upper caste and patriarchy. All this happened because of the help of Muthamma given by her in the elopement of Jayamma and Govind who belongs to Reddy "and Scheduled Castes respectively. Upper caste (Reddy) people Parakala Narayana Reddy, Parvatha Reddy, Ram Reddy, dragged Muthamma from her home and made her nude and her hands were tied with her blouse. After this she was nudely in the village as a procession with beating. These upper caste people had behaved in very brutal manner. This incident reveals about principles of Manusmriti. According to Manu upper caste men could maintain sexual affairs with lower caste women, and there are no social sanctions in Smriti about sexual affairs of Scheduled Castes men with upper caste women[11].

f) Cheemakurthi

Three Scheduled Castes women were raped and murdered by upper caste people in Cheemakurthi of Ongole district. This incident happened in Cheemakurthi on 26th April 1992. Women were asked to clean the lorry by upper caste people with wage of Rs.20/- per hour. Scheduled Castes women Ramulamma, Anjamma, Yesumma and Ramanamma, were brought to the quarry by upper caste people. Among them, three Ramulamma, Anjamma and Yesumma were raped and murdered brutally and they were thrown into water tank. Among them Ramulamma and, Anjamma knew about swimming. But upper caste people Shidda Nageshwar Rao and others argued that women were drowned into water while they were cleaning the lorry. This incident remained as a mark of sexual exploitation by upper caste people towards lower caste people. This brutal action reveals about caste prejudices and sexual exploitation of Scheduled Castes women[12].

g) Pottilanka

Pottilanka is a tiny village of East Godavari district of Andhra Pradesh about 20 km from Rajahmundry town. Upper caste people attacked the Scheduled Castes colony on 21st March 1995 night about 200 people and had beaten to death one Scheduled Castes youth, Palli Veera Pandu. All this happened on account of the caste ego of upper caste people against Scheduled Castes in this village. Upper caste people sowed the seeds for this violent misbehavior of Scheduled Castes man, Ambati Rajaratnam with an upper caste woman who was waiting to board a bus. Thereby upper caste people accompanied the women, beat up Rajaratnam and dumped him at the village Panchayath office. The Scheduled Castes, enraged by the attack on Rajaratnam, thrashed some upper caste youth in the village and this set off another attack on the Scheduled Castes colony by a 200 strong upper caste mob with lethal weapons and killed Veera Pandu[13].

h) Vempeta

The Indian village Vempeta is located in Pamulapadu Mandal of Kurnool District of Andhra Pradesh. There was an incident on 15th July, 1998. It was depicted as clash between Malas and Madigas, clash between two revolutionary parties. This incident observed in closure and in human rights approach by Varavara Rao and Balagopal respectively. But one should observe that incident is anti caste approach to know ground realities. This incident proved that, the marginalised people were affected to carnage if social movements lead in class struggle approach. Vempeta village was seen as a communist village but it has remained for a longtime under the leadership of Reddy communists without any remarkable changes. Now, in Andhra Pradesh, caste (social) consciousness rose against not only to political parties but also communist revolutionary groups. In the course of time Vempeta communist village was transformed into an intra-class war village. Whenever Scheduled Castes questioned the caste lines and communist leadership of Reddys never looked into Scheduled Castes' awareness in anti-caste philosophy. Vempeta massacre was not a result of murder of Bomma Shivaiah. It had a prehistory by five incidents like (1) Bus tickets (2) Agriculture Land gardening (3) Food grains Kanta (4) Problem of endowment land (5) Murder of Mala Devaraju. As Dr. B.R. Ambedkar said, until India is caste based country nobody can change these caste differences with class struggle approach or a religious approach. So all this was not a matter of conflict between the communist groups. In India, caste is a social agent which kept the people in water-tight compartments beyond economic matters. In Vempeta, endowment land was distributed among 76 Madiga families, 56 Mala families and 106 other Backward Caste families under the leadership of Madiga youth by name of Rythu Coolie Sangham. In Kurnool district, struggle for land is not only against the landlords but also against the Armed Gangs (factions). So here both had been worked against. In this situation, Bomma Shivaiah tried to attack the people to stop land struggle. For that, communist revolutionary groups warned

Shivaiah but he never stopped himself. The revolutionary group realized the wicked and crucial mind of Shivaiah and killed him. Madigas have been opposing factions and landlords in every aspect in that village. Upper case landlords here waiting for a suitable time to attack Madigapet. The Death of Shivaiah gave a chance to upper caste land lords to attack Madigapet. Budda Vengala Reddy and others attacked Madigapet and others who supported Madigas in land struggle. In this brutal killing ten people lost their lives including 6 Madigas; Madigapeta was burnt by Vengala Reddy group. All death bodies were thrown into fire to postmortem and depicted as clash between Malas and Madigas[14].

i) Pyapili

In Pyapili, on 1st September 2003, upper caste and Backward Caste Hindus attacked on the procession of Ganesh of Scheduled Castes (Madigas). Upper castes and backward castes made objection to allow the Scheduled Castes Ganesh immersion procession through their streets. Because Scheduled Castes are religiously untouchables and they are not eligible to celebrate the Hindu festivals as caste Hindus celebrated. Upper castes and Backward Castes attacked the procession with stout sticks and stones. They disturbed the procession and destroyed idol of Ganesh and police vehicle that came to protect the Scheduled Castes religious right. After that, Backward Castes along with upper castes raided the houses and shops and exploited, looted the belongings of Scheduled Castes with the help of officials. Finally, district officials arranged another new idol and immersed as the wishes of Backward Castes and upper castes. All this episode reveals that Scheduled Castes have no right to practice their own religious rites against upper castes and other backward castes in an equal manner[15]. Among Backward Castes, Boya caste population have a major portion in the population of that village. But upper castes economically and politically dominated. Scheduled Castes are converted to Christianity and they educated their children and some of them became employees in the Government sector. In 2001 local bodies' elections, K.E. brothers candidate Boya Chennaiah was defeated by the Jangam Suseelamma (Leelavathi). Then they accused Scheduled Castes for their defeat and Scheduled Castes were converted to Christianity, they are not working with landlords families in bonded labour. All these things lead to Pyapili incident[16].

j) Laximpet

On 12th June 2012, 200 Backward Castes people who belong to Turpu Kapu community including 22 women attacked Scheduled Castes with spears, axes stout sticks and stones and killed five Scheduled Castes men and injured 20 members due to the clash about government assigned land in the Ayukta of Madduvalasa Reservoir in Srikakulam District[17]. The village Laxmipet is located in Vangara Mandal of Srikakulam district of North–Andhra. The Government of Andhra Pradesh collected 350 Acres land for Madduvalasa reservoir from Turpu Kapu and other castes with compensation. But only 100 acres were used for reservoir purpose and remaining 250 acres are nearer to new settlement of Laxmipet and among 250 acres 190 acres of land is under the cultivation of Turpu Kapu people and remaining 60 acres of land is cultivated by the Scheduled Castes which was left by the Devakavada villagers. Laxmipet Turpu Kapu people who have economic and political hegemony in the district want to grab the land from Scheduled Castes. But Scheduled Castes resisted the Backward Castes Kapus from the land grabbing. This has resulted in anger of Turpu Kapus against Scheduled Castes. They raided the Scheduled Castes houses and murdered five members and injured 20 members of Scheduled Castes[18].

CONCLUSION

Militant Scheduled Castes struggles in Andhra Pradesh started with the carnage of Karamchedu. Dalit Mahasabha emerged from Karamchedu Balipeetam (after the death). After birth of Dalit Mahasabha, the image of Dr. B.R. Ambedkar entered every Scheduled Castes colony and his anti-caste philosophy spread over the villages and it became the philosophical foundation of the lives of the

Scheduled Castes. Thus, when they tried to get their rights when they were attacked by dominant castes in Andhra Pradesh. The failure of the Indian state and its instruments to cope with the problems arising in the process of socio-economic change in a society with adult suffrage and equality of opportunity and status, among other similar objectives provided in our Constitution, has led to rising expectations on the one hand, and growing consciousness of the exploitation and indignity in social relations, on the other. Such a combination has inevitably led to strong resentment expressing itself in violence. Policies are proclaimed and promises are made but which remain unfulfilled. Laws are enacted which are not fairly and effectively implemented because of strong vested interests combined with the weak political will and inadequacies of the administration.[19] Unless these infirmities are removed and progress made towards the creation of a truly just society and non-exploitative social order, violence is not only likely to continue but may get aggravated.

REFERENCES

1. Emanual Nahar (2007). Restoration of Human Rights and Dignity to Dalits, Mainstream, p. 13.
2. Nandu Ram (1995). Beyond Ambedkar, Essays on Dalit in India, Har-Anand Publications, New Delhi, p. 268.
3. Rajagopal, P.R. (1987). Social Change and Violence, the Indian Experience, Uppal Publishing House, New Delhi, p. 82.
4. Henry Thiagaraj (*ed.*) (2007). Human Rights from the Dalit Perspective, Gyan Publishing House, New Delhi, pp. 79–82.
5. Selvantathan, S. (1989). Status of Scheduled Castes, Ashish Publishing House, New Delhi. p. 193.
6. Bixapathy, D. (2008). Caste Discrimination in Revenue Records-A Study of Erstwhile Warangal p. 36 1911"1976, UnPublished Thesis, Department of History, Kakatiya University, Warangal.
7. Kanchallaiah (2000). The State Oppressions and Weaker Sections, in ChanduSubbarao. Francis, D. (*ed.*), Development of Weaker Sections, Rawat Publications, Jaipur, pp. 205–209.
8. KanchaIlaiah (1994) The Chundur Carnage - The Struggle of Dalits. *In*: Sandeep Pendse (*ed.*), At Cross roads Dalit Movement Today, Vikas Adyana Kendra, Bombay, pp. 95–102.

9. Devarapalli Mastanrao (1997). Dalita Dasabdam, Lokayukta Publications, Ponnuru, p. 48.
10. Bixapathy, D. (2008). op.cit, p. 39.
11. Sa, U. (2005). Dalita Rananinadam, Edureetha Publications, Hyderabad, pp. 129–131.
12. Bixapathy, D. (2008). op.cit, p. 46.
13. Pani (2005). Nalugu Simhala Dadilo Dalitulu (Four Lions attack on Dalits). Sa, U. (*ed.*), pp. 287–288.
14. Fact Finding Report on Pyapili, ibid, pp. 239–244.
15. Ajay Gudavarthy (2005). Dalit and Naxalite Movements in Andhra Pradesh: Solidarity or Hegemony, Contextualizing Dalit Movement in South India, Selfhood, Culture, and Economy, VikalpAlternatives, pp. 27–31
16. Shah, Ghanshyam *et al.*, (2006). Untouchability in Rural India, Sage publications, New Delhi.
17. Chimme John Barnabas (2012). Laxmi Pet Ghatana Em Theliyajestundi. *Veekshanam*, 10(8).
18. Ramachandram, Y. and Ramakrishna Rao, D.V. (2012). Laxmipet Massacre - Land – Caste. *Veekshanam*, 10(8): 12.
19. Rajagopal, P.R. (1987). op.cit, pp. 7–8.

Dr. Nagaraju Vadapalli has been working as Assistant Professor (PT) of Political Science in Kakatiya University, Warangal, India. He has been working for Post-Doctoral Progamme on Social Movements and Social Change: Scheduled Castes Human Rights Movement in Andhra Pradesh-A Study from Kakatiya University, Warangal, India. He pursued his Doctoral Degree for Ambedkarites' Political Participation in Andhra Pradesh and Master Degree in Political Science with Mass Movements and Politics in India as specialization from Kakatiya University.

He has been attended many National and International Conferences and presented Research Papers/Articles on Dalit-Bahujan Philosophers and their Philosophy and its Relevance, Dalit Movement, Education and Social Justice, and Indian Politics. He has been published Twenty Nine (29) Research Papers/Articles in various Journals and Magazines and Edited Books. He was authored for Three Books (1) Democratic Experience of Dalit-Bahujans in India (2) Status of Dalit-Bahujans in India, (3) Dalit, Oppressed Castes-Imperialism). He has membership in Professional Bodies like Indian Social Science Association, Indian Political Science Association, Indian History Congress, South Indian History Congress and Andhra Pradesh History Congress. He has Fourteen years of Teaching Experience. He has been organizing NGO (Centre for Dalit-Bahujan Studies) as founder Director since 2014.

Chapter 9

Social Exclusion, Mobility Strategy and Atrocities Against Dalits in Gujarat

RAJNIKANT PARMAR[1]

INTRODUCTION

The State of Gujarat, which proclaims the unprecedented economic growth 14.70 (GDP) during 2012-13[1] and also a development model of Gujarat, under the then regime of CM Narendra Modi, has a different story to tell about the conditions of Dalits in Gujarat. The Hindutva project of Rashtriya Swayamsevak Sangh in Gujarat has tactically segregated the lower castes from development opportunities and it has filled the various government departments with employees supporting Hindutva ideology (Shani, 2007). According to the RTI query of an NGO Navsarjan Trust in Gujarat, the atrocities against Dalits are very rampant and 8,884 cases of atrocity were registered in the state between 2006 and September 2013. The data revealed that on an average the state recorded 18 murders, 37 rapes, 52 severe injuries and 1,019 cases where families were afflicted with atrocities every year (The Times of India, 2014). And the cases of caste-based

1 Tata Institute of Social Sciences, Mumbai

[1] Business Standard briefed in an article about Gujarat's economic growth on July 2, 2014.

discrimination, arson, atrocity, murder, land grabbing, rape, burnt and seriously injured, social boycott are frequently reported in news papers. Caste-based discrimination rooted in the religion against Dalits has made the life of Dalits more challenging and vulnerable. Besides, the lack of equal opportunities for social development and justice in Gujarat has made the educated people among Dalits lose their faith in all institutions and they foresee their safe future by assimilating in larger Hindu fold. Thus, the educated urban middle class Dalits have started changing their surnames and attempt to access the social needs such as housing and education which are exclusionary in character. Even after changing surnames, the demon of caste still follows them and they become victims of atrocities after revelation of their real Dalit identity. The present paper revolves around the social exclusion of Dalits and its consequences. It also attempts to reveal the resultant effect of changing surnames with social exclusion and the atrocities Dalits face after revelation of their real Dalit identity.

The first section of this paper briefly presents the concept of social exclusion and the practice. The second section comprises social exclusion of Dalits and its consequences in the field of education, employment and housing. Finally, the third section will discuss the risks and atrocities Dalits have to face after revelation of their surnames.

SOCIAL EXCLUSION

The term, social exclusion, was coined in 1974 by Rene Lenoir in France, who published Les Exclus. Un Francais stir dix. He included variety of people who are excluded like not only the poor but also the handicapped, suicidal people, aged, abused children and others (Silver, 1994). The concept became popular in other countries through European Union channels (Silver, 1998). The concept of social exclusion has potential to provide essential insight into the current situation of Dalits in Indian society and challenges faced by them in daily lives. According to Silver (1994) who draws on the work of Weber emphasizes exclusion as a result of hierarchical power relations in the constitution of a social order, group monopolies, social closure by powerful groups to restrict the access of outsider.

Social exclusion is practised through mobilization of institutional bias (Lukes, 1974), through a set of values, beliefs, rituals and institutional procedure that operate systematically to benefit the certain groups and individuals and to exclude others. Parkin (1979) argues social closure is another exclusionary mechanism by restricting access to valued resources and opportunities to a concentrated group and such social collectivities maximize their rewards. It is a deliberate strategy of exclusion and any groups or individuals based on caste, religion, gender, origin, race are seized from accessing opportunities and economic resources. Another mechanism is the unruly practices (Fraser, 1989; Gore, 1993) refer to the gaps between rules and the implementation in all institutional domains. According to Sen's analysis, 'judiciary bends the rules to support particular class, gender or ethnic interests whilst invoking the rules to maintain an illusion of impartiality' (Gore, 1993: 443).

Besides, a comprehensive working definition of social exclusion is as follows. "Social exclusion is a complex and multi-dimensional process. It involves the lack or denial of resources, rights, goods and services, and the inability to participate in the normal relationships and activities, available to the majority of people in a society, whether in economic, social, cultural or political arenas. It affects both the quality of life of individuals and the equity and cohesion of society as a whole" (Levitas *et al.*, 2007: 25).

Since it is a multi-dimensional concept as people may be excluded from livelihoods, employment, property, housing, education and social network (Silver, 1994), people are often deprived of different things at the same time in the economic, social and political spheres. The disadvantages faced by the excluded communities are interrelated, for instance, people belonging to lower castes or school drop-outs may have a greater risk of being unemployed or employed in unstable jobs and hence be low paid, less educated, have little political power and fewer social contacts (Haan and Kabeer, 2008).

Social exclusion focuses on societal relations, institutions and social processes through which people are being deprived. Group formation on the basis of identical social attributes or vested interests takes place in society therefore social exclusion takes place at each level against those who are not part of such association. G.S. Ghurye (1932) also observed the tendency among every caste to form an association of its members to preserve and ameliorate the social status in the hierarchy. Thus a member of such association who get help from such caste-based association is likely to pay back to the association and the resources will likely to remain within the community.

Urban space which is characterised by anonymity and plurality, the caste functions through caste-based associations and networks which tend to exclude castes which are not the 'in-group member' (Parmar, 2014). Disadvantage results in social exclusion when the various social institutional mechanism through which resources are allocated and value assigned operate in such a way as to systematically deny particular groups of people the resources and recognition which would allow them to participate fully in the life of that society (Haan and Kabeer, 2008: 24).

"More pragmatically, to continue to overlook and ignore the needs of the excluded, and their sense of exclusion, is likely to generate a range of unruly practices on their part, from petty crime to organized violence to civil war, activities with negative implications for the security, safety and peace of mind of all sections of society." (Haan and Kabeer, 2008: 35).

Social Exclusion of Dalits and its Consequences

P Sainath (1999) and Parmar (2005) argue that Dalits are changing their surnames to escape their caste tags because it invites prejudices and results into discrimination and exclusion. Bearing a surname that identifies a person as a Dalit can have huge problems in getting a job or purchasing house, for instance. The new generation is widely throwing away the caste indicating surnames and some Dalits keep neutral surname that does not reveal a person's caste identity, certainly not as a Dalit in order to further their life chances and enhance livelihood opportunities. Parmar (2005) on the phenomenon of changing surnames, listed benefits such as social acceptability and better interaction, easier availability of private sector jobs, access to credit, purchasing land and property and even striking office friendships in inter-caste work place. Therefore, Dalits are following this innovative mobility strategy of changing surnames to avoid negative implications of one's caste surname and to further life chances and enhance livelihood opportunities.

Education

A study of Lancy Lobo (1994) reveals that the privileged caste-Hindus were against educating outcastes in government schools and opposed having exclusive schools for outcastes as well. The upper classes do not wish to see sheds taught either in the government schools or by missionaries as they think they will give themselves air and get a rise in the world...' (Ibid, 18). Even today 53.78% Dalit children studying in primary schools are discriminated against in mid-day meals. 'Even as the syllabus teaches equality, students learn lessons in untouchability in practice. All Dalit students are forbidden from participating in cultural events. Valmikis have to also clean up school toilets.'[2] The upper caste students of a government school in Sabarkantha district of Gujarat rejected government's mid-day meal scheme because the utensils used were washed by a Dalit woman.[3]

In higher education sector, the medical field is the most exclusionary for the untouchables and it is also proved by the studies of the Shani (2007) that Dalits are discriminated in medical colleges in Gujarat after riot over reservation since 1980. Dalits face the major challenges after getting admission in medical college. The faculties in medical field discriminate the untouchable students and discourage them to join medical education by making poor evaluation

[2] Times of India reported on Dec. 9, 2009

[3] Firstpost published an article on its website Feb. 6, 2013

of their practical or viva of medical exam. In viva-voce examination of medical students, the toughness of the questions depends on the caste status of the student. As soon as the examiner recognises that the student is from untouchable caste she is likely to ask tough question in order to ventilate one's anger over reservation and caste prejudices on the Dalit student. Such caste-based discrimination is difficult to prove if it is practised in viva or practical in medical exam.

A 65 year old retired tailor-cum*accountant from a government hospital says,

The toughness and criticality of the questions in viva and practical are different as per the student's surname and caste background. It is difficult to prove this type of discrimination in medical institutions because the examiner can ask questions per his desire.

Division of labour along caste lines

People who migrated to urban areas with the growth of the textile industries in Gujarat were mostly Dalits or Muslims. Caste-based discrimination in recruitment and employment in various departments of textile industries was rampant; and the work-force in different departments was composed of and determined by caste groups. For instance, in textile mills of Ahmedabad, the Scheduled Castes were engaged in spinning department which was most laborious and lowest paid whereas privileged caste-Hindus were engaged in more comfortable jobs (Shani, 2007: 42, 44).

The privileged caste-Hindus dominate and monopolise the employment in private sector and Dalits are hardly welcome in private sector jobs. A study conducted by Thorat *et al*. (2009) reveals that a candidate with Dalit or Muslim identity is less likely to get a job in private sector as compared to the caste-Hindus identity. Besides, social recruitment takes place where human resource bosses recruit their relatives and friends belonging to the similar caste (Thorat *et al*., 2009; Goyal, 1990). A study by Thorat and Newman (2007) highlights that human resource managers of twenty five large firms not only swore by merit in their choice of candidates in recruitment but they are also against reservation of jobs. Moreover, this study also highlighted that merit in such firms tends to be distributed by caste and region. Thus, it is unlikely possible for the highly qualified Dalit candidates to be hired for their skills and accomplishments.

The caste-Hindu's prejudices work under the garb of questioning the talent and merit of the Dalits. It hinders the Savarnas to avail the medical services offered by Dalit doctors. As a result the Dalit doctor with his/her caste indicating surname is vulnerable even though he possesses required skills and knowledge. Therefore, this caste-Hindu prejudice forces the Dalits to change their surname in order to run the clinic and earn bread.

A 52 year old retired employee of Reliance, says,

An educated modern Dalit is apprehensive about his future if he becomes a doctor and opens a clinic but the clinic may not run well due to his caste and surname. Patients may feel hesitant to visit his clinic.

Migration and residential segregation pattern

The caste discrimination was also extended to the housing. The gradual development of city also made certain upwardly mobile groups among the privileged caste-Hindus who occupied residential settlements and they formed social and residential segregation from other lower-castes and class. Access to housing opportunities and services were largely limited to the privileged caste-Hindus and upper income groups in the city of Ahmedabad. Co-operative housing societies were occupied through caste membership by Brahmins, Banias and Patels who were dominant and they had monopoly over occupations like business and government services. Thus there was a massive increase in caste based residential patterns and such residential societies were named after the name or caste of their members. Hence, population movement pattern in sheris, poles and housing societies also happened to occur according to caste status and people were also inclined to migrate to similar caste-based residential area (Shani, 2007).

The caste-Hindus are having a strong hold on the real estate property business whereas Dalits, by and large due to their caste and poverty ridden life, have been unable to venture in this business. Many times the caste-Hindu builders quote high prices to untouchables in order to discourage them from buying a house or they directly deny (Parmar, 2014).

Consequences of social exclusion of Dalits

Anti-Dalit ideology has been intensified after the riots over reservation since 1980s in Gujarat and it is a great challenge for the Dalits to access to the main stream society (Shani, 2007: 36). The caste-based nepotism and antagonism have resulted in exclusion and marginalization of the Dalits in the social, economic, political and cultural arenas. Legislation and religious movements have not brought ample change in the lives of Dalits and their social inclusion is still a challenge (Lobo, 1994: 30). Even though there are Scheduled Caste and Scheduled Tribe (Prevention of Atrocities) Act, 1989 and other affirmative action policies in educational institutions and government services for the Dalits, it has been observed that these rights are hardly implemented. 'Legislations relating to the removal of untouchability, control of atrocities and equality of opportunities have, by and large, remained on paper' (Shah, 2001: 20). Increasing atrocities against Dalits and hatred of Hindu militant group is spreading like a wildfire not only among the privileged caste-Hindus but also among the other backward castes.

The negative effect of day to day discrimination, rejection and humiliation is so strong that an average educated Dalit does not remain unaffected by its impact and they have started changing their surnames in search of social mobility. Dalits, who are getting the advantage of the new educational and employment opportunities, have achieved certain economic status and they want to change their identity (Parmar, 2005; Shah, 2001: 202). This phenomenon of changing surnames is very much prevalent in urban areas of Gujarat.

Atrocity Against Dalits

This section deals with risks and atrocities faced by Dalits after changing surnames. Dalits have changed their surnames and they try to experience the mainstream society to get access to social needs supplied by public and private institutions which is highly caste exclusive in character like education, housing, private sector job and others. The revelation brings greater danger for the Dalits in these fields and it creates sense of betrayal among the caste-Hindus.

Education

In education field, if the caste of the Dalits is revealed then it can invite worst consequences, thus Dalit student have to be in constant guard against their victimisation. A Dalit student after changing his surname had mingled with the upper-caste students in a medical college. He was getting all the educational support required for educational and personal development by being in the caste-Hindu group. But eventually, he was exposed as a Dalit and he was beaten up by his friends on false allegations of theft.

A 52 year old, retired Reliance (former IPCL) employee says,

In Baroda, a son of my friend had hidden his caste before the Savarnas in the medical college. But gradually he was revealed as Dalit, as a result he was beaten up by the Savarnas on false allegations.

Dalit students after getting admission to a medical college become victims of torture and atrocities from caste-Hindus over the revelation of their Dalit identity. Dalit student are specially targeted in ragging by caste-Hindus to vent their anger over reservation policy. Dalit students do not prefer to file a complaint before the authority in order to avoid any conflict and to avail smooth education in colleges. Many times Dalit students get hostel in caste-Hindu dominating hostel lobby where they are harassed in various manners so that they leave the hostel. Dalit students change the hostel in order to escape such harassment. Thus in educational institutions, the anti-dalit attitude is so vehement that the caste-Hindu students discourage the entry of Dalits in the medical education.

A 57 year old respondent working as an auditor with Gujarat government says,

Dalit students are specially targeted when ragging takes place in colleges. Many Dalit students become victims of such ragging; they don't raise the issue before the authority since they have to stay together in the same student circle or hostels. Many times Dalits students are harassed in upper caste-Hindu dominating hostel lobby and they are forced to change the room.

Thus, the experiences of caste-based discrimination in medical field take the form of inhuman treatment and violence to discourage the Dalit students to come into such professional education. Once the caste-Hindu faculties or students come to know about Dalits students, they give the worst of their treatment to these Dalits. Dalits are likely to face ragging by seniors in medical colleges.

A 52 year old, retired employee of Reliance, says,

If a student is recognised as Scheduled Caste in medical education, then he can become victim of ragging. A doctor in Ranoli block was killed in ragging. Therefore, you should change your surname at time of birth not later on. Otherwise they (caste-Hindus) would recognise you.

Housing

Thorat (2008) has argued that the exclusion of Dalits is taking place in access to housing. Shani (2007) has also revealed that there has been residential segregation and migration pattern along caste and religious lines in urban areas of Gujarat. In a recent case, a Dalit teacher was denied housing and as a result she had to resign from the job.[4] The Telegraph reported that in Delhi, a girl student had to

[4] A Dalit school teacher was denied access to housing in caste-Hindu locality because she belonged to untouchable caste. This article was published in leading NEWS paper Times of India, in Ahmedabad edition, on 14 Dec 2012.

keep the caste identity secret in order to get a house on rent but when the landlord identified that she is from lower-caste status, she was brutally beaten up by him.[5] Sengupta Anannyya, 2008, A Dalit Student in Delhi? Hide your Surname- Brutal Assault by Uppercase Landlord on Research Scholar Blow Lid off Capital's Can of Worms. Thus the Dalits are hardly welcome in the caste-Hindu dominating housing locality. They are excluded from access to housing in buying or renting a house. Further, the builders of real estate also do not construct the one bedroom, hall, kitchen (1BHK) house in order to keep the Dalits away from purchasing such a cheaper house.

Besides, the builders of the real estate scrutinise the caste of the customer before any sale of the house. And if the customer is an untouchable then the builders openly deny saying that 'we do not sell houses to untouchables'. Many times on the day of the inauguration of the plotting in the housing society, the builders lie to Dalits saying that 'all plots are sold'.[6] Thus they try to diminish the entry of any Dalit into the location to buy a house. By chance if any Dalit has purchased a house in caste-Hindu's locality then he has to face social boycott, harassment and he is forced to leave the housing society. The isolated Dalit rid after revelation does not get any support and he has to leave the place to get rid of the harassment of the caste-Hindus.

A 41 year old, event organiser says,

In 2000,1 wanted to buy a house. The clerk of the builder asked me 'Tame kai caste na? [what is your caste] Are you a Muslim?

I: No. I am Vankar (a Scheduled Caste in Gujarat). Then he told me clearly that- 'Ame Muslim ane tamara samajna vyakti ne ghar nathi aapta '[We do not sell houses to people from your caste and also Muslims].

[5] Sengupta Anannyya, 2008, A Dalit Student in Delhi? Hide your Surname- Brutal Assault by Uppercase Landlord on Research Scholar Blow Lid off Capital's Can of Worms.

[6] An interview with A 57 year old respondent working an auditor with Gujarat government in July 2014.

Dalit assertion and inclusion are challenged by the privileged upper-caste Hindus and any assertive actions "...evoke violent reactions making Dalit assertion a risky proposition for Dalits independent of dominant caste" (Waghmore, 2013: 69). There are Dalits who have managed to buy houses in caste-Hindus locality after changing surnames. In housing societies, such Dalits are living since long times with their neighbours coming from various castes and regions. Dalits after residing in a housing society for so long cannot hide their real caste because their relatives often make visits to their house and they get in touch with the caste-Hindu neighbours somehow. In this way through their interaction, the surname changed Dalit gets revealed. Thus the caste-Hindus look down upon the Dalit not just as a Dalit but also as a traitor. The revelation of a Dalit's identity also creates a sense of betrayal among the caste-Hindus. Sometimes, the feeling of betrayal and cheating among the caste-Hindus leads to execution of humiliation and violence on Dalits.[7] Thus, Dalits are at double disadvantage and risk, that on one hand they do not get opportunity to find house on rent or purchase in caste-Hindu dominated housing society and on the other hand when they live in disguise, they become victims of unprecedented violence from caste-Hindus on revelation.

A 59 year old, retired school principal shares,

One of my relatives was staying in a Patel community dominating area after changing his surname. The real Patels assumed that he is Savarna, but when his relatives started coming to see him, the real Patels knew these relatives and their ancestral background. Then the Patels realized that this Patel is untouchable and not the real Patel. Therefore the doctor had to face violence from the caste-Hindus and he left the house to be safe.

[7] An interview with 59 year old, retired school teacher and a principal August 2015.

CONCLUSION

The practice of caste based discrimination has changed in urban space and it is latently practised through caste indicating surnames. As a result Dalits are excluded from possible opportunities of development; therefore they change their surnames to access to the social needs such as housing and education. But when they are revealed they have to face the social exclusion, social boycott and atrocities from caste-Hindus. Thus there is a cycle of social exclusion, surname change, caste revelation and again social exclusion or atrocity. By perpetrating violence on Dalits, the Caste-Hindus convey their dominance and reject any idea of Dalit assertion. Simultaneously, the failure of the judiciary, lower conviction rate, corrupt investigation officials, lack of financial means with the Dalits to fight for justice seem to be the motivating factors the caste-Hindus' atrocity against Dalits. Caste atrocity against Dalits is so common that it is institutionalised and it is made normative. Thus the 'culture of violence' is prevalent through the use of religious codes of Manu and the caste-Hindus legitimise violence against untouchables through the religious connotations and they make use of violence to control the Dalits. Even the state is also unwilling to curb the atrocity issue due to its political interest. The caste-based binaries of superiority-inferiority and pure-impure is so internalised and institutionalised that any actions of untouchables questioning the dominance of the caste-Hindus are considered as threats to the caste-based social order; and invite atrocities. Thus in such a condition it is a great challenge before the Dalits to exercise their rights and it is also a challenge for the democracy to sustain.

REFERENCES

Fraser, N. (1989). Unruly Practices: Power, Discourse and Gender in Contemporary Social Theory. Cambridge: Polity Press.

Ghurye, G.S. (1969). Caste and Race in India. Bombay: Popular Prakashan. (First published in 1932 by Routledge and Kegan Paul, London in the History of Civilisation Series).

Gore, C. (1993). Entitlement Relations and Unruly Social Practices: A comment on the work of Amartya Sen. *Journal of Development Studies,* 29(3): 429–460.

Goyal, Santosh (1990). 'Social Background of Indian Corporate Executives' *In*: Rao, M.S.A. and Frankel, Francine S. (*eds.*), Dominance and State Power in Modern India: Decline of a Ṣocial Order. Delhi, India: Oxford University Press.

Haan, Arjan De and Kabeer, Naila (2008). Social Exclusion Two Essays. New Delhi: Critical Quest.

Ruth Levitas, Christina Pantazis, Eldin Fahmy, David Gordon, Eva Lloyd and Demi Patsios (2007). The Multi-dimensional Analysis of Social Exclusion. Department of Sociology and School for Social Policy, Townsend Centre for the International Study of Poverty; and Bristol Institute for Public Affairs, University of Bristol.

Lobo, Lancy (1994). Religious Conversion and Social Mobility'. *ICSSR Research Abstract Quarterly*, XXIII(1–2): 17–32.

Lukes, S. (1974). Power: A Radical View, London: Macmillan.

Parkin, F. (1979). Marxism and Class Theory: A Bourgeoisie Critique. London: Travistok.

Parmar, Hasmukh (2005). Na Odhkhavani Navi Tarah: AtakBadlo (In Gujarati) (Literally translated as 'New Way to Disguise Identity: Change Your Surname') Ahmedabad: Jani Publication.

Parmar, Rajnikant (2014). Sanskritisation or Social Inclusion? A Study of Dalits Changing Surnames in Gujarat, Unpublished MPhil Dissertation, Mumbai: Tata Institute of Social Sciences.

Shani, Ornit (2007). Communalism, Caste and Hindu Nationalism: The Violence in Gujarat. Cambridge: Cambridge University Press.

Silver, H. (1994). Social Exclusion and Social Solidarity: Three Paradigms, IILS Discussion Papers No. 69. ILO, Geneva.

Silver, H. (1998). Policies to Reinforce Social Cohesion in Europe, *In*: Figueiredo and de Haan (*eds.*), pp. 38–73.

Shah, Ghanshyam (*ed.*) (2001). Dalit Identity and Politics Vol. 2: Cultural Subordination and the Dalit Challenge. Delhi: Sage Publication.

Thorat, S. and Newman, K.S. (2007). Caste and Economic Discrimination: Causes, Consequences and Remedies. *Economic and Political Weekly*, 42(41): 4121–4124.

Thorat, Sukhadeo (2008). Dalit Exclusion: The Empirical Evidence. (*http://infochangeindia.org/agenda/social-exclusion/Dalit-exclusion-the-empiric.html*).

Thorat, Sukhadeo, Paul, Attewell and Firdaus, Fatima Rizvi (2009). Urban Labour Market Discrimination,' Indian Institute of Dalit Studies, Working Paper Series, 3(1).

Waghmore, Suryakant (2013). Civility against Caste, Dalit Politics and Citizenship in Western India. New Delhi: Sage Publications.

Websites

Sainath, P. (1999). A Dalit by Any Other Name, The Hindu.

mttp://ww.cscsarchive.org:8081/MediaArchive/audience.nsf/%28docid%29/BB8FB39056B^ B60B65256942002AF128) (Accessed on 7 July 2012)

Parmar, Vijaysinh (2009). Dalit kids shamed at mid-day meals. Times of India. (http://timesofindia.indiatimes.com/india/Dalit-kids-shamed-at-mid-daymeals/articleshow/5316960.cms) (Accessed on 5 June 2015)

First Post (2013). Won't eat in vessels cleaned by dalit woman, say Gujarat students.

(http://www.firstpost.com/india/wont-eat-in-vessels-cleaned-bv-dalit-woman-save-children-in-gujarat-school-615541.html) (Accessed on 5 June 2014).

Sengupta, Anannyya (2008). A Dalit student in Delhi? Hide your surname - Brutal assault by uppercaste landlord on research scholar blows lid off capital's can of worms, The Telegraph, (6May) (http://www.telegraphindia.com/1080506/jsp/nation/story_9231504.jsp) (Accessed on 31 August 2014).

Business Standard staff Gujarat GSDP growth at 8%, per capita income up 6.6% (July 2 2014) (http://www.business-standard.com/article/economy-policy/gujarat-gsdp-growth-at-8 income-up-6-6 114070200797^1 .html) (Accesses on June 5 2015).

Rajnikant Parmar is a PhD student at Tata Institute of Social Sciences, Mumbai and his research interest area includes names and surnames, social identity, social mobility strategies, Dalit resistance and caste politics in Gujarat. He has also completed MPhil from TISS, Mumbai with his innovative research focusing on Dalits changing surname in Gujarat.

Chapter 10

Caste-less India? Atrocities and Dalit Activism

SHARVANI NAVANGUL[1]

ABSTRACT

Caste system and assigning of hierarchical status to communities has been a widespread practice around the globe. In the context of the subcontinent, the society was divided into four major castes and Dalits happened not to fall in the much prevalent caste system. They have been accorded with lowest societal status in the community and have been looked down upon for ages. India accommodates a large number of Dalit populations. Over 16% of the total population of India is constituted by this community and any discrimination against them is equal to shaming a class of around 167 million people of the nation. With the various developments which the country has witnessed, a number of laws and policies have been framed in order to protect the community from atrocities of what is well-known as the 'Creamy Layer'. They have been deprived of the basic fundamental rights of education, health, housing, religion and equal treatment before the law. At various instances violence has been inflicted upon this class due to the apparent low societal status they

[1] National University of Study and Research in Law, Ranchi

bear. According to unofficial estimates, more than 1.3 million Dalits are employed as manual scavengers to clear human waste from dry pit latrines without proper protection against toxic substances and various allied infections.

The Indian Government, evidently sensitive towards the issue and has taken a lot of measures to curb this differential treatment, to create mechanisms of enforcement, and to enact policy to combat discrimination against Dalits in government, and education. From the very inception of the Constitution provisions are in place for abolishing caste discrimination and the act of untouchability. These measures have born small but significant gains in the past 60 years, benefitting a small section of Dalits from educational and employment opportunities. India has seen the coming of various Dalit Activists who have profoundly worked in this area. The contribution of Dr. B.R. Ambedkar cannot be left unnoticed in this field. Dr. Ambedkar is considered the messiah for his efforts to bring equal opportunity and social justice to the marginalized communities. He argued for creating separate electorates and reservations for untouchables and other religious communities. India saw the rise of a lot of other Dalit activists like Namdeo Dhasal, Shantabai Kamble, Krishnammal Jagannathan, etc. Mahatma Gandhi also took various steps to put an end to the atrocities inflicted against the Dalits.

Although various policy measures have been taken, the Government has also been supportive in eradicating the discrimination against Dalits and Dalit Activism has taken a stride in the past 15 years, there is still need for stronger laws to protect the interests of these communities and their equal representation in the society. The present study examines how the Dalit movement is functioning at the grass roots level, focusing on the policy measures taken up by the Government for their protection. Also the research focuses towards using of awareness and education as a tool to put an end to the class-based societal discrimination customary in India since the inception of Varna System.

INTRODUCTION

"The blight of caste discrimination, under which millions in India are regarded as 'untouchable', has spread to this country virtually unnoticed."

Thousands of years of oppression has what has left this socially and economically backward community at a still place level. Be it the egregious violence, dehumanizing human activities and a more than prominent system of social exclusion has left such an etch mark on this community that even after about a decade they are termed as backward classes. Indian law, provided for various protections since the inception of the Constitution but this tool has also not succeeded in bringing this community up to the mark with other communities.

The Supreme court in the case of *Indra Sawhney vs. Union of India*[i] laid down the definition of 'backward class'. The definition so provided stated that, the socially backward class of citizens whose educational and economic backwardness is on account of their social backwardness may be constituted as a backward class. A caste by itself may constitute a class. However, in order to constitute a backward class the caste concerned must be socially backward and its educational and economic backwardness must be on account of its social backwardness.[ii]

The acts that have been prevalent against the Dalits, especially the assertion of rights in a common place are the atrocities that these classes have been subjected to Article 14 of the Indian Constitution talks about equality before the law and equal protection of the law. While equality before the law is somewhat a negative protection, equal protection of law provides for a positive assertion. The right to equality guarantees that no person shall be discriminated on the basis of his religion, race, caste, sex or place of birth. A person

[i]. *Indra Swahney vs. Union of India* AIR 1993 SC 477

[ii]. Referred to in Article 16(4): Reservations in Services.

including non-citizens cannot thus be discriminated in public places or in general public matters.

RIGHT TO EQUALITY

This right is an indicative of equality of all persons within the territory of India, implying thereby the absence of any special privilege in favor of any individual. Every person whatever is his rank or post, is subject to the jurisdiction of the ordinary courts. It states that all persons within the territory of India enjoy the privileges under this right. It secures all persons within the territorial jurisdiction of the Union in the enjoyment of their rights and privileges without favoritism or discrimination. Laws which create classification basing on some objective should be protected. By providing the classification they are discriminating which in other right are similar but under the purview of this law which has been raised force certain objectives, they aren't equal.

Equality must be among equals.[iii] For each and every circumstance, the concept of equality changes and evolves. It implies that among equals the law should be equal and equally administered, that the like should be treated alike.[iv]

Thus the Indian Law explicitly provides for equality for those of an equal social stature. It accepts that in a diverse country such as India there exists class difference, and such differences should be abridged by providing for special provisions for the oppressed. But then the question of what should be the reasonable ground for discrimination arises. There once it is established that a caste is a backward class, the doctrine of reasonableness comes into play.

[iii]. *Western U. P. Electric Power and Supply Cooperation Ltd. vs. State of U.P.* AIR 1970 SC 21

[iv]. *Chiranjeet Lal vs. Union of India.* AIR 1951 SC 41

DOCTRINE OF REASONABLENESS

Article 14 forbids class legislation, however it doesn't forbid reasonable classification of persons, objects and transactions by the legislature for the purpose of achieving specific ends. For any classification to be reasonable, the following tests need to be passed:

1. It shouldn't be arbitrary, artificial or evasive. It should be based on intelligible differentia, some real and substantial distinction, which distinguishes persons or things grouped together in the class from others left out of it.
2. The differentia adopted as the basis of classification must have a reasonable nexus with the object sought to be achieved by the statute in question.[v]

Thus, those who actually deserve a discrimination should be united and this gap be abridged. The old belief of untouchability, for a fact, is such an acute expression of psychological violence that right from childhood, a Dalit is made to feel that he or she is an inferior being, a person of low intelligence and a person whose life is worth only the service and the betterment of the dominant caste men and women. The law thus aims at minimizing such atrocities. The main motive behind the establishment of such laws is to deal non-violently with the violent performances.

DALIT ATROCITIES

Article 17[vi] of the Indian constitution deals with the abolition of untouchability. Though, this article does not create a right, yet it is a lease of rescue to the 1/6th of Indian population from perpetual subjugation, humiliation and disgrace of centuries. To incorporate the article in the constitution as one of the most unambiguous articles

[v]. *Laxmi Khandsari vs. State of Uttar Pradesh*. AIR 1981 SC 891.

[vi]. Abolition of Untouchability: Untouchability is abolished and its practice in any form is forbidden. The enforcement of any disability arising out of Untouchability shall be an offence punishable in accordance with law.

of the constitution was the best way to eradicate this evil. To, further strengthen the constitutional provision in Article 15 and Article 17, the parliament of India enacted the Untouchability (offences) Act in 1955. This act was further amended and renamed in 1976 as Protection of Civil Rights Act, 1955. This act lays down that whatever is open to general public (or Hindus) should be open to the members of the scheduled castes. It abolishes the untouchability and its practice in any form is made punishable under the law. The main purpose of the paper is to highlight some of the prevalent practices in regards to the Dalit atrocities. This will be dealt with from two aspects *i.e.*, social atrocities and individual atrocities.

The passing of Land redistribution laws was seen as the benchmark for such atrocities, the government and the dominant caste landlords fought unceasingly to prevent Dalits from actually gaining control over land that is legally theirs. This discrimination is also by far etched in the education system that prevents Dalit children from full participation in classrooms, thereby barring them from accessing the most important tool for social mobility. Moreover, violence against women is on the rise and patriarchal attitudes toward the role of women prevail. This "hidden apartheid" impacts most of the average population in India. The government action to create mechanisms of enforcement, and to enact various policies to combat discrimination against Dalits in government, the workplace, at educational institutions have not completely gained justice. Even after the abolition of the caste system, more than half a century ago, Dalits or 'untouchables' continue to face caste discrimination.

Looking at recent statistics every year, 13,000–15,000 cases of atrocities against Dalits and 3,000–3,500 cases of 'untouchability' are registered in India. Two instances of harassment in the western Indian state of Gujarat have prompted the Asian Human Rights Commission (AHRC), a Hong Kong-based rights body, to urge the Indian government to take urgent action against anti-dalit presentations. The AHRC was seen quoting, "Fifty-six years after India's independence, the country is still suffering from caste discrimination and inequality". The incidences that caught the national eye were when three Dalit teachers were transferred for protesting against caste-wise seating arrangements during lunch at their school. Another stone in the pillar was by the suspected suicide of a Dalit man whose wife Gangaben Maru, an elected village head, was being threatened by her upper caste political rivals. The chain of happenings is endless and uncared for.

Two Dalit boys were killed, allegedly by members of an upper caste community in Saharanpur district of Uttar Pradesh, because they had won a cricket match says a report by the New Delhi based Indian rights group People's Union for Civil Liberties (PUCL). For the past 60 days people have been on a dharna protesting police inaction in the mysterious disappearance of a Dalit sarpanch Karan Singh from the Brahmin-dominated Pehrewar village in Haryana's Rohtak district four months ago has further highlighted the issue. The police allegedly refused to lodge an FIR for over a month after the incident took place. The people are demanding a CBI inquiry. Haryana the not so peaceful land anymore records a whooping rate of Dalit atrocities. In October 2002, five dalits were lynched in Duleena village in Jhajjar district. Two hundred dalit families fled their homes in Harsola village in Kaithal district after being attacked. And, a few months ago, a woman dalit sarpanch was beaten in public in Gandhra village in Rohtak district.

Several campaigns have been launched to curb and control these atrocities. Heads of various institutions such as National Human Rights Commission and the National Commission for Scheduled Castes and Tribes as well as the United Nations, were called for acting and presenting their views for this pressing problem. Action to be taken against those violating the rights of Dalits was the main criterion of discussion. The bodies urged the Indian government to set up an independent body to investigate and try "the offenders of such gross violations of human rights".

A pilot study done at Delhi's Jawaharlal Nehru University has been associated with the National Campaign for Dalit Human Rights, points out the discouraging situation for Dalits. The chief coordinator encourages the efforts put up by the Indian government for registering efforts by Dalit groups and other human rights bodies to highlight the issue of discrimination against Dalits at an international conference against racism held in the South African city of Durban in 2001. The awareness is spreading but not as one would desire. Had this caste-less society been never established, the founding stones of India would have shaped differently. But we cannot necessarily blame it all on the Varna system. It is we, the people, who are responsible for the continuance of such atrocities. Action Aid, a soon-to-be-published report by the global nongovernmental organization, states that Dalits are often harassed if they assert their rights. Social and economic boycotts, murders, and rape- the sequence of violence against the Dalits is endless.

Many cases go unreported as the police means to dilute the seriousness of the offences and shield the offenders thus also indirectly inflicting injustice against the people who are discriminated upon. Police, the role of whom is to protect the society and maintain the civil order drifts away from being 'the professional imposition of a coherent moral consensus on society'. Political activities too lead into the oppression of these minorities, women and children are harassed at an altogether different level. The situation is so inappropriate that the tainted rule of the British colonial rule fetched a far better outcome for these oppressed societies.

CURRENT STATISTICS

The Indian Penal Code provides for strict punishment for subjecting Dalit or so termed, 'untouchables'. The total figure of atrocities against the SCs for the entire period was 127,933 cases, with an annual average of 25,587 cases. The total number of atrocities against STs during the same period was 21,426 cases with an annual average of 4,285 cases.

What is more surprising is that the rate of conviction of all these crimes is only about 10%. The main reason for this is the ignorant attitude of the people. The entire justice system is ridiculed due to some of the common mistakes that are done firsthand by the victims,

Year			***Breakup of offences***			***Total***
	Murder	***Rape***	***Grievous hurt***	***Arson***	***Other***	
1997	513	1037	3860	389	22,145	27,944
1998	516	923	3809	346	20044	25638
1999	506	1000	3241	337	20009	25093
2000	486	1034	3298	260	18664	23742
2001	553	1127	3256	326	20254	25516
Total	2574	5121	17464	1658	101116	127933
Average	515	1024	3493	332	20223	25587

The table above shows the crime records during the year 1997 to 2001.[vii]

like not reporting their plight. A more recent analysis by the National Commission for Scheduled Tribes (NCST) indicates a significant increase in the number of 'atrocities' against tribal people in the central tribal belt of Madhya Pradesh and Chhattisgarh, which has witnessed rapid rise of the Maoist movement. The NHRC and other bodies have made recommendations for reforms in the criminal justice system but with no result. No progress has been made in enforcing police accountability for arbitrary arrests and extrajudicial killings. The NHRC report states that ever since the law against atrocities came into existence, Hindu fundamentalists have launched a campaign against it. Nowhere in the country has the law been effectively used. The police machinery resorts to various machinations to discourage registration of cases, dilutes the seriousness of the offences, shields the accused persons, and often inflicts the violence itself.

People each day get away with such acts the main reason being the adamant behavior of not registering an FIR (First Information Report). The aspect of many police offers belonging to the upper caste and thus not entertaining such complaints cannot be overlooked. The victims are tyrannized and justice is delayed. And the famous quote goes, "Justice Delayed is Justice Denied." The findings of a plethora of reports are not taken seriously mainly due to this reason.

[vii]. *Source*: National Commission for Scheduled Castes and Scheduled Tribes, Seventh Report, 2001-2002 (2004), p.119

PREVENTION OF ATROCITIES ACT, 1989

The 1989 Prevention of Atrocities Act (POA)[viii] is an acknowledgement by the Indian government that caste relations are defined by violence. The Act denoted specific crimes against Scheduled Castes and Scheduled Tribes as "atrocities" and created corresponding punishments. Its purpose was to curb and punish violence against Dalits. The list of atrocities included humiliations such as the forced consumption of noxious substances. Other atrocities included forced labor, denial of access to water and other public amenities and sexual abuse. The Act permitted Special Courts to try POA cases. The Act called on states with high levels of caste violence (said to be "atrocity-prone") to appoint qualified officers to monitor and maintain law and order. In practice, the Act suffered from a near-complete implementation failure. Only two states created separate such courts. Policemen displayed a consistent unwillingness to register offences under the act. This reluctance stems partially from ignorance and also from peer protection. According to a 1999 study, nearly a quarter of those government officials charged with enforcing the Act were unaware of its existence.

DALIT ACTIVISM

Dalit Activism has taken up the mould that is desired today. It has grown in the past 15 years. Major gains have been made by way of international recognitions, especially at the level of the United Nations. At domestic level recent amendments have shaped the constitution in such a way that it extends reservations to private schools, colleges, and training institutions. The economy has started to liberalize towards these backward classes. Implementation and shaping attitudes remain the greater challenges, however, to effect true rights realization. Formulating a dignified social and political

[viii]. An Act to prevent the commission of offences of atrocities against the members of the Scheduled Castes and the Scheduled Tribes, to provide for Special Courts for the trial of such offences and for the relief and rehabilitation of the victims of such offences and for matters connected therewith or incidental thereto.

identity for Dalits is always valued as one of the essential tasks of modern social movements in India. Among all such movements, one can witness a conflicting relationship between "the given" identities and the identities carved by the "Dalit self".

While incremental progress has been made, caste discrimination does remain entrenched and the continuing struggle promises to be a long one. The attention from international bodies serves as a gaining point but the struggle remains at the state and center level policies. The ultimate lesson to be taken from the recent advancements both at national and international level awareness and advocacy efforts is that the Dalit rights movement consists of a profoundly committed base and, as it enjoys greater support internationally and achieves greater organization and reach, promises to continue to make strides towards diminishing caste discrimination and entrenched inequality.

These movements have largely affected the nationalist strategies of the country and now are helping mold a better social-economic policy of change and dignity for all. The activists are widely ranging from the Dalit masses to the non-Dalit masses who in order to uphold the three pillars *i.e.*, justice, equity and good conscience are giving the Dalits what they rightly deserve. But inspite of all this the underlying reasons remains unanswered as to why urban activists do not recruit young men in their movement as active members or activists; and why the young men in the village neither seek out the Dalit movement as a channel for fighting for their rights.[ix]

Urban Dalit activists can hardly represent the numerous Dalit communities that reside across class, caste, religious and regional identities, within social contexts that are contradictory, and in economic settings that are highly heterogeneous. Educated young men and some young women are beginning to organize themselves into associations in an unprecedented way. The formation of such groups can be linked to the experience of schooling and increased

[ix]. Mohd Zia-Ul-Haq Rafaqi, *"Dalit Education and the Government Policies"*, Department of Education, Aligarh Muslim University, Aligarh, Uttar Pradesh, India.

awareness through print and other media. Such actors are often invisible to urbanized forms of activism, and do not appear in the mainstream of political activity in rural communities. They are hidden from view because they do not easily link to mainstream channels of protest or mass mobilization. Such actors provide a vantage point from which to examine how rural people far removed from urban forms of activism draw upon emancipator discourses found in the Dalit movement.

THE DALIT MOVEMENT - CONCLUSION

According to the 2001 Census the Scheduled Caste population of India was 166.6 million people, making them 16.2 per cent of the total population[x]. While lower caste does not necessarily imply lower class, the overlap between caste and class remains strong in contemporary India. While statistically the Dalits remain among the poorest and least educated groups in the country, the prevailing image of them as oppressed and exploited has by now been adjusted by the emergence of a Dalit middle class, and of political parties, scholars, writers and organizations advocating 'Dalit issues' and demanding the attention of the state as well as the rest of Indian society. Recent studies show that the taboo of Dalit professions are now being changed and a humane form of society is emerging. Various fields are witnessing leaders from the scheduled castes and due credit has to be given to the impact of these rightful movements. Various expressions of rights claims and opposition, espoused by representatives of different but similarly placed social groups, constitute what is generally called the Dalit movement in India. The movement has produced formal political parties like the BSP, and it aims to alter existing power structures through redefining identities: 'Resource flows are determined by a field of power within which identities are constantly being reformulated in categorical terms. The power to define reality is an economic and political power'.[xi]

---

[x]. Census of India, 2001

[xi]. The Hindu, *"A rightward shift in Dalit Politics"* : September 13, 2014 10:33 IST

The roots of the Dalit movement can be traced back to the socio-religious reform movements of the late 19th century. The Neo-Vedantik movement was initiated by Hindu religious and social reformers. These movements attempted to remove untouchability by taking them into the fold of the caste system. Dayanand Saraswati the founder of Arya Samaj believed that the caste system was a political institution created by the rulers for the common good of society and not a natural or religious distinction. The Neo-Vedantic movements and Non-Brahmin movements played an important catalytic role in developing anti-caste or anti Hinduism dalit movements in some parts of the country. The Satyashodhak Samaj and the self-respect movements in Maharashtra and the Tamil Nadu, the Adhi Dharma and Adi Andhra movement in Bengal and Adi-Hindu movement in Uttar Pradesh are important anti-untouchability movements which were launched in the last quarter of the 19th and the early part of 20th century. The Dalit movements are dominated by raising issues related to identity and reservations of government jobs and political positions. Their struggles have brought Dalits on the agenda of mainstream politics. They have exploded number of myths created by Brahminical ideology. The Dalit movements have also successfully built up a good deal of pressure on the ruling classes. It was observed by Gail Omved that the post-Ambedkar Dalit movement was ironically only that in the end- a movement of Dalits, challenging some of the deepest aspects of oppression and exploitation but failing to show the way to transformation.[xii]

REFERENCES

1. Janet A. Contursi, *"The Oppression over a million years."* Cambridge Journals Online.
2. Anil Kumar Thakur (2008) *"Impact of Economic Reform Policies on Dalit and Weaker Sections"*, Deep and Deep Publications.
3. Dr. Hugo Gorringe, *"Untouchable Citizens: Dalit Movements and Democratization in Tamil Nadu"*, Sage Publications, Vol. 4

[xii]. Sociology Guide, "Dalit movement: An overview" : http://www.sociologyguide.com/dalit_movement/an-overview.pdf

4. Ojha Jai Prakash, *"DNA of Dalit Movement",* Partridge Publishing.
5. Râmacandra Kshîrasâgara, *"Dalit Movement in India and Its Leaders",* M.D. Publications Pvt. Ltd.
6. Thenmozhi Soundararajan, *"Fighting the Dalit women's fight with art and activism."* The Guardian.
7. Prahlad Gangaram Jogdand, *"Dalit movement in Maharashtra",* Kanak Publications, 1991.
8. Balagopal, K. (1988). *"Probing in the Political Economy of Agrarian Classes and Conflicts,"* Perspectives Publishers, Hyderabad.
9. GOI (Government of India), (1979-81) National Police Commission Reports.
10. Info Change India (2010). *"Why atrocities against Dalits and Adivasis continue."*
11. Info Change India (2004). *"Rising Dalit atrocities in India worry rights groups."* Source: www.ndtv.com.
12. The Indian Express (2014). *"Dark days of violence on Dalits return to haunt Bihar."*
13. Navsarjan, *"Atrocities and Interventions."*
14. Luisa Steur (2012). *"Dalit civil society activism."*

Sharvani Navangul is a student of National University of Study and Research in Law, Ranchi, pursing her BA.LLB (Hons.). With a consistent top of the class academic track, she also has won several college and school level debate and elocution competitions. She has successfully published four research papers in prominent national & international journals, such as 'International Journal of Legal Research'. She also has a paper presentation to her name, in a national conference. An active member of the Legal Aid Committee in her University, she has been assisting economically disadvantaged rural communities in Jharkhand through legal aid, particularly in gender violence and family disputes; and has performed many street plays to promote spread legal awareness. A leading member of the Moot Court Committee she has a few successful competitions in her name.

Chapter 11

Changing Discourses and Experiences of Caste Based Discrimination in Higher Education

ANJALI THOMAS[1]

INTRODUCTION

Caste is one of the most intensively investigated aspects of Indian society. There are many controversies as regards the origins of caste, its relation to the concepts of "Varna" and "Jaati", the relation of caste to the colonial experience and in particular to the colonial exercise of classification and enumeration (Dirks, 2001). There have been several scholars who have sociologically theorised caste (Ghurye, 1969; Dumont, 1908; Bougie, 1958). These seminal works continue to be at the centre of intense debate in Indian and foreign academia. Caste, Caste based prejudices, practices, discrimination and humiliation continue to be part of everyday reality for a majority of the population. Caste discrimination translates into social exclusion from education, employment and other opportunities and venues.

In the early years after Independence, it was popularly believed that modernization and urbanization would lead to a gradual decline

[1] Tata Institute of Social Sciences (TISS), Mumbai.

in the role of caste, especially through a gradual upward movement of key segments of the most oppressed. However, we can now see that caste as a basis of social discrimination has survived. This form of social stratification has combined with other structural forms of inequality like property ownership and access to economic opportunities (Ghosh, 2006). In light of the presence of several constitutional provisions, services and facilities being (on paper) made available to students from the reserved categories, manifestations of caste-based prejudices and discrimination have evolved and become more subtle, more difficult to clearly identify and address.

PREJUDICE AND EVERYDAY REALITY OF CASTE

Allport (1958) defined prejudice as thinking ill of others without sufficient warrant. He explains it as an aversive or hostile attitude towards a person of a certain group and the perception that this person has the objectionable qualities which is presumed to characterise the group and its members. He describes discrimination as the practice of prejudice. Individuals have prejudices but it is not necessary that they practice it. Apart from articulation of prejudice, discrimination also includes avoidance of people who are members of an unfavourable group and exclusion from employment, residence, educational opportunities, social privileges and others.

Gyanendra Pandey (2013) visualises the politics of prejudice as a politics of difference. He argues that prejudice is often masked on the identification of difference. He says that the subordinated and marginalised are marked by difference. He refers to Simone de Beauvoir who says that in the man-woman binary, the difference is not symmetrical rather one becomes the "sole essential" against which the other is evaluated.

Social relationships between people can be understood as feelings of trust, mistrust, fraternity, sisterhood, empathy, sympathy or apathy between people. People are coloured by their plural identities and how these identities negotiate these feelings between supplementary and competing identities. Identities are in themselves imbued with gradients of hierarchies, prestige and stigma. They are often created in difference to another or the other. In an attempt to be neutral we try to define an identity in an affirmative manner but these often fall back on comparison with or negation from others. We make strenuous attempts to create affirmative identities but they often succumb to the morphology of difference between the Self and the Other.

Bourdieu and Passeron's work on cultural reproduction in education and society talks about how dominant culture, which is arbitrary, is reproduced through education. This idea has implications on social and cultural capital of an individual. The social and cultural capital of an individual influences the opportunities and choices available to the individual in higher education. Cultural reproduction of the dominant culture and the habitus that it inculcates in the students within the Educational System also influence the peer interactions and group dynamics within higher education institutes (Bourdieu and Passeron, 1977). Bourdieu and Passeron establish the manner in which educational practices reproduce and thereby legitimise the ideologies of power and control. It examines in great detail how education reproduces social relations of power through symbolic violence (Lardinois and Thapan, 2006).

Goffman (1963) has described stigma as a discrediting attribute. The attribute categorises people into what Goffman calls the 'stigmatized" and the 'normals'. Goffman defines three distinct types of stigma; (1) abominations of the body or deformation, (2) blemishes of individual character inferred from a known record and (3) tribal stigma of race, nation, religion which operates through lineage and family. Rao (2013) is of the opinion that the third form of stigma which is tribal, racial and national in nature fits into the framework of the stigma that is attached to Scheduled Caste (SC) and Scheduled Tribe (ST) groups. Attributes which create the divide between the stigmatized and the normals are established by society and the social settings, according to Goffman social settings also establish the categories of persons likely to be encountered in those settings.

Goffman says that individual stigma arises out of everyday life and experiences and that we exercise varieties of discriminations, consciously or unconsciously, which reduce the life chances of the stigmatized.

Goffman says that the varieties of discriminations that we exercise are based on a constructed stigma-theory or ideology which are often rationalised on differences. (Goffman, 1963)

Bruce Link and Jo Phelan say that people distinguish and label differences. Differences are associated with cultural values and categorisation between "us" and "them". They say that stigmatization rests on access to social, economic, and political power that enables identification of differences, categorisation and discrimination (Link and Phelan, 1998).

The conceptualising of the Self and the Other becomes a significant mechanism through which people are categorised and placed into hierarchical social structures and relations. It becomes a question of what came first, the social structure or social relations, both of which are mediated by the mechanism of identity and difference. The interplay between identity and difference essentially takes us towards a social structure which is fundamentally unequal and social relations which perpetuate these inequalities.

There are a few studies and articles which do look at the dimension of caste discrimination in India and how these dynamics play out in the life of students from primary education to higher education (Velaskar, 2005; Vasavi, 2006; Krishna, 2012; Majumdar and Mooij, 2012; Wankhede, 2013).

Satish Deshpande has highlighted that in India, the dropout rates and examination pass rates are inversely related to class and caste status. He also highlights that the SCs are significantly under-represented in Higher Education Institutions (Deshpande, 2006; Hasan and Mehta, 2006). The Unit for Research in the Sociology of Education at Tata Institute of Social Sciences had conducted a Survey on the SC students in Mumbai in the early seventies and found that a majority of the SC students were enrolled in relatively inferior colleges which have poor academic performance records. This study also revealed a high rate of stagnation and drop outs among SC students; they also have poor academic performance in comparison to their other classmates and a majority of them have a record of declining academic progress (Chitnis, 1972).

This study was followed by another on the character of inequality and disadvantages suffered by SC students in the same colleges and found that most cases of drop-outs and stagnation were due to failure and employment. It also found that participation in extra-curricular activities like watching films and interactions outside the campus was low in both groups but significantly lower among SC students and that social interaction largely remained within caste communities or groups (Aikara, 1980).

There is no lack of examples of social discrimination by professors and authorities. The recent case involving the suicide of a student in Hyderabad is only the tip of this iceberg. N Sukumar has written about the problems faced by Dalit students on an everyday basis in Hyderabad University in 2008. The Anveshi Law Committee findings are indicative of the discrimination and exclusion suffered by Dalit students in the same university from the faculty, staff, and peers'- on a daily basis. S. Omprakash's study on the psychological and social problems faced by socially disadvantaged groups in IIT Kanpur revealed social problems which emerged out of the social status, lack of confidence, poor academic performance and language barriers (Omprakash, 1986).

AR Vasavi briefly discusses the covert nature of discriminatory practices and policies at higher education institutions and that, "most upper caste [UC] students are insouciant about the disadvantages and differences of Dalit students and form opinions about them primarily on the basis of competition, resentment and apathy towards them" (Vasavi, 2006: 3769). This situation makes the situation harder for students from the reserved categories to survive the challenges and hurdles of the grinding education system in India.

Wankhede has theorised that there are four distinct forms of social discrimination around caste and the social discrimination and exclusion faced by students and academicians from the reserved categories. He especially talks about caste-imposed discrimination and self-imposed discrimination and how the concept of caste allows individuals from the dominant castes to enjoy more power and allows them to successfully impose their cultural worldview on the marginalised castes; and how the marginalised castes internalise and misrecognise caste inequalities and accept the unequal treatment and worldview imposed on them. In light of this, there is need for research on the Upper Castes category groups and social discrimination (Wankhede, 2013).

Discrimination on the basis of caste is additionally influenced by dimensions like gender, language, religion, class identity and the rural-urban divide. Discourse on reservations within classrooms, peer groups and in the media, especially post-Mandal commission have become a key site where caste based prejudices and discrimination is being enacted and voiced by the Upper Castes.

The issue at hand is not whether the Indian policy of caste-based reservation of seats in higher education is desirable or not. What is of greater material significance is how the implementation of this policy of affirmative action, however perfectly or imperfectly it has been executed, has played a role in the construction of caste-based prejudices and biases and how they have played out among students and across student groups.

Anoop Kumar Singh (2013) finds that for Dalit students, "their toughest battles have to be fought inside higher education, the very place they have struggles so hard to reach". He is of the opinion that words like reservation and inclusion represent desirable and progressive social goals but are by themselves flat and one-dimensional. Singh identifies four areas wherein discrimination is experienced - (1) social and economic environment prior to higher education, (2) attitude and actions of teachers, (3) animosity and exclusion from fellow students, and (4) apathy or sometimes active opposition of administrative officials (Singh, 2013).

In India the issue of reservation and social inclusion has received a little bit of attention in Media where the focus is usually on isolated incidents of discrimination. It has been contested that this is because of asymmetrical representation in the media industry and intelligentsia. This discourse has implications on the student body and can be reproduced within university campuses. Thus it is imperative to study the discourse on caste based discrimination and the social backgrounds which breed these discourses, especially among the dominant groups.

There have been very few studies which look at the issue of caste, experiences of caste based discrimination and higher education. However these studies do not look at the experiences of caste based discriminations of students in an institution. They have looked at experiences of individuals from different generations and institutions. The few studies which have focussed on students within the same institution have not explored the discourse of the students from the Upper Caste groups in the same campus or university. This study attempts to address this gap. Such a focus is required to develop a comprehensive perspective and understanding of issues and social dynamics in higher education institutions.

METHODOLOGY

Qualitative data was collected through twenty four In Depth Interviews (IDIs) and three Focus Group Discussions (FGDs) in one of the colleges in South Campus of the University of Delhi. The IDIs and FGDs were conducted and recorded after receiving informed consent from all the participants. All the data was recorded, translated and transcribed. The data was then coded and analysed by the researcher using the Atlas.Ti software.

A couple of informal discussions were also conducted with lecturers and professors in the colleges to briefly explore their perspective on the social background of their students, their issues, academic performance and social discrimination. Additionally, non-participant observations recorded by the researcher were used to add depth to the findings.

Three interviews were also conducted with Post-Graduate students of Social Work at the Department of Social Work. Although the researcher had managed to have interviews with students from the Schedule Caste background in the college, it was felt that interviews with more mature post-graduate students might add depth to the researcher's own understanding of their issues and experiences as undergraduate students while in college.

The Participants and the City

New Delhi has been a civic, political and economic epicentre of the country. The study explored the social background and experiences of students from one college in the University of Delhi. The University of Delhi has seventy seven colleges spread across two campuses in the city. The North Campus has a majority of the elite colleges which are located adjacent to each other within an open campus area. On the other hand, the South Campus has few elite colleges and many other colleges which have middle or low educational status.

The college was purposively selected from the South Campus. The sample college is among the colleges which are of a lower education status. For this study at present only one college was selected due to the limited amount of time and resources available. The elite colleges in the University have a majority of students who are the creme-de-la-creme of students from the various private schools, convent schools and residential schools across the country. The colleges which are not elite and are believed to have a lower educational standard have students with lower percentages in their high school graduating examinations and are more likely to be from middle class and lower middle class families.

Educational History of the Participants

A major aspect of the educational history of the participants is the history of their family's education. It was observed that most of the

Schedule Caste participants were either first or second generation learners whereas the Upper Caste students were second or third generation learners. None of the general or Upper Caste students were first generation learners. Scheduled Caste participants have parents who were not educated at all whereas almost half of the non-scheduled caste participants have parents who have either graduates or post-graduates degree. The number of non-scheduled caste parents increased with every level of education, but this was not so with scheduled caste parents. The only exceptions were observed in the social background of Scheduled Caste participants from socially active Ambedkarite families.

Socio-economic Background of the Participants

A majority of the parents are involved in medium level jobs like teaching, government, service, Police and others. A majority of the women, especially among the non-Scheduled Caste communities are engaged as Housewives or Homemakers. Here, gender dynamics are intersecting caste based social inequalities. A majority of twenty participants had mothers who were Homemakers. And among the mothers who were working, three out of five mothers are from Schedule Caste families. Here too it is important to note that these Schedule Caste mothers are an Asha Worker, an Anganwadi worker (AWW) and a social activist. The latter is from an elite Mahar Ambedkarite family and therefore seems to have the cultural backing and support that enables her to be a social activist.

It was noted that non-Schedule Caste parents who are usually in high level occupations like Doctors, Management and Business, Army, Police, Criminal Investigative and Intelligence Agencies, Doctors and Government Service; there are no Scheduled Caste parents having high level professions or employments. The Scheduled Caste participants have fathers engaged in occupations like small scale vendors, and Cook. One of the participants had an unemployed father who was suffering from chronic alcoholism and health issues while another Scheduled Caste participant, who is from an elite Mahar Ambedkarite family, has a father who is an Education Officer.

Looking at the Family income, the range is wider when it comes to Upper Caste families there are only three Upper Caste participants which have annual family income less than Rs. 3,00,000. There is a great degree of income overlap but the difference social status and educational capital between participants from Scheduled Caste and Upper Caste families are nevertheless wide.

Experiences of Caste-based Discrimination

The educational history and financial background of the students impacted the degree of awareness and experiences of the students. First generation learners have shared experiences of confusion and missed opportunities even at the time of admission, especially with regard to fulfilling bureaucratic requirements and paperwork. One of the Scheduled Caste participants had shared that he had got admission in English honours in a discouraged him saying that considering his "background" it would not. This participant also alluded to his status as a Scheduled Caste student from a poor background and also shared difficulty in interacting with the opposite sex.

The classical conceptualisation of caste and caste abased discrimination also limits understanding to documented practice of untouchability, verbal and physical labelling and segregation put blinders into the students' recognition of casteist prejudices and discrimination today. One participant did not have experience where people have told him that he is very "smart" and does not seem to be from a Scheduled Caste family. Another Scheduled Caste participant expressed that some Upper Caste students feel that if they interact with students from the lower caste it would adversely affect their reputation and status in the college. One Scheduled Caste participant shared that sometimes Upper Caste students felt that the Scheduled Caste students are privileged due to the system of reservation and hence don't want to be associated with Schedule Caste.

The Upper Caste reaction to reservation or affirmative action is largely based on ideas of merit and eligibility. This also affects the self confidence and the emotional and social life experiences of the Scheduled Caste students. One Scheduled Caste student shared that his dream is to build a college only for the scheduled caste students so that he can prove that they are of equal if not more merit and capabilities.

The Scheduled Caste participants' social background, especially the educational and cultural capital of their parents influenced their consciousness of caste dynamics and caste* based discrimination. Social and cultural capital when associated with Ambedkarite philosophy made the participants from Scheduled Caste communities more aware, confident and assertive about their rights, experiences, challenges, and needs.

Caste based prejudices and discourses

While claiming to be blind to casteist considerations and identities, the Upper Caste participants were immediately, able to identify friends, classmates and teachers who were from the Scheduled Caste communities. The discourses of the Upper Caste students were often insensitive to the social context and hardships faced by their friends and classmates from Scheduled Caste communities. Casteist prejudices often were disguised on the basis of identification of difference. Difference in economic, cultural and social capital and habitus were described with terms like "nature" of the individual.

The idea of education being opposed to sustained presence of casteism and classical understanding of caste and discrimination has allowed the Upper Caste students to claim to be non-casteist or blind to casteist considerations and prejudices. All of the Upper Caste participants shared that they never enquired about the caste of their classmates while making friendships and instead focussed on the "nature" of the person and whether they are "a good being". One being probed it was found that the term "nature" manner of speaking, of bearing, of eating and drinking. Some of the Upper Caste participants from wealthier and more privileged backgrounds also used terms like poor quality of the "crowd" in the college or "cheap crowd".

Relationship with Teachers

Padma Velaskar has been very sceptical of the idea that education will solve issues of social inequality and exclusion. She stresses, "The dominant cultural, social and economic values, both Brahmanical and capitalist, of the ruling classes are deeply embedded in the hierarchical design of the institution (education), making it the most significant source of inequality." She argues that the dominant and influential castes are served by hegemonic processes and mechanisms of the institution which are embedded in its internal and external structure. They consolidate and perpetuate inequalities. She has in fact highlighted the role of social reproduction of schools in India which have 'created and strengthened new inequalities' (Velaskar, 2005). This is visible in the experiences and narratives of the Scheduled Caste and Upper Caste students in the college.

This can be seen in the difference in the Scheduled Caste and Upper Caste students' relationship with their teachers. Instances of partiality and being scolded in the classroom are identified by the Upper Caste students as the result of the student being a "back-bencher" poorly participating in the classroom. Partiality from the teacher for the Upper Caste and wealthier students are often explained as the students' ability to build a good rapport or relationship with the teacher. Some students also identified regional alliances between the students and teachers as the root cause of partiality in the classroom. It is clear that the cultural capital and habitus of the wealthy and middle class Upper Caste students enable them to build better rapports and relationships with their teachers. This also makes insouciant (A.R. Vasavi, 2006) to the problems and challenges faced by their Scheduled Caste classmates and friends.

Although the participants were as a rule reluctant to criticise any of their teachers, in one of the FGD the Upper Caste students argued that since the UGC has made passing NET mandatory the quality of teachers from the reserved, categories do not suffer much:

They argued that NET is tough and even if you do not want to, you have to study. One of the post-graduate Scheduled Caste participants reiterated his idea that the wealthy Upper Caste students have 'scanning machines' in their eyes which help them identify people from the reserved categories.

Discourse on Reservation

Ideas of "Merit", "Deserving" and "Eligibility" dominated the Upper Caste students' discourse on reservations. There was often a sense of personal grievance and apathy. Some even called it a "curse" to be from the general category. They expressed the feeling that their rights have been snatched away from them and that the system is unfair. A couple of students who were more tolerant about this also reverted to saying that at present the exemptions and services being provided are too many and should be less or limited. Some said that it is acceptable only in cases of severe economic and regional deprivation.

The Upper Caste participants vehemently deny practicing casteist prejudices but were not averse to voicing discourses against reservations and upholding ideas of merit and eligibility. "Deserving" was one term which was frequently used in these narratives. The Upper Caste discourse often expressed resentment against the provisions, services and facilities being made available to Scheduled Caste students during school, college, employment, and promotions in government jobs and services. These kinds of caste-based discrimination and narratives were more vocally expressed by more privileged or wealthy Upper Caste participants who born and went to the private English medium schools in the city. Upper Caste students who have migrated to the city for educational and economic reasons later in their lives were found to be more sensitive and empathetic. This questions the validity of the belief that education resolves social stratification and issues like casteist and sexist prejudices and discrimination. This is therefore of great significance to educational administrators, planners and policy makers both at the national and international level.

CONCLUSION

Undergraduate students, both Scheduled Caste and Upper caste are in general hesitant to identify caste as a factor which influences their college life experiences and activities. However this hesitation is absent when probed to identify dynamics of class, gender, religion or region. Among Scheduled Caste the students, the age, maturity and the social and cultural capital (especially associated with Ambedkarite philosophy) has facilitated the post-graduate participants to be more acutely aware of their rights and conscious and vocal about caste*based discrimination around them.

Casteist prejudices and discriminations today have become more subtle and can be found in the Upper Caste students' choice of friends and in their narratives and discourses on issues such as Reservations, the quality of education and social life in the college and the skills and eligibility and the capabilities of teachers from the reserved categories.

Difference is marked with difference of cultural capital and habitus. This reproduces the arbitrary dominant Upper Caste and Upper Class culture. The socio-economic and political power enables the Upper Caste and Upper Class students to define terms like "nature", "deserving", "eligible" and "merit" with Brahmanical and elite cultures and values.

Caste based prejudices were observed when Upper Caste participants talked about their experience seeking admission in the University. This often led to a discussion on the system of Reservations. The Upper Caste students banked their arguments on the idea of "merit" and how they themselves or other "deserving" or "eligible" students were denied admissions to a more elite college. There was a sense of resentment against this and also apathy to the problems and hardships experiences by the Scheduled Caste students.

A Konrad Adenauer Stiftung (KAS, Germany) and CSDS study in 2007 to investigate the attitude of Indian Youth (from 15-35 years of age) suggested that social borders continue to be strong and crossing the borders of religion, caste and gender while making friends is discouraged. This was interpreted as an illustration of "a lack of opportunity for interaction in a situation of greater opportunity, both spatial and material conservative mores would not hold young people back from making friends across traditional borders." (deSouza, Kumar and Shastri, 2009). The study concludes that education is significant and that those who are better educated exhibit greater willingness in "plural settings" to cross borders of social mores. The study conducted by the researcher in the University of Delhi questions the validity of these conclusions. Social borders of caste, class, gender and region persist in this college in spite of being located in the capital city, a metropolitan city; in an institution of higher education where youth are receiving education. Persistence of social inequalities due to conscious and unconscious prejudices, discrimination and exclusion in institutes of higher education is an issue of great concern not only in India but globally.

REFERENCES

Aikara, J. (1980). Scheduled Castes and Higher Education: A Study of Students in Bombay, Pune, Dastane Ramchandra and Co.

Allport, G.W. (1958). The Nature of Prejudice (abridged), USA, Addison-Wesley Publishing Company Inc.

Anveshi Law Committee (2002). Caste and the Metropolitan University. *Economic and Political Weekly*, 37(12): 1100–1103

Bourdieu and Passeron (1977). Reproduction in Education, Society and Culture (Second Edition), London, Sage Publications.

Chitnis, S. (1972). Education for Equality: The Case of Scheduled Castes in Higher Education, *Economic and Political Weekly* 7(31-33).

Deshpande, S. (2006). Exclusive Inequalities: Merit, caste and discrimination in Indian higher education today. *Economic and Political Weekly,* 41(24): 17.

deSouza, P.R., Kumar, S. and Shastri, S. (*eds.*) (2009), Indian Youth in a Transforming World: Attitudes and Perceptions, New Delhi, Sage Publications.

Dirks, N.B. (2001). Castes of Mind: Colonialism and the Making of Modern India Princeton University Press, Princeton, NJ.

Ghosh, J. (2006). Case for Caste based Quotas in Higher Education. *Economic and Political Weekly*, 41(24): 17.

Goffman, E. (1963). Stigma: Notes on the Management of Spoiled Identity, N.J. (USA), Prentice-Hall Inc.

Hasan, R. and Mehta, A. (2006) Under-representation of Disadvantaged Classes in Colleges: What Do the Data Tell Us? *Economic and Political Weekly*, 41: 3791–3796.

Krishna, M.M. (2012). Pedagogic Practice and Violence against Dalits in Schooling *In*: Sleeter, C., Upadhyay, S.B., Mishra, A.K. and Kumar, S. (*eds.*), School Education, Pluralism and Marginality: Comparative Perspectives, Hyderabad, Orient Blackswan Pvt. Ltd. pp. 54–82.

Lardinois, R. and Thapan, M. (2006). Reading Pierre Bourdieu in a Dual Context: Essays from India and France, New Delhi, Routledge.

Link, B.G. and Phelan, J.C. (2001). Conceptualizing Stigma. *Annual Review of Sociology*, 27: 363–385.

Omprakash, S. (1986). Caste and Politics in Indian Education, New Delhi, Deep and Deep Publications.

Pandey, G. (2013). A History of Prejudice: Race, Caste, and Difference in India and the United States, New Delhi, Cambridge University Press.

Rao, S.S. (2013). Structural Exclusion in Everyday Institutional Life: Labelling of Stigmatized Groups in an IIT *In*: Nambissan, G.B. and Rao, S.S. (*eds.*), Sociology of Education in India: Changing Contours and Emerging Concerns, New Delhi, Oxford University Press. pp. 182–198.

Sen, A. (2000). Social Exclusion: Concept, Application and Scrutiny. Social Development Papers No. 1, Office of Environment and Social Development, Asian Development Bank.

Singh, A.K. (2013). Defying the Odds: The Triumphs and Tragedies of Dalit and Adivasi Students in Higher Education in Deshpande, S. and Zacharias, U. (*eds.*).

Sukumar, N. (2008). Living a Concept: Semiotics of Everyday Exclusion. *Economic and Political Weekly*, 43(46): 14–17.

Sukumar, N. (2013). Quota's Children: The Perils of Getting Educated *In*: Deshpande, S. and Zacharias, U. (*eds.*), Beyond Inclusion: the Practice of Equal Access in Indian Higher Education, New Delhi, Routledge.

Vasavi, A.R. (2006). Caste Indignities and Subjected Personhoods. *Economic and Political Weekly*, 41(35): 3766–3771.

Velaskar, P. (2005). Educational Stratification, Dominant Ideology and the Reproduction of Disadvantaged in India, *In*: Dahiwale, S.M. (*ed.*), Understanding Indian Society: The Non-Brahmanic Perspective, Jaipur, Rawat Publications, pp. 221–258

Wankhede, G.G. (2001). Educational Inequalities among Scheduled Castes in Maharashtra. *Economic and Political Weekly*, 36(18): 1553–1558.

Wankhede, G.G. (2013). Caste and Social Discrimination: Nature, Forms and Consequences in Education. *In*: Nambissan, G.B. and Rao, S.S. (*eds.*), Sociology of Education in India: Changing Contours and Emerging Concerns, New Delhi, Oxford University Press. pp. 182–198.

Anjali Thomas, is currently a Ph.D. student in Tata Institute of Social Sciences (TISS), Mumbai. This article is based on her M.Phil. research study on Caste based discrimination in a college in Delhi University. The research was conducted in 2014 under the guidance of Professor G.G. Wankhede in TISS, Mumbai. Anjali is also interested in the studying gender, religion, culture and Identity in contemporary India. She has a Masters in Social Work from Delhi University and has worked with CORD, Delhi on an impact evaluation project to map the changing value of the girl child in Haryana. During her masters she has worked with different NGOs in New Delhi working on issues of juvenile justice, child labour, integrated school education, education of children with disabilities, minority issues and communal harmony.

Chapter 12

Denial of Dalit Access to Water in Marathwada: Multi-Case Study Approach

RAJU ADAGALE[1]

1. INTRODUCTION

The fingers of thirst get peeled off as they hull beans.
    And man begs compassion of his own barren body
An earth-mouthed bowl widens its jaws
    How your secular regimes turn into toadies
Upstream, the water is all for you to take
    Downstream, the water is for us to get
Bravo! Bravo! How even water is taught caste system.

(*Source*: Namdeo Dhasal, Golpitha, 1972; translated from Marathi by Dilip Chitre 2007: 17)

Water is one of the vital means of human existence. Yet, the availability and accessibility–both in quantity and quality–has not been the same everywhere and for every section of society. Thus the right to water emerged as one of the major concerns world over including India, necessitating legal intervention both globally and

[1] Tata Institute of Social Sciences (TISS), Mumbai.

locally. The Constitution of South Africa explicitly endorses right to water through a Free Basic Water policy. This policy aims 'to provide a supply of 6000 litres of safe water per month to all households free of charge' (Joy *et al.*, 2011: 29). The right to water became one of the major concerns in the agenda of United Nations (UN) which highlights that the State should guarantee the right to water and it should be enjoyed without discrimination on the grounds of race, colour, sex, age, language, religion, political or other opinion, national or social origin, property, birth, physical or mental disability. Even in times of severe resource constraints, the vulnerable members of society including the Dalits must be protected (United Nations, 2002: 4-7). Thus, the UN acknowledges that clean drinking water is essential to the realisation of all human rights.

Therefore, the right to water is indeed a global issue, to be recognized in every nation including India. According to the Twelfth Five Year plan of the government of India (2012-2017), the current per-capita water availability is estimated at around 1,720.29 m^3 (Planning Commission, 2013: 79). Although there have been no direct constitutional provisions guaranteeing every citizen right to water, the judicial system supports that water is the basic need for the survival of the human beings and it is part of right to life guaranteed under article 21 of the Constitution of India (Banerjee, 2010: 5; Joy *et al.*, 2011). While supplying water, exclusion of unauthorised slums in Mumbai was challenged recently in the high court of Bombay. The court 'explicitly disapproved of the policy as a violation of the fundamental human right to water, as understood in the context of the Constitution of Inda.' (Forum for Policy Dialogue on Water Conflicts in India, 2015: 6). Moreover, the National Water Policy 2012 focuses on 'The Centre, the States and the local bodies (governance institutions) must ensure access to a minimum quantity of potable water for essential health and hygiene to all its citizens, available within easy reach of the household.' (Government of India, 2012: 4). The Article 15 (2) (b) of the Indian Constitution declares:

'no citizen shall, on grounds only of religion, race, caste, sex, place of birth or any of them' be subject to any disability, liability, restriction or condition with regard to the use of wells, tanks, bathing ghats...maintained wholly or partly out of State funds or dedicated to the use of the general public'

The right to water of Scheduled Castes (SCs)/Dalits is reinforced also in the special laws such as the Protection of Civil Rights Act, 1955 (PCR Act) and the Scheduled Castes and Scheduled Tribes (Prevention of Atrocities) Act, 1989 (henceforth PoA Act). For instance, Section 3 (b) of the PCR Act declares:

*'...bathing in, or using the waters of, any sacred tank, well, spring or water-course river or lake or bathing at any ghat of such tank, water-course, river or lake in the same manner and to the same extent as is permissible to the other persons professing the same religion or any section thereof, as such person; shall be punishable...*5

Section 4 (iv) of the PoA Act also emphasises that Dalits are equally entitled to have access to any sources of water which other members have a right to use or have access to. Besides, Section 3(1) xiii of the PoA Act declares: whoever, not being a member of a Scheduled Caste or a Scheduled Tribe: 'corrupts or fouls the water of any spring, reservoir or any other source ordinarily used by members of the Scheduled Caste and the Scheduled Tribes so as to render it less fit for the purpose for which it is ordinarily used' would be considered guilty of a crime.

Some of the recent incidents of crimes against the Dalits in Maharashtra were most inhuman and shocking. When the Dalits of Ansurda village in Osmanabad district demanded access to water from the common wells, a social boycott was declared against them. When the Dalits of Pimpalgaon Dakbangala in Washim district dared to fetch water from the village common well, they were brutally attacked by the Caste Hindu villagers. Most unfortunately, both these incidents of atrocities happened in 2015 just after the 125th birth anniversary celebrations of Dr. B. R. Ambedkar.

2. THEORETICAL FRAMEWORK

Historically, the Dalits were denied access to water as they were considered as agents of pollution and legitimised through religious sanctions. This situation has not changed even after 68 years of independence. Thus there is a need to explore what are the bases on which some people are denied access to water? To explore this one could use the following four different theoretical perspectives: 1) Theological or Brahmanical perspective, 2) Human rights perspective, 3) Marxian perspective and 4) Ambedkarian perspective, which is locally evolved but based on universal values. According to the Brahmanical perspective, Caste is God-given and therefore its validity and relevance cannot be questioned. The God created the Shudra to be the slaves of people of other Varnas ~ Brahmin, Kshatriyas and Vaishyas. The Dalits should be prevented from accessing water as their very touch would pollute water and make it unusable for others. For instance, the Hindu law-giver Manu declares: 'When Shudra touches a well or any other stagnant water source, the source and the water is polluted'. Manu went to the extent of elaborating rituals to be performed to purify such polluted water (Joshi and Fawcett, 2001: 4). The Brahmanical perspective indicates that the denial of water to the Dalits is not a crime. Even it is the God-assigned duty of the caste Hindus even to resort to violent means to prevent the Dalits accessing water. Therefore it cannot be challenged. Under human rights perspective, every human being is entitled to get access to water being a human being. The General Comment No. 15 of the UN Committee on Economic, Social and Cultural Rights describes the human right to water in which it emphasises that, 'water should be treated as a social and cultural good, and not primarily as an economic good.' The human right to water can be realized through the legal means in which the state has prominent role to play. Marxian perspective is based on class conflict between bourgeoisie class owning the means of production or those with economic power–is greedy for generating private properties, which is the foundational truth of exploitations of the proletariat class–and those who do not have the means of production

(Marx and Engels, 1848). Bourgeoisie class controls the natural resources including water ultimately to generate profits. Therefore to the question why the Dalits are denied water, the answer within the Marxian perspective would be that the Dalits are denied water because they are poor, not having the required purchasing power. Beyond such theoretical conclusion that one can arrive at, the Marxian perspective does not have scope to understand how caste plays a role in preventing Dalits from accessing water from common sources of water.

India is a country where most people are more aware of the caste rules. And value them more than the rule of law including human rights. Human rights are those that every human being for the simple reason of being a human being is entitled to and for every human being is the creation of God and to be respected. Marxism and human rights prespectives help to understand the denial of access to water to the Dalits in a limited manner.

Here, Ambedarian perspective is adopted as it brings Caste to the centre. As long as Caste exists, denial of access to water to Dalits would also exist. Ambedkar said that 'turn in any direction you like, caste is the monster that crosses your path. You cannot have political reform, you cannot have economic reform, unless you kill this monster' (Ambedkar, 1979: 47). The reality is: most of the water sources in India are either owned or controlled by the caste Hindus, and therefore the plight of most of the Dalits is such that they have no option but to depend on the caste Hindus to meet their daily water needs. Ambedkarian perspective based on universal values considered access to water as their basic human rights. According to Ambedkar, one cannot expect the Dalits to establish their rights and utilize public water resources since religious sanctions, traditions and customs are deeply embedded in society (GoM, 2008:25). Ambedkar's views on access to water are based on the principle of social justice, equality and human rights. Mahatma Phule also aimed for the complete destruction of caste system by linking his thought with a movement of opposition to the Brahmanism (Omvedt, 2004: 5-6). In pre-independence period of India, while formulating of new water policy, Ambedkar emphasized the absolute necessity of the benefits of the irrigation filtering right down to the grassroots (Thorat, 2006: 127).

Many scholars have brought this out in their empirical studies Mosse (2003) explains how water is controlled and powered historically and culturally by the dominant communities in Tamil Nadu. Tanks irrigation systems were embedded in 'Caste Prejudices' among the cultivators. Tiwary and Phansalkar (2007) show that caste identities strongly affect daily interactions around water in India. The discrimination and deprivation of the Dalits regarding access to water, particularly for domestic use is more prevalent in the rural area. Even, the socio-cultural rules play a larger role in accessing water for domestic use. Joshi (2011) brings out the peculiar behaviours of younger Caste women towards Dalit men who are older than them. These women look down on the Dalit men including offering them food or water from a distance, and also requiring them to wash their own cups and plates after use. Some times Dalit families get access to water through stealing. Guru (2009) shows that conversion of water from a natural (pure) substance into a polluted substance should not be considered as objectionable. The use of water for maintaining physical hygiene should not be considered as objectionable. The Brahmanical theory of purity-pollution is consciously created by the privileged sections of society. It legitimizes that some bodies as being ritually pure, and others as being eternally impure. Thus water determines scale of untouchability (Guru, 2009: 50-52). Joshi and Fawcett (2001) describes that the Varna system operates in a form of purity and pollution while accessing water particularly in rural settings. Thorat (2002) shows that discrimination and deprivation around access to water is regularly practiced and also Dalits have to face humiliation while accessing water in rural areas of India. Navsarjan Trust's Study (2010) brings out how and to what extent untouchability is practiced at water sources or while accessing water in Gujarat. Paranjape *et al.* (2008) have shown that untouchability has been closely linked to water. Dalits have to face atrocities while gaining access to water. Such studies did focus on water-caste linkages, but their focus does not seem to be adequate enough to understand the socio-political complexity of water related caste conflicts. Geographical focus of most of these studies was also not fallen in Maharashtra or they were very site specific and limited. Also most of these studies do seem to have methodological gaps. Unit of analysis, limited tools and single source of data collection were used.

Therefore, there is a need to study the denial of Dalit's access to water irrespective of the fact that there are a number of legal measures and special laws guaranteeing Dalit's access to water. The fact is that the Dalits still find it difficult to access water for their cultivation, domestic and other needs in rural India and any attempt on the part of Dalits asserting their right over water is often met either with overt and covert forms of discrimination including brutal violence against them. In this context, there is a need to study how the Dalits' socio-economic status, political connections and numerical strength in their village have helped them in negotiating their right to water.

3. METHODOLOGY

A multi-case study method has been used. Robert Yin (1984) argues that every selected case serves a specific purpose within the overall scope of enquiry, each case had been carefully selected to ensure that 'it either (a) predicts similar results (a literal replication) or (b) produces contrary results but for predictable reasons (a theoretical replication)' (Yin, 1984: 47-53). Multiple cases give a comprehensive historical understanding of the context; for instance, the occurrence of violence while asserting the right to water (Gerring, 2007: 27-29). The choice on cases to be chosen for the study has been based on a theoretical sampling method (Strauss, 1997). Fourteen cases have ultimately been selected for the study. The universe of the study constitutes all registered and unregistered cases of water-caste crimes in Beed district (Maharashtra, India). Primary and secondary sources of data are used. Unstructured interview guide, checklist for Focus Group Discussion and observation are used to collect primary data.

The data has been collected during the period from September 2, 2012 to July 19, 2013. Thematic analysis has been made for analysis. This was done using Bryman's four stages of analysis–reading, again reading, categorizing the text and linking the text to the theoretical premises (Bryman, 2008: 550-552). While analyzing the data, an attempt has been made to establish a link of evidence between the different data sources.

4. STUDY SETTINGS AND PROFILE OF CASE STUDIES

The state of Maharashtra falls in the western central part of India and is the second largest state in India in terms of population and geographical area, spread over 3.08 lakh sq. km. Out of six administrative divisions, the area covered under the Aurangabad division is traditionally known as 'Marathwada', particularly in the socio-cultural context (GoM, 2010: 1-2). Beed district is situated in the central part of Maharashtra. According to Census 2011, the district has around 13.58 per cent SC population. In the rural areas of the district, out of 4,46,114 total rural households, 35 per cent households have a tap water connection, about 25 per cent have well water availability, 38 per cent avail water through handpump/ tubewells, whereas 3 per cent use water available through other sources of drinking. About 58 per cent household level tap connections are treated whereas 42 per cent household level taps are untreated. Approximately, about 6 per cent household level wells are covered while 94 per cent wells are uncovered which does not help prevent water contaminations. Figure 1 shows the location of the study area. The details of each selected case-village are given below.

In Dagdi Shahajanpur, water crisis is a usual issue for the Dalits in the village and they get the least priority in access to water for their everyday lives. Sometimes, they have to face cruel violence and conspiracy over accessing water. For instance, the village Gram Panchayat (GP) functionaries along with some other Maratha men mixed poison in the water tank of the village but put the blame on the Dalit family of Dhutadmal, a Mang by caste. In Ghodka Rajuri, There was a water conflict between a Dalit lady and a Maratha woman in which the Maratha woman's brother-in-law, one Raosaheb Ghodke, damaged the vessels belonging to the victim and also threatened her with physical assault. It was resolved in the police station in 1995. In 2013, yet another water-conflict erupted, involving the same family, but this time, the husband of the Dalit lady was the victim who was badly beaten up for accessing water which was used mostly by the upper castes. Gawandara village also has plenty of water facilities. It comes under the command area of the Upali Medium Irrigation Project, which provides irrigation water to more than 250 hectares. The farmers used to lift water directly from the canal system. During one such operation under the jurisdiction of Kari village, near Gawandara, physical violence took place against a Dalit woman, Sangita Shirsat, who was the resident of Gawandara village in 2007. While she was irrigating her leased farmland, the motor-pump was switched off by the perpetrators who objected to a Dalit woman irrigating the land prior to them. In Wantakli, an atrocity took place against Mangal Kharatmal, a 40 year old educated woman from the Dhor caste. She had married someone from the Vanjari caste and stayed in the village/she was prohibited from accessing water from the handpump installed in front of the Maruti temple. Both the woman and her husband were brutally beaten up by five Vanjari caste men and women on the issue of accessing the handpump. In Ranmala Dajiba Bhole, a Mahar was a waterman who used to perform all the tasks pertaining to water distribution and management in the village. One day the waterman was unable to release water as there was a technical fault in the electricity supply. The water supply from the Pipe Water Supply (PWS) Scheme therefore got stopped and, and the sarpanch's family could not get water. On this issue, the waterman was attacked and injured by the sarpanch's husband and others from his caste called Laman (Denotified Tribe). In Mali Pargaon, Laman Chopade, a Mahar having eighteen acres of land, was murdered in 2003 while accessing water from his Maratha neighbour's well. Chopade was thirsty and he was unable to draw water from his own well because of the inconvenient structure of the well and water depletion. In Kuslamb, while accessing water, a young Dalit girl's vessel was spat on by a Maratha woman who then asked her to drink that contaminated water as the Dalits have been traditionally required to do. When the girl refused to do so, physical violence erupted in which the Dalit girl's entire family was beaten up very badly and the Dalit community was terrorised by unleashing a riot on them in 2004. In Ashti, Kanta Walhekar, a Mang, was murdered over the issue of accessing water for his ruminants in 2001. In Ganjpur, prior to 2008, most of the Dalit households were prohibited from accessing the common source that was claimed to be on private land therefore the source was considered to be the part of private property. In Kiti Adgaon, a common well located in front of the Maruti temple was off-limits for the Dalits. Instead, they had to collect water from one of the upper caste people by paying them Rs. 2 per vessel, the price being hiked in periods of scarcity. The waterman was appointed by the village whose duty it was to draw water from the well and then further pour it into the vessels belonging to the Dalits. In Rui Dharur, while accessing water for drinking, a Mahar caste man was abused in the name of his caste and badly beaten up by Vanjari caste men in 2008. The primary reason for this physical assault was that the Dalit man had unknowingly bumped into the vessels owned by the perpetrators. In Vanjarwadi, while accessing water from this common well, a young man from Mang caste was physically assaulted and orally abused in the name of caste by Maratha men. In Jategaon, while accessing water, a Mang sugarcane-cutting worker was brutally attacked with a chopper, in an attempt to murder. The reason for the attack was that his ruminants had drunk some of the water from the vessels belonging to Laman caste men. Rearing goats was the major source of his livelihood. In Rajegaon it is about atrocity committed on the Dalits when they tried to establish their rights over fishery. The Dalits were attacked as they were attempting to gain a government contract of fishery from the dam.

Each of the above mentioned cases explains the unique nature of denial of access to water for survival. According to Census 2011, the average SC population of the state is 11.81 per cent. Out of the fourteen case villages, the Dalit population in seven Villages is more than 11.81 per cent, but none of the villages studied were found to have above 21.26 per cent Dalit population (See Table 1). These cases highlight the different types of violence encountered by the Dalits in accessing water—the violence ranging from verbal to physical brutality like murder. The oppressors were not only from the Maratha community but also from other dominant caste groups in the region like the Laman (DNT), Vanjari, Salgar (NT) and Muslim (religious minority) communities. These castes are also fairly active in discriminating against the oppressed castes. The oppressed Dalits hail from the Mahar, Mang and Dhor communities. Two cases–Kiti Adgaon and Ganjpur were unregistered, in which no formal complaint had been filed with any police station.

Table 1: Demographic profile and water availability of the selected cases

Case	*Village*	*Total population (2011 census)*	*% of SC population (2011 census)*	*Water availability as on 1/4/2012*
Case 1:	Dagdi Shahajanpur	1103	7.43	40 lpcd[3]
Case 2:	Ghodka Rajuri	2257	12.54	Out of 3 habitations, 2 habitation 10 bed
Case 3:	Gawandara	2253	8.88	40 lpcd
Case 4:	Wantakli	2004	21.26	40 lpcd
Case 5:	Ranmala	1044	18.97	Out of 3 habitations, 1 habitation 20 bed
Case 6:	Mali Pargaon	2529	20.13	40 lpcd
Case 7:	Kuslamb	2760	8.99	40 lpcd
Case 8:	Ashti	243607	10.20	Out of 13 habitations, 1 habitation 20 bed
Case 9:	Ganjpur	1255	8.76	Out of 5 habitations, 1 habitation 10 bed
Case 10:	Kiti Adgaon	4767	16.15	40 lpcd
Case 11:	Rui Dharur	2866	21.11	40 lpcd
Case 12:	Vanjarwadi	989	2.22	25 lpcd
Case 13:	Jategaon	4564	17.81	Out of 8 habitations, 1 habitation 20 bed
Case 14:	Rajegaon	The case details have not been mentioned here.		

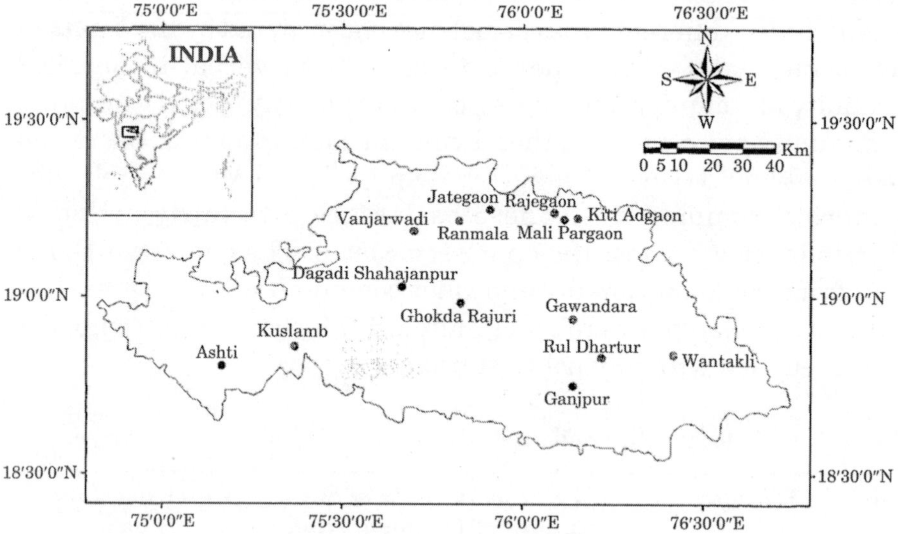

Fig. 1: Showing cases selected from the villages, Beed District *Sources*: 1) Census of India, 2011, 2) Website of NRDWP, Ministry of Drinking Water and Sanitation, Government of India.

5. FACTORS RESPONSIBLE IN NEGOTIATING 'RIGHT TO WATER'

Tiwary and Phansalkar (2007) and Paranjape *et al.* (2008) argue that the Dalits encounter tremendous hardships in periods of water scarcity. Joshi and Fawcett (2001), Guru (2009), Paranjape *et al.* (2008) and Navsarjan Trust 2010 revealed that the Dalits are still considered as agents of pollution, therefore they are denied the access to water. Ramaiah (2007) argues that the numerical strength of the Dalits matters a lot in their negotiating the right to water in the villages. Prakash and Sama (2006) and Tiwary and Phansalkar (2007) showed that Political connection with the village power structures decides the exclusion of the Dalits from the water domain. The Dalits are mostly dependent on public sources of water. In addition, they are frequently recipients of poor quality of water. They are excluded from water management at the village level in which the Gram Panchayat plays a decisive role. Kulkarni *et al.* (2007) and

Tiwary (2006) also examined the economic factors in the shape of the water market which often excludes the Dalits. They face water deprivation for their livestock and agriculture needs as well. Therefore, in this section, on the basis of literature review, social status, numerical vulnerability, political connections and economic status are discussed as the factors to explain the attrocities while accessing water.

5.1. Social Status

The Dalits face extreme hardships when they are denied the access to water. For instance, Ghodka Rajuri, Ranmala, Ashti, Ganjpur and Jategaon cases showed that water availability was less than 40 lpcd in some pockets of the village (Table 1). In such pockets, it was the Dalit families who were the residents. 40 lpcd has been the norm over the last 40 years in rural areas. Contrary, under Twelfth Plan, the Central Government has set the goal of providing 135 lpcd for urban area and 55 lpcd for rural area for domestic use (Planning Commission, 2013b: 301-360)

The notion of purity and pollution continues to be attached to water in the contemporary context. Impurity revolves around practices of death, birth, marriage, food habits, giving and receiving water among multiple caste groups–from superior to inferior. Water is considered as a 'purifying' agent to destroy impurity imposed by such practices. But the untouchables may not use the same well as the others (Dumont, 1999: 46-61). The Dalit's touch can, apparently, defile the natural status of water, making it unfit for further utilization. For this reason, discrimination against the Dalits was practiced around sources of water by the non-Dalits. The Hindu scriptures fundamentally define the rewards and punishments for this sort of defilement. For instance, the Manusmriti legitimises the discrimination that is practiced against the Dalits. It was observed that irrespective of whether it was a registered crime or an unregistered one–in all the cases, the Dalits were denied access to water on the basis of 'purity and pollution'. Such social practices were closely associated with the temple affairs as well. For instance, the Maruti temples and common sources of water were closely related. These sources were designated as holy by the temple authorities. Therefore, the water was considered as sacred and denied the access to water. In Wantakli, the victim's husband said:

'There was a temple near our house. It was a Hanuman Mandir which had a stone idol. They used to offer water to this idol. Also, the water was used for Satyanarayan puja, Abhishek and other such rituals. The non-Dalits would claim that the Brahmin priest does not allow them to use the 'polluted' water or that that they would not want to use such water for cooking. For these reasons, they never allowed us to draw water from the well.' (In-depth interview, 31 October 2012)

It was observed that the non-Dalits followed the social distinction between superiors and inferiors. In some of the cases (Kiti Adgaon, Gawandara, Ranmala, Vanjarwadi and Wantakli) it was still the practice that the upper castes poured water to the Dalits when they requested. For instance, in the Gawandara and Kiti Adgaon cases, the non-Dalits had argued that denial of access to water from the Maruti's well was their tradition which was more important to them than the Constitution of India which they were rather apprehensive about. The caste prejudices seem to be fully loaded in the mindset of the people. Dalit women from Ashti said that the non-Dalits decided that when the Dalits approached for taking water, they should close the gate to 'protect' the well. The intention was: 'Dhed-Mang ko pant nahi denekcf (Mahar-Mang should not be given access to water). Dalits were treated as degraded in status. Therefore, the study findings negate the premise of Gupta (2000: 80-81) that the notion of purity and pollution is inactive in many rituals and symbols in society which are prominently considered to be separating the castes. On the other hand, the findings in this study corroborate the study by the Navasarjan Trust (2010) that the Dalits experience untouchability while collecting water from the various sources. The Brahmanical notions of hierarchy among the castes were persistently practiced in the case of collection of water.

5.2. Numerical Vulnerability of Dalits

The Dalits' numerical vulnerability was the prime determining factor in the commission of violence when they attempted to gain access to water. Ramaiah (2011) says that along with socio-economic vulnerability, the Dalits always face 'numerical vulnerability' which leads to social exclusion in village settings. Out of the 14 cases studied, in 7 case villages the Dalit population was not more than 11.80 percent which is the average Dalit population in the state of Maharashtra. The case villages where the population of the Dalits was relatively large–for example, in Kiti Adgaon, Jategaon, Ranmala–there the Dalits had resisted the perpetrators. It was also observed that they could build up the strength to struggle for asserting their right to water. In the case villages like Ganjpur, Vanjarwadi, Kuslamb, Gawandara and Dagadi Shahajanpur, the proportion of the Dalit population was significantly low (Table 1). This resulted in violence on the Dalits when they asserted their right to water and this violence was quite extensive. Even, the structure of the village settlement had changed over a period of time in Ghodka Rajuri. As per their convenience, most of the Dalit landed households had shifted to their farms because daily travel from the village to the farms was time consuming. Also, some of the Dalit families had shifted from old Maharwada to a new settlement colony called Khadi-Machine. In those villages where the Dalit population was significant, there was comparably no oppression. Perhaps this was why Dr. Babasaheb Ambedkar had suggested, 'leave the village and proceed to the cities'. His idea was to concentrate on the numerical strength of the Dalits. Therefore, the findings of this study confirms the findings of Ramaiah's study (2007) which states that lesser population of the Dalits in a village setting is responsible in instigating violence upon them whereas larger numerical strength implies them occupying a focal position in village affairs and in the overall power domain.

5.3. Political Connections

The study showed that the Dalit communities had very little say in gaining access to water in the political domain of the village. The Gram Panchayats (GPs) were in the hands of the dominant castes who mostly contest such elections. They also mainly regulated the available water supply and augmented the water resources at the village level. These finding are slightly in contrast to those in the Tiwary and Phansalkar (2007) study. For example, it was observed that in the Ganjpur case, though the Dalits held prime power positions in the Panchayat Raj institutions (both in the Gram Panchayat and the Panchayat Samiti), still, the Dalit communities remained deprived from getting access to the common well. Denying the Dalits access to water seemed to be a matter of political interests'. Moreover, the Gram Panchayat functionaries also neglected to provide water facilities to the Dalits. They occasionally displayed caste prejudices while implementing the water schemes. Political leaders played an important role in both instigating violence and as well as in conflict resolution. In the Kuslamb and Vanjarwadi cases, the victims of caste violence around water were popularly active in local politics although they had been targeted and caught in through a political conspiracy of attributing a crime against them. Even the Dalit youth from Dagadi Shahajanpur were politically suppressed. It was seen in the Ranmala case that the ML As too mostly supported the non-Dalit castes and only occasionally the Dalits (and that also only to defeat their political rivals). In Kuslamb, the MLA made the statement to save his caste brothers: [For caste, the politics would be thrown into the stove. I would agitate on the road for caste.]' One Dalit pointed out how the political leaders stood by the side of the Savarnas with great enthusiasm (Field notes, 26 October 2012).

The Dalit habitations received least priority in water management at the local level. They release insufficient water and that without keeping to any given time, for drinking and domestic use. In Dagadi Shahajanpur, the Dalits used to collect water from a low pressure water supply which was supplied for a short time as well. Though there was shortage of water in Ranmala, the Dalit waterman used to manage water distribution as effectively as possible. However, in Dagadi Shahajanpur, the waterman, who was Maratha by caste, was found to be mostly irresponsible while supplying water, especially to the Dalits. Often the 'community' that dominantly consists of the non-Dalits excludes the Dalits from accessing water. For instance, in Gawandara, water was supplied through a common water tank. Most of the time water was supplied to the main village habitation and the least priority was given to the Dalit vasti (habitation) which had a small independent water storage tank, catering only to the Dalits. One of the Dalits said:

'If we could switch it off, then who would take the risk? If water is supplied to their area and we switch it on here, why should we create a foundation for a conflict? Therefore whatever we could receive, we adjusted with that less quantum of water.' (FGD, 25 February 2013)

The Dalits were largely dependent on the public sources of water. In the absence of the availability of public sources of water, the Dalits had to beg for water from the non-Dalits who were known as the water resource rich people, owning the sources of water. The Dalits mainly roamed about far and wide in search of water. The Dalits' situation worsened when the public sources of water would become non-functional. Moreover, as was seen in Dagadi Shahajanpur, Gawandara and Ranmala, the public sources of water were predominantly regulated by the non-Dalits, particularly in water scarcity periods.

Chandane, Regional President of Democratic Party of India, pointed out:

'Those people [the non-Dalits] have wells on private land while our people have no wells. First thing is that we have no agriculture land in the village, no house in the village. This is the Dalits' situation...Since there were no wells for the Dalits, they had to collect water from public sources of water–wells, borewells in the village. The government had planned some schemes which have not been implemented on a large scale in the Beed district yet. Therefore, the Dalits are more vulnerable as compared to the other villagers.' (In-depth interview, 17 January 2013).

Also, the Gram Panchayat by and large, regulated the Dalits' demand for water (for instance, in Ashti, Mali Pargaon, Ganjpur and Kiti Adgaon). The cases studied proved that discrimination was practiced when water was supplied in the villages. The Gram Panchayat functionaries seemed to be reluctant to distribute water equally among all. In the Vanjarwadi case, the Gram Panchayat openly supported the Maratha oppressors on the issue of the water conflict, instead of taking up any stringent actions. In Ganjpur, the Gram Panchayat was reluctant to provide the Dalits separate access to water. Being a leader in the village, Dattatray demanded a separate installation of a motor-pump on the well for the Dalits so that they could gain access to water, which the Gram Panchayat did not agree to. Members in the Ashti FGD stated that the Gram Panchayat had not been taking much initiative to make water available to the Dalit communities. The Gram Panchayat released water once a month. Its representatives were also not keen to even speak on the issue. They only came during the election period including the Sarpanch of the village (FGD, 18 March 2013).

The public sources of water were either located at inconvenient places or the sources of water were in very bad condition. For instance, in Dagadi Shahajanpur, the village water tank was located at an elevation which easily catered water only to the non-Dalit households. In Gawandara, handpumps had rapidly become non-functional in the post-monsoon period as groundwater table got depleted drastically. The Dalits from Ghodka Rajuri had to face deprivation of water because of being settled in different locations in the village. It was seen in the Kiti Adgaon and Kuslamb cases that though the perennial sources of water were created for the Dalits, the non-Dalits had hijacked those sources.

Poor quality of water, which was particularly available to the Dalits, was a major issue. For instance, the Dalits in Ranmala preferred to purify water as they found it to have bacterial contamination. But the Dalits from Dagadi Shahajanpur and Ashti had to use unclean sources of water as their degree of water deprivation seemed to be too high. The unclean water deteriorated their health too. The victimized family from Wantakli was also helplessly using contaminated water from the riverbed as the family was socially excluded from all other sources of water. The water in Ganjpur was saline. The district laboratory also indicated that water used by the Dalits had chemical contamination more than the permissible limits and was also contaminated by bacteria which made it unfit for drinking in Ganjpur, Ghodka Rajuri and Gawandara (Table 2 and Table 3).

Table 2: Report on chemical examination of water for drinking purposes

Test parameter Location	***Sample 1 (Bore well) Gawandara Vasti***	***Sample 2 (Public well) Gawandara Maruti Mandir***	***Sample 3 (Public well) Ganjpur-Mangwada***	***Sample 4 (Public well) Ganjpur-Gaon***	***Sample 5 (Handpump) Ghodka Rajuri Rajwada***	***Sample 6 (Public well) Ghodka Rajuri Gaon***	***BIS Specifications 10500: 2012 Normal values Desirable Limits***	***Permissible Limits***
Physical Observations	Clear	Clear	Clear	Clear	Clear	Clear	- .	-
Odour	Odourless	Odourless	Odourless	Odourless	Odourless	Odourless	Unobjectionable	-
Turbidity (N.T.U.)	0.77	0.62	o.58 ;	0.42	0.67	0.5	1	5
pH value	7.7	7.4	7.3	7.1	7.3	7.3	6.5 to 8.5	No Relaxation
Chlorides (as Cl)	166.0	140.0	220.0	284.0	74.0	142.0	250	1000
Nitrates (as NO_3)	121.9	122.05	176.9	261.7	35.52	71.2	45	No Relaxation
Total Hardness (as $CaCO_3$)	448.0	512.0	744.0	720.0	400.0	480.0	200	600
Alkalinity (as $CaCO_3$)	336.0	344.0	472.0	464.0	336.0	300.0	200	600
Permanent Hardness (as $CaCO_3$)								
Iron (as Fe)	0.1	0.11	0.15	0.06	0.23	0.03	0.3	No Relaxation
Fluoride (as F)	1.03	0.62	0.46	0.75	0.64	1.30	1.0	1.5
Total Dissolved Solids	1320.0	1160.0	1696.0	1630.0	744.0	962.0	500	2000
Calcium (as Ca)						75	200	
Magnesium (as Mg)							30	100
Sulphate (as SO_4)						200	400	

Source: District Public Health Laboratory, Beeo! 26 July 2013.

Table 3: Report on the bacterial examination of water for drinking purposes

Test parameter	*Sample 1 (Bore-well)*	*Sample 2 (Public-well)*	*Sample 3 (Public-well)*	*Sample 4 (Public-well)*	*Sample 5 (Hand-pump)*	*Sample 6 (Public-well)*
Location	Gawandara Vasti	Gawandara Maruti Mandir	Ganjpur-Mangwada	Ganjpur-Gaon	Ghodka Rajuri Rajwada	Ghodka Rajuri Gaon
Chloroform	More than 16	More than 16	More than 16	More than 16	More than 16	More than 16
Thermo-tolerant	09	06	16	16	04	09
Remarks	Unfit for drinking	Unfit for drinking	Unfit for drinking	Unfit for drinking	Unfit for drinking	Unfit for drinking

Source: District Public Health Laboratory, Beed, 22nd July 2013

5.4. Economic Status

The violence on the Dalits had an economic basis. The Dalits were exploited in such a way that the non-Dalits could gain some economic benefits. As per the 'Class' analysis, the different classes in society have differential access to the means of production. Water is one of the means of production when it is used for agriculture and livelihoods. But, when it is used for domestic purpose it can be considered as a part of reproduction. It was observed that while controlling water resources, the upper castes execute their economic interests. For instance, in the Jategaon, Rajegaon and Rui Dharur cases, the victims were physically assaulted by the oppressors merely on account of economic transactions. These water-caste conflicts occurred on the issue of shrinking of the balance money in Jategaon, mortgaging land in Rui Dharur, and seeking tenders of fishery in Rajegaon, Commodification of water was prevalent in the rural areas, resulting in exclusion of the Dalit communities. Sometimes, in many water stressed rural areas, water is pumped by farmers from deep borewells and sold to the water tankers (Kulkarni *et al.*, 2007: 13). It was seen that a water market had rapidly emerged in the study area. The water-lords, predominantly from the non-Dalit castes, sold water. This was an extensive practice and it specifically mushroomed during the periods of water scarcity. The Dalits were economically exploited and water was used as a commodity. The Dalits had to purchase it for their drinking and domestic needs. Since the Dalits were economically socially disadvantaged this worked against them. Ashti and Kiti Adgaon showed adequate glimpses of this. In Kiti Adgaon, the Dalits were denied access to water as they were considered impure. It caused harm to the Dalits in many ways and one of them was through the 'water market' that was in full swing. The water was sold only to the Dalit communities at Maruti's well. The Maratha ex-Sarpanch said that Gujar, a Maratha man, used to earn money through this activity.

The violence took place in the Gawandara, Ashti and Jategaon cases because the victims had attempted either to irrigate their land or feed their goats which were their means of livelihood. Water-caste conflict had a link with land ownership as well. Those Dalits who had at least some land were deliberately targeted in the Dagadi Shahajanpur, Ashti, Rui Dharur, Gawandara and Ganjpur cases. The resource poor Dalits hardly had ownership of water resources. For instance, late Eknath Awad, former President of Manavi Hakk Abhiyan, said that water-caste discrimination was also experienced around irrigation and economic activities:

'If a Dalit has a water facility, he has to bring pipelines *via* other people's land. Generally it is seen to it that the pipeline should not be made available to him. One of the Dalits in Tad Sonana, Beed tehsil, was awarded 3 acres of land that was taken out from a landowner under the land ceiling act by the government. A well was dug. Then the previous landowner claimed: "the land belongs to me; therefore, the well also belongs to me." The atrocity took place in such a context...' (In-depth interview, 10 May 2013).

In Gawandara, the violence against a Dalit woman was carried out on the issue of who could first gain access to water for irrigation in the command area of the Kundalika Project. The victim stated that most of the farmers had access to water for irrigation by installing their own motor-pumps. The state or any other apparatus like the irrigation department did not distribute water for irrigation to the users, which as per rules, they are supposed to do. As part of the pumping race, there was a possibility of gaining access to more quantity of water by the powerful farmers in the command area. In Rui Dharur, a Dalit victim said:

'My parents had been labourers at Motiram Solanki's [Maratha] house for 16 years. They cleaned and smeared Solanki's house with cow dung. My brother and I, by cutting sugarcane, and our parents by labouring at their place, had bought Solanki's four-acre land. We mortgaged this land to Darade [Vanjari], who later on gave it to Solanki [original owner—the Marathas]. He did not return it to us.' (In-depth interview, 5 October 2012).

It was observed that the well owners were predominantly from the non-Dalit castes. Searching for water consumed plenty of time particularly for the Dalit women. This affected their economic and livelihood opportunities as well. Caste still mattered while asserting right to water in the everyday life in rural areas. Yet, the Dalit's touching of water was non-permissible. Whether it happened consciously or unconsciously, the Dalits had to face dire consequences. All the 14 cases studied were the living examples of water-caste linkages–just for touching water, the Dalits were murdered. The perpetrators were annoyed at how the Dalits had dared to utilise water for economic gains. Manusmriti still ruled over the society. The Dalits were denied access to water not on class basis, but on caste basis. Caste became important in such a scenario. The non-Dalits did not want the Dalits to gain economic prosperity; rather, they wanted the Dalits to sustain their lives continuing the hereditary occupation assigned to them by the caste system. Though the Dalits may have captured some prime positions of power in the Panchayat Raj Institutions or had become economically prosperous as compared to the non-Dalits, they were still discriminated against at the sources of water or while taking water. Classical 'class' analysis therefore offers limited interpretation of this complex issue of access to water by the Dalits.

6. CONCLUSION

In short, this article, through multiple cases, explored the various factors that came into play when negotiating the right to water by the Dalits. The Dalits had to face hardships in collection of water in which productive time was consumed. The non-Dalits were unwilling to break the orthodox rules laid down by the caste system. The Dalits were not considered as equal fellow citizens. Untouchability was persistently practiced while the Dalits tried to access water. They were denied access to water on the basis of 'purity and pollution'. The fact that Dalits were numerically smaller contributed to the commission of violence on them when they tried to access water; in populations where there was a significant Dalit presence, they were much better able to negotiate with the village caste groups. Panchayat Raj Institutions were usually in the hands of the non-Dalits who often times misused that power to target the Dalits. As part of political connections, water resources were predominately controlled by the non-Dalits and as a result the Dalits did not have much say in water management and their concerns were not attended to Gram Panchayat neglected the water requirements of the Dalit households. On the other hand, it paid more attention to the supply of water to the non-Dalits, the dominant section. The Dalits were dependent on public sources of water which were by and large non-functional or inconvenient to access. Apart from this, the Dalits mostly had to rely upon poor quality of water as compared to the non-Dalits. The Dalits were also economically exploited and water became an instrument to do so. Water was used as a commodity and the Dalits had to purchase it for their drinking and domestic needs.

Thus, there is a need to take up this issue for policy level intervention and various measures should also be taken up at the local level as the poor quality of water affects the health of the Dalits significantly. In that sense, one of the areas of research in the future is to explore to what extent the Dalits have to rely on contaminated water as compared to the non-Dalits and what are the measures to deal with the issue.

Untouchability was persistently practiced as the non-Dalits had a mindset that the Dalits were contemptible people who were born to be inferior and therefore were eligible for only hate and negligence. However, there is now an urgent need to change such caste based mentality which is distinctly still the foundation of social relations in the rural areas. The change cannot take place overnight. It requires constant efforts in the long run and direct immediate actions in the form of effective implementation of water policies and programmes from the perspective of access to water as a fundamental/ constitutional right of everybody. Awareness can be initiated through the planned campaigns that assert that the Dalits are our fellow citizens and they are equally entitled. Like others to realize their right to water without any discrimination and barriers. Dr Babasaheb Ambedkar had said that annihilation of Caste is way to deal with such issues of caste based discrimination and exploitation. Indian society requires to internalize this path to create a just world.

ACKNOWLEDGEMENTS

The author is sincerely thankful to his Ph.D. guide, Prof A. Ramaiah, Centre for Study of Social Exclusion and Inclusive Policies ofTISS and K.J. Joy, a Senior Fellow with Society for Promoting Participative Ecosystem Management, for their extensive comments on the draft article.

REFERENCES

Ambedkar, B.R. (1989). "Dr. B.R. Ambedkar–Writings and Speeches (Vol. I)," Mumbai: Government of Maharashtra.

Banerjee, Taposik (2010). "Right to Water: Some Theoretical Issues," *Contemporary Issues and Ideas in Social Sciences*, 6(1): 1–17.

Bryman, Alan (2008). Social Research Methods, 3rd Edition, Oxford: Oxford University Press.

Census of India (2011). "The Primary Census Abstract," Mumbai: Directorate of Census Operations Maharashtra.

Dhasal, Namdeo (2007). A Current of Blood: Poems Selected and Translated from the Marathi by Dilip Chitre, New Delhi: Navayana Publishing.

Dumont, Louis (1999). Homo Hierarchicus: The Caste System and Its Implications. Complete Revised English Edition (Second Impression) Translated by Louis Dumont and Basia Gulati Mark Sainsbury, New Delhi: Oxford University Press.

Forum for Policy Dialogue on Water Conflcits in India (2015). Right to Water in India: Privileging Water for Basic Needs, Pune: Forum for Policy Dialogue on Water Conflcits in India.

Gerring, Jonh (2007). Case Study Research: Principles and Practices, Cambridge: Cambridge University Press.

Government of India (2012). "National Water Policy 2012," New Delhi: Ministry of Water Resources. *http: / /wrmin.nic.in / writereaddata / NationalWaterPolicv / NWP201.pdf*. Accessed on 13 April, 2015.

Government of Maharashtra (2008). "Dr. Babasaheb Ambedkar yanche Bahushkrut Bharat Aani Muknayak," Mumbai: Department of Higher and Technical Education.

Government of Maharashtra (2010). "Economic Survey of Maharahstra 2009-10," Mumbai: Directorate of Economics and Statistics, Planning Department.

Gupta, Dipankar (2000). Interrogating Caste: Understanding Hierarchy and Difference in Indian Society. India: Penguin Books.

Guru, Gopal (2009). "Archaeology of Untouchability," *Economic and Political Weekly,* XLIV(37): 49–56.

Joshi, Deepa (2011). "Caste, Gender and the Rhetoric of Reform," *Economic and Political Weekly*, XLVI(18): 56–63.

Joshi, Deepa and Ben Fawcett (2001). "Water, Hindu Mythology and an Unequal Social Order in India," Paper Presented at the Second Conference of the International Water History Association, Bergen, pp. 1–12. http://www.wateraid.org/documents/hindumh.pdf

Joy, K.J., Sangameshwaran, Priya, Latha, A., Dharmadhikary, Shripad, Prasad, M.K. and Soma, K.P. (2011). Life, Livelihoods, Ecosystem, Culture: Entitlements and Allocations of Water for Competing Uses, Pune: Forum for Policy Dialogue on Water Conflicts in India.

Kulkarni, Seema, Ahmed, Sara, Arya, Swamalata, Joy, K.J. and Paranjape, Suhas (2007). Women Water and Livelihoods, SOPPECOM: Pune.

Marx, Karl and Frederick, Engels (1848). "Manifesto of the Communist Party," http://www.marxists.org/archive/marx/works/download/pdf/Manifesto.pdf (accessed on 5 May 2014).

Mosse, David (2003): The Ride of Water: Statecraft, Ecology and Collective Action in South India, New Delhi: Oxford University Press.

Navsarjan Trust and Robert F. Kennedy Center for Justice and Human Rights (2010): Understanding Untouchability: A Comprehensive Study of Practices and Conditions in 1,589 Villages. Robert F. Kennedy Center for Justice and Human Rights. Retrieved December 2, 2015, from http://www.esocialsciences.org/Download/repecDownload.

Omvedt, Gail (2004). Jotirao Phule and the Ideaology of Social Revolution in India, New Delhi: Critical Quest.

Paranjape, Suhas, Adagale, Raju and Pomane, Ravi (2008). "Mahad to Mangaon: Eighty Years of Caste Discrimination: What Caste is Water?" *In*: Joy, K.J. (*ed.*), Water Conflicts in India: A Million Revolts in the Making, New Delhi: Routledge.

Planning Commission Government of India (2013). Twelfth Five Year Plan (2012-2017) Economic Sectors Volume II, New Delhi: SAGE Publications.

Prakash, Anjal and Sama, R.K. (2006). "Contending Water Uses: Social Undercurrents in a Water-Scare Village," *Economic and Political Weekly*, XLI(7): 577–579.

Ramaiah, A. (2007). Laws for Dalit Rights and Dignity: Experiences and Responses From Tamil Nadu, Jaipur: Rawat Publication.

Ramaiah, A. (2011). "Relevance of Dr. Ambedkar's Demand for Separate Settlement," *Mainstream*, XLIX(17): 1–4. http://www.mainstreamweekly.net accessed on 11 June. 2011.

Strauss, A.L. (1997). Grounded Theory in Practice, London: Sage Publications.

Thorat, Sukhadeo (2002). "Oppression and Denial: Dalit Discrimination in the 1990s," *Economic and Political Weekly*, pp. 572–578.

Thorat, Sukhadeo (2006). Ambedkar's Role in Economic Planning, Water and Power Policy, Delhi: Shipra Publications.

Tiwary, Rakesh (2006). "Explanations in Resource Inequality: Exploring Scheduled Caste Position in Water Access Structure. *International Journal of Rural Management*, 2(1): 85–106. http://irm.sagepub.eom/content/2/l/85 accessed on 2 November 2011

Yin, Robert (1984). Case Study Research: Design and Methods, New Delhi: Sage Publications.

Raju Adagale is pursuing Ph.D., from Tata Institute of Social Sciences (TISS), Mumbai. He has more than 12 years' experience in development research. His major assignments and involvements are in the areas related to caste,land, water and renewable energy. Presently, he is working as assistant professor at Dr. Babasaheb Ambedkar Research and Training Institute (BARTI), Pune.

Chapter 13

Exclusion of Dalit and Atrocities in Celebrating Hindu Rituals

ARVINDKUMAR S. MARDAN[1]

INTRODUCTION

The overall progress (including political) of Gujarat is not only remarkable but it also got attention of the whole country. The leadership of Gujarat had not only crossed boundaries of the state but also spread its wings over the country. Gujarat is believed to be a model state of development and progress among Indian states. It is interesting to know. Is the fruit of progress equally distributed among all the people of society? What are real facts about social sector? What is the condition of the Scheduled Castes, Scheduled Tribes, women, minorities and the poor? Naturally, it is a subject of research for social scientists. The present researcher is interested to know about the changing conditions of weaker sections. It is known as that caste is the basic unit of the Indian society and hence the people of Scheduled Castes are more vulnerable than other groups. Time moves constantly without taking a break, but incident of dalit atrocity is also continuing (without ending). It has no relation with ancient or modern times. A number of caste-based atrocities against

[1] Gujarat University (Ahmedabad).

them have increased not in a particular state, but all over India. However there is no difference of inhumanity between the developed state and less developed states. Even Gujarat is not an exception as a state in continuing dalit atrocity. There were many atrocities which have been committed against dalits and only few of them were published in media. They were totally caste-based; and related with social norms and behavior of traditional caste structure. "*In a written reply to an unstarred question of Congress. MLA Raghavji Patel, the Chief Minister Anandiben Patel stated that dalits had been given police security in 116 villages of Gujarat due to the threat to their lives from powerful local communities. Further, according to information provided by the state government, a total of 6385 cases of atrocities against dalits had been registered in the past five years.*" These types of incidents showed that Discrimination and untouchability still present in India. After passing sixty five years of a new Constitution, social exclusion of the dalits is still continued. They were related with social and religious norms; and behaviour of traditional caste structure. The members of the dalit communities were trying to access to such rights but they were obstructed and attacked. Therefore, the present researcher has decided to do some work in this field and has chosen social exclusion as topic of the present study. The researcher should study both exclusion and inclusion of dalits in various fields of society. This research paper attempts to find out the relation between '*Exculsion of Dalits and Atrocities in Celebrating Hindu Rituals*'. There is also relation between celebration of rituals and caste system. There are some rules and regulations of traditional caste system which have still prevailed. Some ritual celebrations are selected for the present study. An attempt is made to find out which types of inclusion and exclusion still prevent in the celebration of Hindu rituals. It is a fact that Indian society is still standing on pillar of Caste system. Moreover 'Purity and pollution' concept is very important in the Indian culture. It reflects in practical behaviour of life. While India has ushered into the technological age, it has also become important for a social scientists to know that types of changes have been noticed in the conduct of rituals in the Indian society. The members of dalit can access to a place of public or common property, which other members have right to access. These results will help to know Exclusion of Dalits and Atrocities in Celebrating Hindu Rituals.

Aims of the Study

(i) To find out relation between Exclusion of Dalits and Atrocities in Celebrating Hindu Rituals.

(ii) To know what types of changes have been noticed in the conduct of rituals in the Indian society.

(iii) To find out inclusion of dalits in various fields of society.

RESEARCH METHODOLOGY

The present study was a survey type study. It selected three districts of Gujarat for this survey. A self made questionnaire was used for the study. The district, where dalit atrocities had been committed more were selected purposefully for this study. There were selected some ritual celebrations as variables for the study like marriage, navaratri, funeral rites, diwali, holi and others. There were and used some secondary sources of information like internet, news paper, social media. The data was analyzed with simple statistics.

Importance of the Study

In the days of Smart City and Mars Yatra (Chandrayan), India has really achieved a great technological development, but the mind set of people still has not changed and is still influenced by religion and traditional social behavioural rules, The man importance of this study is to draw attention to social sector and to shed light on the dark side of social exclusion. This research shows that only getting technological development or economic growth is not sufficient to improve the quality of life of such excluded group. It requires a sensitivity and change in the social structure. The study tries to highlight how deep is 'Caste Discrimination' and 'Social Exclusion' in Gujarat. It is representative of the overall situation as India. It will help in making a policy of social development for Government and various other agencies.

Meaning of Discrimination

According to Pocket Oxford Dictionary, the word 'discriminate' (verb) means

1. '(often followed by between) make or see a distinction.'
2. '(usually followed by against or in favour of) treat unfavourably or favourably, esp. on the basis of race, gender, etc.

Means it is a matter of individual distinction and unfavorable or favorable treatment on the basis of gender, colour, religion, ethnicity, minority, nationality, caste, race and others etc. When an individual is treated unfavorably or favorably on the basis is of such a particular ground is called discrimination. If and individual belongs to a particular disadvantage group in the society, he/she is treated unfavorable and *vice versa*. Hence, discrimination is an 'unfavorable treatment based on racial, sexual, etc. prejudice'.

Meaning of Social Exclusion

According to Pocket Oxford Dictionary, word, 'exclude' (verb) means: 'keep out (a person or thing) from a place group, privilege, etc.'

Exclusion is a group concept. It is a matter of concerning the whole group and an unfavorable treatment to the whole group on the basis of gender, colour, religion, ethnicity, minority, nationality, caste, race by the other group/groups. When the whole group in the society is treated unfavourably by dominant or major or other groups on the particular base is called exclusion. The group which is a victim of unfavourable treatment is known as 'excluded' or 'marginalised'.

Definition

1. Amartya Sen says "the situation where some people are kept out and where some people are being included and the two

situations are ascribed as unfavourable exclusion and favourable inclusion. The acts of exclusion which excludes people from having an access and entitlement to certain social groups that are based on the recognized and accepted principles, rules, norms, practices of fairness can be considered as unfair exclusion, similarly the inclusions which provide access and entitlement to person from certain social groups but on different terms and conditions can be termed as unfair inclusion."

2. "Social exclusion is about the inability of the society to keep all groups and individuals within the mainstream and the tendency to push vulnerable and difficult groups or individuals into the periphery as though they do not belong to that society (Silver, 1994; Estivill, 2003)
3. The social exclusion can also be defined as "On the basis of religion or social rules, one group/some groups who believed oneself/themselves superior to other groups; and for maintenance of their hierarchical order (privileges and rights), superior group/groups not only try to control behaviour of other groups but also allow limited interaction to them is called exclusion. There is no participation of excluded group in all fields of life and their social relationship is limited by duties. If any individual or group does not follow rules of this social (special) relationship, he is severely punished without looking at the dignity of his being a human being. The number of superior group is more than one, because there is hierarchical order and every higher group is believed to be superior to other lower group."

Hence, the concept of social exclusion is understood through the different variables like Access, Rights, Disadvantage, Birth, Denial, Marginalisation, Rupture, Distance, Activity etc 'Social exclusion is the denial or disadvantage of rights or access to resources to develop for the disadvantaged or marginalised groups on the basis of caste, birth, place or process.' 'The publication of Les exclus by Rene Lenoir in 1974 was a milestone in the emergence of social exclusion as a concept. He employed it to raise alarm at the inability of an expanding economy to include certain physically, mentally and socially disabled groups.' Four elements:

According to Atkinson (1998) there are four elements that recur in any discussion of social exclusion.

1. Multiple deprivation,
2. Relativity,
3. Agency and
4. Dynamics. Multiple Deprivations

'It implies that social exclusion is about more than simple poverty, more about the absence of community or social interactions. There is no absolute social exclusion; relativity refers that people are excluded from a particular society in a particular place at a particular time. Since exclusion is an act, there are agents who undertake it; an act by the majority against the minority. It is dynamic as it is perpetual.'

Marginalization

'Marginalization of individuals or groups can be defined as the denial or lack of opportunity for these individuals or groups to fully participate (economically, politically and socially) in the society to which they belong. The lack of full participation means that the marginalized have less ability to even access basic societal resources, such as food, clothing, shelter, and health services. Often the marginalized are seen as outsiders, out-casts, or second-class citizens in the state or country of their citizenship. It stands to reason that if there is a marginalized group then there is also a non-marginalized group. This coupling cannot be dismissed in a discourse on marginalization because the main organizing principle in marginalization is the uneven distribution of employment, development, privileges, power, infrastructures and opportunities of all kinds in favor of the privileged, the advantaged, or the sociological majority (Tunga, 2009).'

Social Exclusion in India

Indian Society is divided into four Varna which is known as Chaturvarna vyavastha'. Hence, caste is the basic unit of Indian society and this caste system was originated from the 'Rig veda'. The following is the hierarchical order of the caste system, or four Varna.

1. The Brahmins, or priests.
2. The Kshatriyas, or warriors.
3. The Vaisyas.
4. The Shudras.

The Untouchable fall completely outside of this system and they also known as 'Varna' or pancham varna. But today the 'varna' was unused and replaced by the 'jati'. Hence there is a clear distinction between varna and jati. Verma has groups of Jatis, and Jati is a local system of ranking. Some groups of jati combined with one varna. 'Jati' specifies rank in the Hindu social hierarchy. Generally jati is related with occupation. Jatis which belong to the three highest varnas are considered more pure than the Jatis of Shudras and Outcastes. According to Hindu scripture, Brahmins, Kshatriyas and Vaisyas are believed to be 'twice-born'. They are believed to be pure and can participance in the Hindu rituals, while Shudras and untouchables are considered impure and can not participate in various ceremonies and rituals of Hinduism. The difference between the higher caste and the lower caste is the concept of purity and pollution. This concept is the base of interaction among those castes or caste groups. The purity and pollution concept of Hinduism allows inequalities among different castes which is based on mythological theory of Hinduism. The Hindu individual is faithful to this theory and it is considered very important for this part of the divinely ordained natural order. Some scholars believed that caste system is an ideal division of labour.

"Since the caste system attaints sanctity in religious writings, emancipation from the rigid classification was very difficult to achieve for the lower groups. The belief in religion has singularly contributed to this difficulty. The Scheduled Castes (SCs), as they came to be described in the Government of India Act 1935, have suffered social, economic, cultural and political inequalities for centuries. Under the customary rules of the Hindu social order, the untouchables were denied rights to property, pursue business (except the polluting occupations), education and employment (excluding the manual labour). The consequences of these traditional restrictions in the past are to be seen, even today in terms of lack of ownership of agricultural land, business or non-land capital assets, in education and ultimately in high incidence of poverty among them."

This inherent structural inequality between the excluded group and advantageous group has created a special social relationship which leads to high level of poverty, reduced benefits from development processes of the excluded groups. There is no involvement of these excluded groups in decision making and meaningful participation in public and civil life.

Hindu Ritual and Social Exclusion

Yet, the legal framework has guaranteed the rights against untouchability and caste-based discrimination. According to article 17 of the Indian Constitution, untouchability was abolished and its practice in any form had been abolished. Untouchability means all the practices of social restrictions and denial of access to basic services on the base of sex, caste, colour, race, religion, lineage etc. had been abolished. The law has defined such practices to be punishable.

On the legal basis it is true that untouchability was abolished but it reflects the theoretical view. Hence in real life the practice of untouchability is still prevalent in India. According to Indian Human Development IHDS) Survey 2011-12 of NCAER, a third of rural respondents and a fifth of urban respondents admitted to practicing untouchability. The practice was most common among Brahmins, followed by Other Backward Classes and then non-Brahmin forward castes. 'The IHDS, conducted by the National Council for Applied Economic Research (NCAER), and the University of Maryland, also reported that 30 per cent of rural and 20 per cent of urban households said they practiced untouchability.'

Every society has some kind of social inequality and some form of division of labour. There are some groups which are united on the basis of occupation. Yet, occupations are passed on from one generation to another, but there is also the freedom of changing occupation. While in India, occupation has passed on from one generation to another but there is no freedom. Hence, caste system is not only an extreme form of this, but also it is hereditary occupational division, which was sanctioned by Hindu rituals. Most of the behavioural rules and regulations surround it. And caste regulates access to resources of various kinds.

Rituals are ceremonies of birth, death, marriage, initiation, healing, harvest, or religious observance which found in all known cultures, and appear to have been performed for thousands of years. They speak to people's core emotions and reveal values that a society holds dearest. Because their expression is conventional and obligatory, they join the individual in solidarity with the group. Rituals bear an obvious relationship to norms and can even be conceived of as forms of norms.

Hindu Rituals is a sum of puja, samskaras, vrats and customs, which are not only related with religion but also behaviour of life.

Hindu rituals combine the following practices

(1) Sanskars: Sixteen samskaras and four Ashrams.

(2) Vratas: Vrataas are observance of sacred Tithis such as Amavasya, Pournami, Chaturthi, Sashti, Ekadasi, Trayodashi etc

(3) Pujas: Pujas are for deities like Ganesha, Krishna, Saraswati, Durga, Shiva, Rama, Hanuman, Skanda, Durga, etc.

(4) Customs: Customs depend on regional climate and available materials.

(5) Festival and fair ceremonies.

Dalit Atrocity in Gujarat

Gujarat is the westernmost state of India and is surrounded by a long sea-coast on its west and south. Geographically, the location of Gujarat is very important for our country. Because the border of Pakistan lies along its northern border. Gujarat is also a birthplace of Gandhiji and is believed to be a peaceful state. The population of Gujarat is more than six crore and the population of the Scheduled Castes (SC) is 7.1% of the total population.

There are main four religions practiced in Gujarat: Hinduism, Jainism, Islam and Christianity. Hence, Hinduism is the dominant religion of Gujarat. There is seen an established hierarchical social structure which comprised of a number of castes. These caste groups are divided into four groups:

(1) Dominant Castes: The Brahmins, Patels, Darbars (Kshatriya), Koli Patels, Ahirs, and Mers etc..

(2) Other Backward Castes: Thakor, Chaudhari, Koli, Ahir, Bharwad, Mers etc.. (it includes 146 castes)

(3) Scheduled Castes: The Chamars, Vankars, Garodas, Nadiyas, Senva, Turi Barots, Valmikis, Hadis etc.

(4) Scheduled Tribes.

The Dominant Castes and some Castes of Other Backward Castes always try to oppress the Dalits. Hence the Dalits are discriminated and excluded by both the Dominant Castes and Other Backward Castes. Even though Gujarat is believed to be a progressive and developed state, but the mindset of people has not changed. They believed in old social structure and religious rules which are practiced in various rituals. Dalit atrocity is very common and has seen a long history of Oppression. Gujarat is a state where dalits have faced twice a long anti-reservation movement (1981 and 1985). In these movements Dalits were not only targeted in cities but also in villages. Recently "In a written reply to an unstirred question of Congress MLA Raghavji Patel, The Chief Minister Anandi ben Patel stated that dalits had been given police security in 116 villages of Gujarat due to the threat to their lives from powerful local communities. Further, according to information provided by the State Government, a total of 6385 cases of atrocity against dalits had been registered in the past five years."

DISCUSSION

There were twenty questions used for getting data. The following is the discussion.

Marriage Ceremony Can

(1) While you are observing 'marriage samskaras', Can the groom ride on a horse and varghodo of groom pass through the main street of your village?

Marriage is an important ritual of every society. When asked this question was asked to respondents, about 74% respondents told that they can ride on a horse and varghodo procession of the groom can pass through street of their surrounding area. Hence about 50% told that they can pass through the main street of village and 24% respondents prefer their surrounding area. Hence about 26% told that while they are observing 'marriage ceremony', the dalit groom cannot ride on a horse and varghodo of groom can not pass through the main street of the village.

(2) Can you play Bandvaja over the main street of your village in marriage? About 84% of the respondents were told that they can play Bandvaja (Band Party) surrounding area. But 50 % of them told that they can also play over the main street of their village. About 16% respondents told they have not freedom of Bandvaja. Hence they are using traditional 'dhol' (drum) at the time of marriage and it is limited to their maholla (locality) and streets.

(3) Are you using the fire-crackers on the main street of your village?

To the question regarding the use of the fire-crackers the answer is the same question number two. About 84% of the respondents told that they use the fire crackers during the marriage ceremony, but they prefer use them their surrounding only. However 16% respondents told that they cannot using the fire-crackers on the main street.

(4) In Marriage ceremony of open castes, do you providing traditional occupational services such as providing 'toran', 'Dhol Service', 'Cleaning place' and others?

Occupation service is the main indicator of caste-system and it is closely related with untouchability. About 86% respondent told that they are providing tradional occupation services such as 'toran', 'Dhol Service', 'Cleaning place' and others. While 14% respondents refused to provide such services. The percentage is higher but there is noticed remarkable change. Some sub castes of the scheduled caste like Valmiki Nadiya and Senama are engaged in these traditional services.

(5) If you are invited in Marriage ceremony of other castes is there a different arrangement of food (bhojan) for your community? Can you take food with them?

It is very interesting to know that which type of interaction will be there between the individuals of dalits and non-dalits during invitation of marriage ceremony. While 30% respondents told that there were an arrangement of 'Bhana system' (Full dish). The dalits have to go with their vessels to the place of marriage and the food is served in their vessels to carry for them home. About 26% said that there is a separate arrangement for taking food, Hence 56% of the respondents can not take food with nondalits. About 44% respondents told that there were common arrangements for marriage food for them. And they can take food with the nondalits.

Antyeshti (Funeral Rites)

(6) Is there separate funeral house for scheduled castes in your village?

It was not surprising that every respondent told that 'there is a separate funeral house for them.

(7) Is the practice still continued to carry out carcasses of animals by the scheduled caste?

The carcass of animals were carried out by the scheduled castes, Most of the respondents about (64 %) told that the carcass by the scheduled castes. But, its forms has changed. Some sub-castes of the scheduled castes like Nadiya and Senama are doing that some villages. Hence there are limited persons who told that they can play **'***Garba***'** at the main place of their village. While 22% respondents told that *they are avoiding to play a garba at the place of other casts.*

(8) *Do you celebrate Navaratri separately in your society (Mohalla)? Do you play Garaba in your resident area only*?

The respondents (78%) answered that they were playing *'Garba' in their residential area (Mohalla) only*. While about 6% respondents told that they can play **'***Garba***'** at the main place of their village. While about 16% respondents told that their villages do not celebrate *Navaratri.*

(9) *Are you allowed to take part in the 'aarati rite'*?

About 98% respondents told that they are not allowed in the 'aarati rite'. They can see the 'aarati' but cannot worship the goddess with the 'aarati rite'. Some respondents told that they can play 'Garba" at the main place of their village, but they are not participating in the aarati rite. 2% of the respondents told positively their village have the *Scheduled castes in majority and* some other village where *the Muslims are in majority*.

(10) *Can you participate in the 'havan rite' or 'aarati rite' in your village*?

The response to this question was not different from the **'***aarati rite.***'** Most respondents told that they do not *participate in the 'haven rite***'** or take part in any religious activities.

(11) *Can you worship 'Holy fire' with all member Holi of your area without casteism*?

About 64% of the respondents gave the answer of this question that they *were not worshiping 'Holy fire' with the members of other castes.*

(12) *There is a separate arrangement of Holy fire for your community*?

They were not worshiping at 'Holy fire' of the other castes, so they have to make separate 'Holi fire' for their own caste. About 64% of the villages of the respondents have separate celebrations of 'Holi fire.'

Some villages where the numbers of the scheduled castes are less not try to, they do celebrate Holy separately.

(13) *Can employee of the scheduled caste get house or hire a house in nondalit residential area of your village*?

Every respondent told that the employee of the scheduled caste can not get house or hire in nondalit residential area in their village. They are required to live in Dalits residential area only.

CONCLUSION

The following conclusions are arrived at from the above discussion.

- From the data it is observed that there was a clear social exclusion and discrimination was notice in some Hindu rituals. These Hindu rituals are related with death, marriage, Navaratri, residence etc..
- The interaction between dalits and nondalits is very limited and it is still controlled by rules of caste system. Hence its forms has changed, but its soul is still living. Dalits can get entry in temple, but cannot participate in 'Havan' or pray in the form of 'aarati'. Hence, there is an absence of community or lack of any social interaction in celebration of Hindu rituals.
- Some Hindu rituals are performed by dalits in their society or their separate places with their community only. For example, every village has a separate funeral house for dalits and it

has been facility. Some of them are too much for a reach. One funeral house of one village near Kadi is situated in such a place, where water logging is common in the monsoon, While dalits have to go to the funeral house, they have to walk through muddy and water-logged street. For the solution of this problem, dalits have stopped to carry out the carcasses of animals from the village. They are demanding for road, to the funeral houses but as yet they were not successful in getting such a road to their separate funeral house.

- Gujarat is famous for 'Navaratri festival' and 'Garba' all over the world. Most of the villages celebrate Garba, but Dalits celebrate it separately in their Mohalla. (residential area) in most of the villages. Hence dalits can play Garba in some villages, but are totally excluded in Havan and aarati rites.
- Food is also seen as a main indicator of social exclusion and discrimination. Except in some villages in most of the villages, dalits are separated directly or indirectly in the sitting arrangement of food in marriage or 'baramu' rituals. (food after twelve days of death). Some villages have adopted a system of taking food in orderly. First nondalits take food, then OBC and lastly dalits.
- These conclusions clearly establish the prevalent relationship between Hindu rituals and social exclusion and discrimination. Hence there is a clear notice absence of community or social interactions.
- So, the caste system is an extreme form of the division of labour and the caste system is still concluded that hereditary occupational division which was sanctioned by Hindu rituals. It is finally Cast still regulates access to resources of various kinds.

REFERENCES

(1) Bhatta Narayan: 'Citizenship and Caste based Discrimination: A Study of Dalit Communities – Case Studies from Western Nepal.'

(2) IHDS 2011-12, The Hindu, Dt. 13-11-14

(3) Pradeep B. Kadun, Prop. Ravindra D. Gadkar, Social Exclusion-Its Types and Impacts on Dalits in India (www.iosrjournals.org)

(4) OJDS 2011-12, The Hindu Dt. 13-11-14

(5) SCSP_TSP Guideline, 2006, Page: 1, (The Scheduled Caste Sub Plan for the Scheduled Castes (SCs).

(6) Lakshmanasamy, T. (2013). 'How deep is Caste Discrimination and Social Exclusion? Methodologies for Measuring Economic Deprivation of Dalits., Indian Journal of Dalit and Tribal Studies and Action, Vol. 1.

(7) The Times of India

Arvindkumar Marden Research Scholar of the Gujarat University (Ahmedabad), pursuing Ph.D in Scoiology. He has done M. Phil (Sociology) from the Gujartat University on 'An Imagination of an Ideal State from the Literature of Sant Rohidas.'He is active in social activity, education and career counseling activities. He has worked with several N.G.Os which are engeged with social movemnt; economic and educational empowerment of Dalit. He has published two books in Gujarati language, one is the biography of Saint Rohidas entitled 'Param Manav Rohidasji ni Jivan Gatha' in novel form and other is the short story book based on untouchability ('Whent Chhete'). He has published more than thirty articles in various Gujarati magazines.

Chapter 14

Mapping the Movements and Atrocities A Study of Dalit Movements in Gujarat

RAJESH LAKUM[1]

ABSTRACT

This study attempts to critically examine the notion of movement and atrocities on Dalit movements in Gujarat. How Caste operate within modern notion of discrimination and protected ignorance of movement and atrocities? In different notion form of discrimination, growing human rights violation apart from the society and a menace to the unity and integrity of the Indian people. Caste violence to examine the atrocities incident and their relation to response with the state and society that the result in multiple victimizations of Dalit at historical and structure levels. The rights based perspectives that the measure of able to facilities of the growth of social democracy has been inspiration of Ambedkar ideology to development of the Dalits. The particular focus of present study is caste violence that the productive role of in the dynamics of caste relations, its power grown up by dominant castes has been to use weapons against Dalits.

[1] Centre for Study in Society and Development, School of Social Studies, Central University, Gujarat.

Politics in Gujarat has been traditionally dominated by upper castes. Thus, they indirectly control the administration, media etc. Therefore, there is rise in violence against Dalits. But there is also assertion among the Dalits against this violence.

INTRODUCTION

The caste system is an obnoxious and hard reality of Indian societal system. The system is itself stands and survives on the basis of hierarchy and discrimination. Due to having lowest strata in this system, Dalits have to face different types of discriminations. They are marginalized and socially excluded. Dalit movements have emerged to fight against inequality and discrimination. One of the form of discriminations is atrocities on Dalits which can be seen as caste violence. In the view of violence, B.R. Ambedkar argued that, "Caste has killed public spirit. Caste has destroyed the sense of public charity. Caste has made public opinion impossible. A Hindu's public is his caste and his responsibility is only to his caste and his loyalty is restricted only to his caste. Virtue has become caste-ridden and morality has become caste bound. There is no sympathy to the deserving and there is no appreciation of the meritorious and there is no charity to the needy. Suffering as such calls for no response. Though there is charity, however, it begins with the caste and ends with the caste. There is sympathy but not for man of other caste" (Ambedkar, 1979, 2014: p. 56). Caste violence erupted involving various caste groups to fight for their share in the resources of production and power in society. While caste conflicts might have existed for centuries, it has become heavily accentuated and has assumed endemic properties in contemporary times. The growing politicization of the socially backward, economically aspiring, politically ascendant and traditionally weaker castes of Indian society, especially the scheduled castes, had led the members of these castes to assert and secure their lawful right and to resist any oppression by the dominant upper castes. Caste violence is a violence of the oppressed against the oppressor and demand for equality and justice (Verma, 2011, pp. 52-3).

Therefore, the paper intends to analyze atrocities on Dalits in Gujarat. The paper is divided into three section. First sections focus on context of movement and atrocities. Second part deals with historical caste system and untouchability and Dalit movements in Gujarat. The final section analyses three recent atrocities incidents occurred in Gujarat.

MOVEMENT AND ATROCITIES

A Social Movement can be described as collective enterprises to establish a new order of life. They have their inception in a situation of unrest and derive their motive power. As a social movement develops, it takes on the character of society. It acquires organization and form, an extra-institutional of a culture, established leadership, a social organization, social rules and social values, customs and traditions (Blumer, 1995: p. 60-83). Here, my concern about social movement is, comparing it to Dalit movements that erupted for many reasons. First, it assists to emphasis on radical movement which aims to annihilation of caste. Second is, the voluntary institutions which involve members from different castes, but only small part of the group have joined the movement. Third is New Social Movement which highlights the contemporary nature of this demonstration of caste. It is often argued that in Indian context, material deprivation is the primary motivation for participation in movement activity (Gorringe, 2005: p. 38-40).

The atrocity is an inhuman and barbarous act, a crime, against the victims. If the victims are poor, illiterate or ignorant, the police and administration can hardly listen to them, what to say of taking any action against culprits who may eventually happen to be the powerful ones. However money makes the major go cannot be possible, because the poor, illiterate or ignorant persons have no money (Jatava, 2007: p. 13). Atrocities have not been defined in law. The term of 'Atrocities', according to the Ministry of Home Affairs, Government of India, implies offences under the Indian Penal Code perpetrated against scheduled castes and scheduled tribes by those not belonging to either community, where caste consideration is really the root cause of the crime even though caste consciousness may not be the immediate motive for the crime (Aloysius Irudayam S.J., Jayshree P. Mangubhai, Joel G. Lee, 2011, p. 7).

Violence could take place on individuals and groups such as domestic abuse, homicide, threats, robbery and so no. however, in the legal institutions, very often, carry out organized violence based on the notion of racist and sexist principles. The institutional violence in the world persists systematically which is more powerful. Institutional violence takes place on the weaker sections who are usually weak. The rich powerful elites are rarely subjected to institutional violence because of their dominant position. The atrocities and violence carried out by powerful institutions but they don't defend atrocities by the claim of self-defense (Chomsky). Therefore, it argues that by using democratic space and with the help of political weapon, the violence could be reduced (Schwarzmantel, 2011: p. vii). The violence is not limited to areas of militarized violence. However, it expanded gender violence, class and caste violence; social violence; political instability; state-sanctioned intimidation; structural violence; unorganized crime and genocidal violence (Kenneth Bush, Colleen Duggen, 2013: p. 7). According to Beatrice Heuser, concept of atrocities means needlessly painful and/or humiliating treatment of enemy combatants, beyond action needed to incapacitate or disarm them. Atrocities also include the act of violence against vulnerable (civilian) populations, for instance non-combatants, especially where substantial numbers are ignored. They include rape, mutilations, torture and killing in any way (Heuser, 2012: p. 3). Kancha Ilaiah says that the atrocities happen for two reasons: Firstly, the oppressed fight for equality and equal rights, the upper caste enraged with this. Secondly, the upper caste can commit atrocity and get away. There is resistance of rape. Therefore, it is a transitory situation in a culture of rape and religious relationships which are projected into sexual relations (Ilaiah, 2015: p. 9).

The prevention of Atrocities act thus offers legal safeguards against caste violence and discrimination. There are two types of atrocities. One is personal atrocities and another one is social atrocities. Furthermore, different forms of atrocities include political atrocities and economic atrocities against protection members of SCs and STs. The appointment of special courts and special public prosecutors under the act of atrocities, the rules of POA act has been stated to identify atrocity prone areas, states to constitute a high powered state- level and district-level vigilance and monitoring committee, setting up the scheduled castes and the scheduled tribes protection cell, nomination of nodal officer of the level of secretary, amount of relief etc. (Narwani, 2011: p. 69-76). The prevention of atrocities act in Gujarat state government identified atrocities prone areas in eleventh (11) district of Gujarat. The year of 1989 from 2012, total incident of 30,692 offences against SCs in Gujarat such as murders, grievance, Hurt, rape, arson, O.I.P.C, PCR etc. The year of 1990 from 2012, total incident of 456 murders and 548 rapes of Dalits in Gujarat.

CASTE SYSTEM AND UNTOUCHABILITY IN GUJARAT

The Hindu social order is based on three interrelated elements, namely, predetermination of social, religious and economic rights based on birth; the unequal and hierarchical division of and provision of strong social, religious and economic ostracism supported by religious ideology to maintain order. It is argued that as like other parts of the country, social evils like the caste system, hierarchy and discrimination very much persists in the state. They are trying to be assertive about their rights and need to live with dignity. The Hindus in Gujarat are divided into several castes- *Brahmins* (priests), *Vanias* (traders), *Rajputs* (warriors and rulers), *Kanbi*, and *Kathis*, *Kolis* (peasants) *Sonis* (goldsmiths), *Suthars* (carpenters), *Valands* (barbers), *Chamars* (leather workers), *Vankar* (weavers), and *Bhangis* (scavengers). The communities like *Brahmins*, *Vanias* and *Rajputs* are known as upper castes, while *Chamars*, *Vankar* and *Bhangis* are known as lower castes. Other castes like *Valand*, *Suthar* and *Kumbhar* etc. are included in the list of other backward castes (OBCs). It is found that there is a division among *Brahmins*, *Vanias*, *Kanbis* and *Patidars* (*Patels*) are considered as peasants. Within the

Patel community, the *Kadva* and *Leva* sub-communities exist. *Brahmins*, *Vania*, and *Rajput* communities control the economy and polity of Gujarat state. Total thirty one castes are included in the list of Schedule Castes in the state of Gujarat (Shah, 2010).

The domination of upper castes on the lower castes have been continuing for centuries but after the independence, it further gained the momentum as the economic development is confined merely to urban areas and upper castes. The caste system further accelerated in rural areas of Gujarat. Due to uneven development, it had an adverse impact on Dalits. Hence, it further continued the caste system, hierarchy and social inequalities in Gujarat. Inter-caste marriages in the villages are discouraged. Many couples who entered into inter-caste marriages were subjected to violence and often have had to leave the village. It is even difficult for them to get houses on rent, particularly, in upper caste localities as it is found that the upper castes practice the principle of purity and pollution. Though Dalits were asked to serve the upper castes, they were never allowed to enter and celebrate the religious ceremonies in villages. The *Panchayat* members elected by the voters from Dalits were served tea in separate designated cups and in some villages; Dalits were not even allowed to have tea along with upper caste men. If they were allowed, they have to wash their cups and keep them separately. Even in the government schools, Dalit children were served food separately and there was no clubbing of upper caste students with Dalit students (Kennedy, 2010: p. 1-59).

There have been agitations against this type discrimination they are strong enough to fight the upper castes as term Dalit give them confident self-respect and dignity. Martin Macwan argues that the term Dalit is rather a moral position of people who believe in equality of all human beings and freedom from oppression (Fernando Franco, Jyotsna Macwan, Suguna Ramanathan, 2004: p. 314). The study in Gujarat in the year of 1971 and 1996 found that rural villages in Gujarat practice untouchability, 75 per cent Scheduled Castes are not allowed entry beyond the threshold and they have to worship from a distance. The Scheduled Castes members of village society do not get entry beyond the outer room of the upper castes. A number of villages observe untouchability in public spaces. As many as 30% of the village *Panchayats* still observe open or subtle discrimination with their elected members belonging to Scheduled Castes. The practice of untouchability has strikingly declined in occupational activities, for example, in buying and selling commodities. In 1971, 85 % of the villages, the Scheduled Castes members were barred from entering shops. This figure came down to 30% in 1996 (Thorat, 2007: p. 107-110). Every year in Gujarat state around 1100 of such cases are arising. The Scheduled Caste Commission Report is that 3.5% cases are only getting resolved.

A survey on untouchability in Gujarat, conducted by I.P. Desai, found this to be widespread in the rural areas in public places like buses, school seating arrangements and seating at *Panchayat* meetings (Fernando Franco, Jyotsna Macwan, Suguna Ramanathan, 2004: p. 6-8). I.P. Desai observed that "There may be less untouchability cases between the Savarnas and the untouchable workers engaged in the similar work, but the personal relations among them are based on their social status (Shah, 2000: p. 467).

DALIT MOVEMENT IN GUJARAT

The Bombay state was bifurcated into Maharashtra and Gujarat on 1st May 1960. More than half of Gujarat's population lives in the rural areas and is engaged in agriculture. The state of Gujarat is divided into three regions: Kachchh and Saurashtra, Central and North Gujarat, and South Gujarat. Dalit Movements occurred in Gujarat like temple entry, hotel entry and bus entry movements and so on. However, important movement was Dalit Panther movement. The unity and fury of the Dalits in Bombay took the shape of the Dalit *Panthers* in reaction to Worli massacre case in Bombay. Its ripples were felt in Gujarat. The seeds of the Dalit panthers were sown in Gujarat where Dalit leaders invited the Dalit Panthers leaders *Raja Dhale* to Ahmedabad on 14 April 1974 and organized a large procession to mark the birth anniversary of Dr. Ambedkar. Dalit activists of Ahmedabad and Dalit leaders organized several public meetings for the spreading the ideals of the Dalit Panthers. *Ramesh Chandra Parmar* and *Naran Vora* of the Republican Party were attracted to the Dalit Panthers and all those leaders strengthened the foundation of the Dalit Panthers in Gujarat. These leaders worked to establish the reputation of the Dalit Panthers in Gujarat as a powerful and militant organization. Its aim was to reach the remotest village, even at the risk of death and help the victims to get justice (Gurjar, 2004, p. 375-77).

The narratives or histories were recorded at a time when atrocities on Dalits have risen, a phenomenon that bears witness to the growing power of that voice from below, for it is precisely this growth the invites the violence (Fernando Franco, Jyotsna Macwan and Suguna Rammanathan, 2004, p. 18). Another movement was anti-reservation agitations of 1981-82 and 1984-85. As a part of this movement, anti-reservation movement directly confronted the Dalits. Whatever the frustration of the upper castes had on Dalits got reflected in this movement. They attacked Dalits, during the movement, Gujarat witnessed caste hatred and communal violence. First incident concerned *Shakarabhai Premabhai Sonar*, a Scheduled Caste man employed as a watchman in the local Gram Panchayat He was locked up in the *Gram Panchayat*. *Kerosene* was poured on him and he was burnt to death by a mob of local residents. In the second incident, a Scheduled Caste lady teacher, *Ushaben Bhalchandra*, who ran away from the back door was caught by the mob and virtually stripped naked. In the third incident, the village main light switch was put off at night and a mob in thousands attacked the locality of Dalits and three pucca houses were broken into, a few others were forced to migrate to the villages. The shops of the *Muslims* and a *Sindhi* were also put to fire. The Dalits ran away from the village for a quite some time due to atrocities on them. In another incident, the anti-reservation stir turned into anti-government agitation in Gozaria village in *Mehsana* District. There was a clash between the police and the upper caste mob. As a result, two persons were killed in the police firing. The whole anger of upper castes got reflected in stopping milk supply and vegetables (S.Rana, 2008: p. 123-125). This is an example of how the upper castes who opposed reservations and did not tolerate the overall development of Dalits. Hence, it is imperative to critically look at the anti-reservation movement. Most of the districts in the state were affected by the anti-reservation agitations. The *Kheda*, *Ahmedabad* and *Mehsana* districts became the epicenters of the anti-reservation movement where many atrocities on Dalits took place. These three districts were having very high rate of education and urbanization. The number of Scheduled Castes also more, therefore, educational and economic progress of scheduled caste was enviously noticeable. One more feature of their widespread atrocities on scheduled Caste was that these three districts are having commonly highest population of Patel community among the upper castes. This community was in the forefront of the anti-reservation movement in the state. Another movements like fight for self-respect of Sambarda in 1989, and also atrocities incident of Golana massacre in 1986, the atrocities against Dalits of Kadi in Gujarat in 1995 indicate that Dalits of Gujarat have been fighting against the undemocratic nature of social system, negative approach of the state and society.

CASE STUDIES

5.1 Case Study-1: Massacre of Dalit Youth in Police Firing and their Assertion

The town fair of *Thangadh* is organised every year by the *Thangadh* Municipality in *Surendranagar* district. It is found that Dalits are not allowed to put up any stall in the exhibition. It was the first time Dalits resisted the denial of stalls. When they resisted, there was a verbal clash between Dalits and upper castes and Dalits were beaten up by the upper caste youth. Dalits as a group went to the Police Station and gave the complaint against the upper caste men who manhandled them but the police did not register any case. The police sub-inspector with his police constables came to the location where the incident occurred and fired on the group of Dalits. *Pankaj Amaratbhai Sumera* (16) was shot at the neck without any prior notice by the police other Dalits took the injured person to the *Rajkot* Civil Hospital where he passed away. It is understood that instead of arresting the upper caste person who indulged in killing of *Pankaj*, they arrested the Dalits who went to the police station for seeking justice. The news of *Pankaj's* death provoked the Dalits. A group of Dalit youth started the rally to the police station but the police intervened and instead of controlling the situation, the police fired indiscriminately on Dalits once again. It resulted in killing of two more Dalits. A few Dalits were severely injured and they were admitted in the *Rajkot* Civil Hospital. Seven Dalit youth were falsely accused of participating in rioting and murder. In this case, the officers have shown their hatred against Dalits and did not tolerate the resistance and assertion of Dalits.

Activists and political leaders visited the village and demanded justice for the family of the Dalit youth who passed away and for those injured in the police firing. There was a statewide protest against the upper castes and the government. After the incident, the Ministers have visited the town and convinced the victims that they would support them and punish the culprits as soon as possible. The government of Gujarat declared a compensation of Rs. 2-2 lakh to the family of the person who passed away in the police firing. It is interesting to note that the local Member of Parliament tried to protect the concerned officers who were involved in police firing. It understood that the death of Dalit youth was sought to be compensated with material benefits. The families of victims were compensated and the four police officers were suspended. The case had sent to the CID Crime and their report came in favour of Dalits and it recommended a huge amount of fine on the police officers who were involved in the firing. But it is found that the government has not taken the action against, the officers who are involved in the killing of Dalit youth. Further it is found that government promoted the officers.

5.2 Case Study-2: Atrocities on Dalits and their Assertion in Rethal Village

In *Rethal* village, three persons were manhandled, one was killed and five others were injured. In fact, the Dalits were divided in this village based on their sub castes and there was no unity among them. *Yuvrajsinh Dodiya* has close links with politicians and administrators. *Himmatbhai Rathod* who was driving a bike overtook *Yuvrajsinh*. The latter considered it as an insult and stopped *Himmatbhai* and manhandled him. Himmatbhai filed the case and similar incident took place once again when the son of *Motibhai Manabhai Rathod* was going to *Sanand* by *'Chhakado'*, there was a quarrel between them. *Himmatbhai* was beaten up and he gave the complaint in the police station but the police did not take the complaint seriously. Third time, he slapped *Vasharambhai Dungarbhai's* son and went to police station to file the complaint. They could not register their complaint. Next, when they were returning, after the submission of complaint, the nephew of *Vasharambhai* was found at the bus-stop. *Yuvrajsinh* and other *Rajput* youth quarreled with *Manubhai* when Manu's brother and Atul heard about this quarrel, he rushed to the bus-stop to cool them but the people were in anger and threatened people not to interfere in this matter. Meanwhile two persons, *Sureshbhai* and *Laxmanbhai* (who were working in *Dalit Shakti Kendra*) telephoned the police. The police took this incident lightly. Still the investigation is going on against *Yuvrajsinh*. In this quarrel, the injured person was sent to *Sahiyog* Hospital where he died after a few hours. Next day, more than 2,000 persons gathered near the dead body, which was later given to *Vasharambhai*. He did not take the dead-body to his village but brought it to the police station and informed the officers that they would not bury the dead-body until they got justice and demanded that the police officers responsible for the death should be suspended, file the SCs/STs atrocities case against them and arrest the culprits.

The officers and politicians tried to persuade *Vasharambhai* to take the body but *Vasharambhai* did not agree. *Narendra Modi* telephoned him and promised him that he would take action against the culprits and the officers as well but he has not changed his stand, the police had lathi charged *Vasharambhai* and other activists and dispersed the mob that gathered there and shifted the dead body to the civil hospital. The news of the death was covered by all the news channels at the state and the national levels. At last, the dead-body was taken by the police to the *Rethal* village and buried. Eight persons were injured, one person died and other four Dalits were severely injured. The activists argue that Deputy SP was responsible for this incident. Though the victims got some compensation, but that is not enough and they argue material benefits cannot be compensated with the respect and dignity.

5.3 Case Study-3: Dalit Women Fight against Upper Caste Masculinity

Gajaraben Himmatbhai Parmar works in *Nirma* Company limited (Ltd) and stays with her family members in the staff quarters allotted by the company. There are also others who live in the same quarters. The company has 480 quarters and more than 1500 workers stay in the quarters. *Gajaraben* is in the senior scale as she has been working in the company for the last nine years. There are more than one thousand women workers in the company but there is only one security guard deputed to look after the security of women. It is found that starting from the supervisor to the Manager, they take the work forcefully from the women workers. It is general trend that the new women workers get recruited and the senior workers are replaced with new workers to exploit the new workers and assuming that there would be no resistance from newly recruited workers and senior women may resist, if were asked to do more than eight hours of work. It is understood that when *Gajaraben* resisted against the Management, her leave had been sanctioned and the officers have harassed her sexually and physically. She continuously protested against sexual violence of the supervisor. When she refused to cooperate with him, she was being transferred to the other department. Since she has been constantly opposing the negative behaviour of the supervisor, she was removed from the job permanently but she did not disclose the harassment that she faced due to the constraints that are involved if she reveals the facts but she had informed her relatives and lodged the complaint.

Against the Supervisor and the Management there was no positive response from the Police department. The police authorities did not take the complaint seriously since she hailed from the Dalit community. After seeing the harassment, her son committed suicide. She left the job in the company and joined another company. After some time, her husband also left the company but his provident fund amount was not paid to him. They had to fight for the provident fund. *Gajaraben* approached the local political leaders and explained the injustice being done to her and her family. The police officer has telephoned the supervisor and suggested to the victims to leave the police station. It later emerged that the police officer had asked the complainant to withdraw the case. The police officers did not take the investigation seriously. It was found that the attitude of the police was negative towards *Gajaraben*. It is seen that this kind of negative response is not merely confined to *Gajaraben*, but is the trend in majority of the cases in Gujarat in particular, and India in general. Dalit women are facing economic, social and psychological trauma. *Gajaraben* and her husband went to the police station for the second time and gave the complaint. Due to her continuous pressure and resistance, the police registered the complaint but did not do anything substantial. *Gajaraben* wrote a letter to the Chief District Police officer, *Ahmedabad* and explained the negative response of the police officers. Due to her relentless resistance, at last the police went to the Industry where she worked earlier and interviewed the eyewitnesses and arrested the guilty persons. After contextualizing the case, it is argued that though other workers are also working in the industry, she has been one of the few women who protested against the injustice meted out to her. However, she did not get much support from her fellow workers. It is also reveals that whenever there is resistance, the rich elite classes or the persons from the upper strata do not tolerate the resistance and create problems for the lower class by using their caste, gender an economic disability.

This trend has been reflected in this case. Because of her continuous struggle, she was taken into the job and allotted the quarter, but industry did not provide other facilities which she was entitled to. She had approached *Navsarjan* Trust. The trust urged the managing Director of the company to provide the basic facilities. After repeated requests and protests of *Navsarjan* Trust, *Gajaraben* got the facilities and her husband was called back to his duty.

ANALYSIS

The first case study shows how police playing role against Dalit youths. Even the police has been influenced by feudal mindset and also been used as power against the Dalits. Police supported perpetuators of caste violence. State government managed caste politics through SCs MLA. Dalit activist seems not fulfill the objective of the movement but they are continuing legal fight for their rights. Second case study shows social, economically and powerful castes and their link between politicians so they use their power of the weapons against the Dalits. In third case study incident of caste violence happened against Dalit women at the work place in industry but owner of industry and higher authorities dominated by upper castes. In this case police also involved with factory authorities and use their state power against the Dalits women.

The analysis of above three different cases indicate that, first police or state atrocities and like political pressure against the Dalit youths atrocities. Second, domination and economic hierarchy through use power of weapons against Dalits may be called social atrocities. Last, Dalit women how sexual harassment at work place and owner and officer use power against the Dalits. This part further critically analyzed the negative response of the state and the authorities towards the Dalits and the negative behaviour of upper castes or mindset of the upper caste not merely in the rural but also urban Gujarat. After asserting critically, it is understood, wherever, there was resistance against Dalits there was rise in atrocities on Dalits. The state which is supposed to help Dalits and punish the culprits, is actually creating problems by booking false cases against the Dalits, arresting them and putting them in the jails. Even political leadership tends to be biased toward upper castes and supporting and protecting them in several instances.

CONCLUSION

This study appraised the caste atrocities on the formation of Gujarat state and assessed that there were anti-caste violence movements from Gujarat. These movements gave the scope for Dalit assertions in Gujarat. Hence, Gujarat witnessed several Dalit movements against the caste system, exploitation and the domination by the upper castes. The movements like Dalits Panthers, Anti-reservation and fight for self-respect of Sambarda in 1989, and also atrocities incident of Golana massacre in 1986, the atrocities against Dalits of Kadi in Gujarat in 1995 indicate that Dalits of Gujarat have been fighting against the undemocratic nature of social system, negative approach of the state and management of industries. In other words, this paper has explained the violence against Dalits in Gujarat and argued that all these movements are the basis for Dalits assertions in Gujarat and made Dalits aware of their rights and encouraged them question the dominance of upper strata or the state in any form, with this understanding of Dalits movement in Gujarat such as cases like atrocities or massacre of Dalit youth in police firing and their assertion, Dalits and their assertion in Rethal village, Dalit women fight against upper caste masculinity. It seems that if Dalits use the collective resistance against the atrocities perpetuated upon them in a systematic manner, then they can utilize this assertion to challenge the existing mindset of the society.

REFERENCES

Aloysius, Irudayam S.J., Mangubhai, Jayshree P. and Lee, Joel G. (2011). *Dalit Women Speak Out: Caste, Class and Gender Violence in India.* New Delhi: Zubaan.

Ambedkar, B.R. (1979, 2014). *Annihilation of Caste, Dr. Babasaheb Ambedkar: Writing and Speeches Vol. 1* (Vol. 1). New Delhi: Education Department, Govt. of Maharashtra and Dr. Ambedkar Foundation, Ministry of Social Justice & Empowerment, Govt. of India.

Blumer, H. (1995). Social Movements. *In*: Lyman, S.M. (*ed.*), *Social Movements: Critiques, Concepts, Case-Studies*. London: Macmillan, pp. 60–83.

Chomsky, N. (n.d.). Institutional Violence. *Democracy is coming to the USA" a film by Walter Miale,* (S. McLeod, Interviewer).

Fernando, Franco, Jyotsna, Macwan and Suguna, Rammanathan (2004). *Journey to Freedom: Dalit Narratives*. Kolkata: Samya Publications.

Gorringe, H. (2005). *Untouchable Citizens: Dalit Movements and Democratisation in Tamil Nadu: Cultural Subordination and the Dalit Challenge* (Vol. 4). New Delhi: Sage Publications.

Gurjar, N. (2004). Dalit Movement in Gujarat. *In*: Fernando Franco, J.M. (*ed.*), *Journey to Freedom: Dalit Narratives*. Kolkata: Samya Publications, pp. 375–377.

Heuser, B. (2012). Atrocities in Theory and Practice: An Introduction. *Civil Wars,* 14(1): 3.

Ilaiah, K. (2015). Dalits are not definitely a block, and there is an intellectual blossom. 9. (e. "Ajmal Khan and Anish, Interviewer) Mumbai: TwoCirles.net.

Indian Express News, Newspaper, Ahmedabad, Gujarat, 24 February 2013.

Jatava, D.R. (2007). *Violation of Human Rights: facts and Foes.* Jaipur: ABD Publishers.

Kennedy, R.F. (2010). *"Understanding Untouchability: A Comprehensive Study of Practices and Conditions in 1589 Villages",* Navsarjan RFK center Publications.

Kenneth, Bush and Colleen, Duggen (2013). Evaluation in conflict zone: methodological and ethical challenges. *Journal of Peace Building and Development,* 8: 7.

Mani, Braj Ranjan (2005). *Debrahmanising History: Dominance and resistance in Indian society,* Manohar Publications, New Delhi, p.13.

Narwani, G. (2011). *Atrocities against Scheduled Castes and Scheduled Tribes.* New Delhi: Rawat Publications.

Rana, S. (2008). *Reservations in India: Myths and Realities,* Concept Publishing Company, New Delhi, pp. 129-34.

Schwarzmantel, J. (2011). *Democracy and Political Violence.* Edinburgh: Edinburgh University Press Ltd.

Shah, A. (2010). *Structure of Indian Society: Then and Now.* New Delhi: Routledge.

Shah, Ghanshayam (2000) *Hope and Despair: A study of Untouchability and Atrocities in Gujarat,* Indian School of Political Economy.

State Crime Records Bureau, Gandhinagar (year -2001 to 2012) RTI Act-2005 and *Balatkaragrasta Dalit women: aadhyana (Do. Hasmukha Parmar),* this information was provided by Kirit Rathod - Navsarjan Trust, Gujarat.

Thorat, Sukhadeo (2007). *Human Rights of Ex-untouchable in India: Violations and Enforcement,* Vol. 10–11(1–2). Jan. 2006- Dec. 2007, *Indian Journal of Human Rights*, pp. 107–110.

Verma, J.M. (2011). Social Justice in India: A case for equality through privilege. *In*: Pais, M.M. (*ed.*), *Backward Classes and Social Justice*. New Delhi: Rawat Publications. pp. 52–53.

Rajesh Lakum is a Ph.D candidate at Centre for Studies in Society and Development, School of Social Sciences, Central University of Gujarat. His research focuses on caste violence, atrocities and human rights issues in larger contexts of Indian society.

Chapter 15

Casteist Media and Atrocities on Dalits

TRUPTI RATNAPARKHI[1]

INTRODUCTION

Media are the important institutions in a democratic state, considered as its fourth pillar. Media play a major role in creating and generating public opinion. In Today so called 'civil society' media have gained unprecedented significance. They can immensely affect the public mindset through the amount of time and intensity they provide to any issue. In India, even today media are overwhelmingly populated by the upper castes. The presence of Dalits and Adivasis is negligible in the decision making posts in the media. The lack of Dalits and Adivasi representation is a serious issue demanding some examination and analysis. This lacuna has resulted in the one-sided, highly partial, prejudiced and casteist presentation of the issues related to the Dalits and Adivasis. The unlimited and uncontrollable power exercised by the upper castes on the Indian media results in the unequal balance of power. This has been reflected, so far, in the insensitivity towards the Dalit issues in media and their (intentional) lack of understanding of the issues. Prejudiced presentation of the Dalit and Adivasi issues ranges from negligible coverage to misinterpretation of the issues. The present paper attends to focus

[1] Tata Institute of Social Sciences, Tuljapur

on the domination of casteism on Indian media and uninstituted control by the upper castes and its reflections in the coverage of the atrocities on the Dalits.

The media have an important role to play in the society. They are one of the prominent agencies in shaping the public opinion. In a democratic set up like India media can be the crucial agent in bringing about social justice and can be an active, vocal institution against discrimination in any form. As is seen in many cases media have promoted and led many social protests, in some instances even raising some issues to the national level debate. In his seminal work 'Development As Freedom' Amartya Sen (2000) also reinforces the role of the media in the process of democratization, as it contributes to the right of freedom of expression and provides a pluralist platform and channel of expression for multiple groups and communities. But as one looks deeper into the Indian media industry, one is able to observe certain discrepancies, fissures and discrimination. When these gaps are dissected and analysed the age old Indian reality comes to the fore, which is casteism.

Caste has always played a very significant, dominant and pernicious role in the foundation and structure of Indian society. As Annie Nama rightly points out, "The caste system not only peripheralizes the Dalit communities, but also excludes them, defining a line between the so-called untouchable communities and the other social groups. The physical phenomenon of untouchability is linked to the deep set notions of purity and pollution and the caste mindset. Thus different layers of civil society and its institutions can exclude and neglect the concerns of these communities from the purview of their duties and responsibilities" (Namala, 2007). It is a lamentable fact that along with other such institutions the caste consciousness has also infiltrated the fourth column of Indian democracy, that is, media. An institution which could have become a weapon, a way of expression for millions of the oppressed has become the tool of oppression itself. As media are owned by the upper caste section of the society in the two basic aspects-financial and intellectual, instead of becoming the voice of the oppressed section of society the media are subverting them by sidelining their issues and covering up the casteist, discriminatory reality of the so-called Civil Society.

The corporate face of media had been predicted by several influential thinker long back. 'The role of the media has been particularly highlighted by Habermas in forming a crucial constituent and catalyst for the existence of the public sphere. In general, the media have been characterized principally through their perceived evolution from a fourth estate guarding the public interest into media that commodity news and are more interested in people as consumers than as citizens" (Deane, 2005). While talking about the media's role in capitalist society E.H. Carr (2006) says, that media are, "...powerful instruments to inculcate desirable tastes and desirable opinions - the standard of desirability being found in the accepted tastes and opinions of the society....Professional advertisers and campaign managers are not primarily concerned with existing facts. They are interested in what the consumer or elector now believes or in events only so far, as this enters into the end-product, that is, what the consumer or elector can by skillfully handling be induced to believe or want."

As is clearly said above, the media try to appease the sentiments of the class on which it depends by covering the gaps in the societal structure. They try to hide or distort the reality to create a pseudoreality which would appeal to the sophisticated taste of their major consumers and capitalists who provide them with the necessary finance. Apart from this business interest of today corporate media, there is an apparent bias towards the Dalit issues in the media coverage. It can be a result of various reasons including negligible number of the Dalit media persons at the decision making level. Majority of the media personnels being upper caste the proper representation of Dalit issues including serious crimes like the atrocities on Dalits are not given proper space as well as unbiased coverage. Again the issue is not limited to atrocities, it is reflected in almost all the issues concerning Dalits including reservations, suicides of Dalit students, Dalit movement and other problematic issues.

Dr. Babasaheb Ambedkar was well aware of the importance of the media as the weapon and the casteist nature of the Indian media as well. He had said, "It is depressing that we do not have enough resources with us. We do not have money; do not have newspapers. Throughout India, each day our people are suffering under authoritarianism with no consideration, and discrimination; those are not covered in the newspapers. By a planned conspiracy the newspapers are involved full-fledged in silencing our views on socio-political problems" (Ambedkar, 1993). It is unfortunate that what Dr. Ambedkar said many decades ago still holds true that, "The untouchables have no press" (Ambedkar, 1993). It was expected that after the unparalleled growth in the media the voice of the common man will be noticed more and more, but this has not happened. "(But) while the proliferation of media in the wake of liberalization in many countries was initially marked by an upsurge of public debate on a whole range of issues, evidence is growing that, as competition intensifies, content is increasingly being shaped by the demands of advertisers and sponsors who pay for the newly liberalized media, and an increasingly intense focus on profitability. The result is more urban biased, consumer oriented media which have diminishing interest in or concern for people living in poverty" (Deane, 2005). The market also influences the coverage of media through the advertisers. "The advertisers also shape the media content of those media which they use to carry their messages. Both directly by lobbying newspaper editors and television schedulers, and indirectly, by choosing not to advertise certain media content, advertisers powerfully shape the media agenda. Their principal interest is in finding media environment that will not be detrimental to the feel good, aspirational messages that they want to attach to the advertised products" (Wayne, 2003).

The newspaper owners and the owners of electronic media have to bond with the advertisers who provide them with the money necessary for production and circulation of their product. In case of India the newspapers and the news channels are principally owned by upper caste propertied class of people who have vested interests in silencing the voices of the depressed section of society. The media did not want to acknowledge the discrimination and injustice prevailing in the society, it also did not want to displease its patrons by making them aware of their caste realities. Even though the market and advertisers as well as public mindset shapes the media coverage, if observed in depth the casteist mentality has also seeped in the mostly upper caste media personnel. Today Indian media are not the institution ensuring social justice, they are nothing but corporate houses seeking profit, marketing whatever is possible. But this corporate house finds it difficult to sell the Dalit issues because it creates conflict and disillusionment in its sophisticated Indian middle class audience. Indian media's casteism has become apparent in the several issues related to the Dalits. It was for the first time seen in the history that media were not only supportive of but actively contributed to coordinating and guiding the protest campaign against Mandal Commission's recommendations about OBC reservations. Media are equally silent about Dalit students committing suicide in the top institutions. If it gives space to such news items the scope remains at the level of reporting, it never goes as far as analyzing the actual basis of the conflict. In case of suicides of the Dalit students media also stand guilty of popularising the view that, due to the lack of the necessary talent the Dalit students are not able to cope.

The casteist prejudice of the media against the Dalits clearly shows in their continuous ignorance about the yearly gathering at Diksha Bhoomi and Chaitya Bhoomi. Teltumbde rightly comments that, "One does not know of any other person in history whose ideology brings such a huge number of followers as Babasaheb Ambedkar's does to his memorial.... Even 'secular' market considerations might indicate the unwisdom of ignoring such a massive congregation. But caste prejudice can be stronger than market logic" (Teltumbde, p. 145). Raja Sekhar Vundru also commented in 'The Times of India', "Sadly enough, Indian television, which scours for stories to pack each minute of air time, lost the golden opportunity to bring this unique event into the public domain. It did not report a minute of it. Is it a case of marked indifference?"

(Vundru, 2006). In the year 2015 this occasion was given some space even in the national media to a considerable extent because of the elections due in Bihar. Every major national party was claiming a share of the person that Dr. Ambedkar is. But as Jyoti Punwani (2015) points out, even though Ambedkar was in the media coverage, Dalits are still not, as the caste crimes are still not taken account of in a justified manner. Ravish Kumar (2015) takes the same stand about the biased media saying, "Why do the norms of the caste conclave feel threatened when a Dalit issue is covered? Ambedkar is the country's most potent political brand, but in the 'media there is not even an inch of space for him. How can there be such a disconnect between society, politics and the media? And why does this disconnect manifest itself only when it comes to Ambedkar? If one wants any proof that our media is casteist, then all one needs to do is investigate who it excludes."

The media try to dilute the intensity of the caste crimes by giving particular kind of treatment to such news. Media may tone it down through using specific kind of language or tone. The way it is presented by the media normalizes it because when they give negligible space and less importance to news related to discrimination against Dalits, it also shapes the attention and attitude of the viewers for the same. This apartheid on Dalits and their issues truly comes to the fore when one looks at the space and coverage given to the heinous and most serious crime like the atrocity. By taking stock of the coverage of the major atrocities which have happened in the past few years one can easily observe the purposeful indifference and misrepresentation of Dalit issues in the mainstream media. The coverage given to the Khairlanji massacre which stands as one of the most cruel, vicious attacks on the Dalit dreams and determination showed how the media can distort and hide the true picture from the viewers. The sum total of the intensity of this crime is evident in the remark of Nagsen Sonare, President of Ambedkar Center for Justice and Peace when he said, "The Khairlanji incident is the end of imagination for us." It was a very evident caste crime but it was initially picturised by the media as a culmination of the moral villagers' rage over an illicit relationship of a lower caste woman with an outsider. The news was first covered by a local newspaper 'Deshonnati' on 1st October and one of the widely read Marathi newspapers 'Lokmat' carried around the news with special emphasis on the built-up 'illicit relationship' story. On the same day the English edition of the same paper ran a six-column news along the same line. This is the common strategy used by media to cover atrocities on Dalits by giving them some other hue or by covering them up with some other vein. By harping on this false cover-up media ensures that the victims of such crime would not invoke sympathy among the people. It has become an unwritten rule for the fourth pillar of our democracy.

This kind of biased reporting continued in the following days. Except a few dailies and weeklies no other national newspaper or news channel considered the incident in its true light of caste atrocity. When there was a reaction from the Dalit population about the suppression of the incident and administration's effort to protect the perpetrators media concentrated on the 'disruptional these rallies demanding for justice caused. They did not criticize the repressive measures taken by the state and the overall lapses in the investigations. The media invested their energy in enthusiastically pursuing the irresponsible statement made by Maharashtra's deputy chief minister and home minister R.R. Patil about naxalite hand behind the protests. This was a sure fire way of the government for distracting people's attention from the actual nature of the crime. Even after Patil took back his statement, the media kept harping on it for several days. They never tried to take the comprehensive view of the situation causing that much anger in the Dalit agitators in the Maharashtra about the desecration of a statue of Dr. Ambedkar in Kanpur on 30 November 2006.

Khairlanji is not an isolated incident of such misrepresentation. Journalist Sunil Dudhe (2015) points out the casteist murder of ACJP (Ambedkarite Centre for Justice and Peace) activist Sanjay Khobragade in Gondia. To protect the upper caste murderers Powars, the police officials fabricated a false account of an illicit relationship between the murdered Sanjay's wife and another ACJP activist Raju Gadpayle. Like it happend in Khairlanji case here this false story was accepted as it is by the media without proper inquiry into the actual angle of a caste crime. Another bizzare incidence of false and fabricated reporting came to the fore in this particular case when several acknowledged newspapers published different accounts of the caste crime, instigating the rage and protests of the Dalit organizations. Pradeep Khobragade, late Sanjay's son started a petition against the arrest of his mother on the false grounds, media ignored this and kept on with the false story. The media did not persuade the truth, never made an inquiry into the facts. Nalini Raj points out that, "Even the major atrocities like Kilvenmani, Chunduru, Karamchechu, Khairlanji, to the more recent Laxmipet incident, the media never covered them with objectivity; Journalists are supposed to be active processors and however encoded their received realities, they may decode it different ways" (Rajan, 2007). But contrary to what Rajan says the journalists not only do not have the will to decode such caste crimes but are trained and motivated to decode it in the opposite way. Marxist analysis considers media as being "locked into the power structure, and consequently as acting largely in tandem with the dominant institutions in society. The media thus reproduces the viewpoints of dominant institutions not as one among a number of alternative perspectives, but the central and "obvious" or "natural" perspective" (Curran, Michael, Janet *et al.*, 1982).

This is where the under-representation of Dalits in the media and near about no representation at the decision-making posts in the media industries plays a role. Our national media fail to represent the social diversity. According to the 2001 census Dalits and Adivasis constitute 24% of the population but have negligible presence in the media. When Kenneth J. Cooper, the former New Delhi bureau chief of The Washington Post and an African- American asked Indian journalist Unniyal to arrange a meeting with a Dalit journalist, to his surprise Unniyal found out that in his career of 30 years he had never met a Dalit journalist and more shocking to him was that he had failed to recognize it before. He published an article on 16 Nov, 1996 describing this incident as 'In Search of a Dalit Journalist. Cooper also wrote a piece entitled as 'India's Majority Lower Castes are Minor Voice in Newspapers' on 5th Sept, 1996. The leading journalist Ravish Kumar points out this condition in his article 'Absent Dalit: the Indian Newsroom (2015) - "There are no Dalits in the Newsroom. This has been revealed through numerous surveys. Yet there is little discussion on what might be a solution to this problem. If everyone makes it to the newsroom based only on merit and chance, then surely some Dalits should also have made it. There is a serious lack of diversity in the media. Perhaps that is why the media sometimes ends up taking a stand against diversity. It begins to see all answers in one leader and his/her leadership."

This is not only a grave condition created by the numerical lack, but the basic perception of the national media is casteist in nature. Shivam Vij's feature on The Hoot from June 2004 titled 'Gate in the Newsroom?', " Opens with a question he asks Dilip Awasthi, a senior editor of 'Dainik Jagran': Why there are so few Scheduled Caste and Backward Caste journalists? Awasthi answers: "They do not go to school.' The next question: has Awasthi ever met a single SC/OBC journalist worthy enough of a job? He replies, "Never. They cannot write a single sentence properly." This typical discriminatory, prejudiced attitude of the editor says it all and is representative of the caste-ridden perspective of the upper caste Indian media. A field experiment done by Sukhdeo Thorat and Paul Attewwel uncovered the same attitude in case of the so-called modern job sector in India. To quote them, " This field experiment study of job applications observed a statistically significant pattern by which, on average, college-educated lower-caste and Muslim job applicants fare less well than equivalently-qualified applicants with high caste names, when applying by mail for employment in the modem private- enterprise sector" (Thorat and Attewwel, 2007). They very correctly conclude in the end that, "Our findings suggest that social exclusion is not just a residue of the past clinging to the margins of the Indian economy, nor is it limited to people of little education. On the contrary, it appears that caste favouritism and the social exclusion of Dalits and Muslims have infused private enterprises even in the most dynamic modern sector of the Indian economy" (Thorat and Attewwel, 2007). Due to the upper caste control over the resources media reflects the so called caste Hindu perspective as the "obvious" or "natural" perspective. Today Dalits have become conscious of their rights. They also have realized how media downplays their issues and contributions. This has alienated Dalit youth from the media and media's power to democratize opinions. Even if they try to enter it, the environment affected by the caste bias and the subjugation of the reality which is very immediate to them results in their disillusionment and they lose the hope, if they had any in the media's role about bringing the social justice to the marginalized and the oppressed section of the society.

Many atrocities have taken place on Dalits after Khairlanji, ranging from rape to murder, but not a single case has been highlighted by the national media. In recent years several cases took place in Maharashtra alone, a state which prides itself on its so called "forwardness1. In Jamkhed of Kharda talukas in Ahmednagar a 17 years old Dalit boy named Nitin Aage was murdered by the upper caste people from the village on 24th April, 2014. His only mistake was that he was in love with an upper caste girl from the same village. The family members of the girl's family killed him for the sake of their honor, as the girl was in love with him too. Hardly one month afterwards, on 25th May, 2014 a Dalit named Umesh Aagade was murdered because of his alleged affair with an upper caste girl, in Kannad, Aurangabad. Manoj Kasab, a Dalit sarpanch was attacked by the upper caste former sarpanch in Nanegaon village of the Jalna district. He died due to sustained injuries in a hospital after one month. A Buddhist youth in Chikhli from Pune named Maanik Udage was murdered by the upper caste OBCs from the same village. Shockingly, the reason was that he was aware enough to celebrate the birth anniversary of Dr. Babasaheb Ambedkar.

The cases are endless. If this is the condition in a single state in India then one can imagine the status of Dalits all over. In spite of the killings, rapes, molestations, incarcerations which are continuing on a daily basis the media fail to recognize this. The attention is limited to reporting only. No news channel perseveres the progress of the cases which are filed under atrocities. It never lobbies support for promoting justice in such cases. It never highlights the lack of conviction in the atrocity cases. They do not want to conduct an open debate on this very basic violation of the right to live. Media had shown their responsible face in many public protests in the past, for instance in the case of Priydarshini Mattu, Jessica Lai murder case or the recent Delhi Gang rape. They also organized standard debates on the prime time slot about the status of women in India and mentality of Indian people towards women. But when it comes to the day to day persecution of the basic human rights of the Dalits media chose to remain silent, as if the plight of this section of the society will not appeal to them or is not worth taking notice of. It is 'normal'.

If one observes the schedule of the news channels or the space given to different kind of news items in the print media, one can realize that the media cater to the popular demand of sensational turn of their audience's mindset. Special slots are given to sensational and disturbing crime stories and the media reporters do all the efforts to fill in more and more details in the reporting to gamer more number of viewers. But when it comes to caste crimes media lose interest in spite of all the gory violence involved in it and limits itself to one line mentioned somewhere on the screen. May be caste crime reveals that face of Indian society which people do not want to see or media do not want to focus on. The power of media support was clearly evident in the protest against 'Delhi Rape'. But the same media without any kind of scruple sidelined the rapes of Surekha and Priyanka Bhotmange, because it was not as salable/ marketable news item/ product as its basis was the caste. Anand Teltumbde (2010) says it well while talking about media's reluctance to cover atrocities discussing caste crimes and the everyday murders of Dalits does not offer the consumers of television any pleasure. On the contrary, it reduces the pleasure factor by inducing guilt. Viewers could not feel entertained if the media were to remind them of their own fundamental consciousness-caste.... Since this is disturbing it lacks amusement value." It is the caste discrimination which the media try to avoid highlighting.

The quite shocking case of the serial murders in Nithari has a Dalit undercurrent, because 15 out of the 17 murdered children were from the Dalit families. According to Annie Namala (2007), a member of the fact finding committee, "The perpetrators presumed that by choosing victims from the socially excluded and marginalized communities, they would escape the consequences." She has also observed the same kind of caste discrimination in the relief operations in the tsunami affected areas. She poses very pointed questions at the end of her article? Killing by Default'. To quote her-" One can legitimately ask: Would these killings have been possible had a majority of the victims been from any other community other than Dalits, the untouchables?" While covering this sensational news item not a single news channel paid any attention to this aspect of that heinous crime.

The scale of atrocities against the Dalits says it all. India's national crime record says that everyday, while three Dalit women are raped and two Dalits are murdered, two Dalit homes are incinerated. This is the statistics of the reported cases, if one considers the cases which go unreported or are rejected to be reported by the police the picture looks quite grim. These are the same questions one has to ask in each Dalit atrocity continuously. It is unfortunate that every time the answer remains the same. There is no doubt that this so-called civil society and its media have failed and are continuously failing the Dalits and that "too by default."

REFERENCES

Ambedkar, B.R. (1993). Writings and Speeches: Volume 17. Delhi: Government of India.

Ambedkar, B.R. (1993). Writings and Speeches: Volume 2. Delhi: Government of India.

Buckwalter, Sabrina, 'American Experience of Caste Virus', https://atrocitynews.wordpress.corn/2007/09/25/a-story-full-of-hatred-american experience-of-castevirus.

Carr, E.H. (2006). What is History? London: Penguin Books.

Cooper, Kenneth J. (1996). India's Majority Lower Castes Are Minor Voice in Newspapers; Few Journalists, Periodicals Advocate Interests of the Underclass. The Washington Post.

Curran, James, Michael, Gurevitch and Janet, Woollacott (1982). The Study of the Media: Theoretical Approaches. In: Gurevithch *et al.*, Culture, Society and the Media. Methuen and Co. Ltd.

Deane, J. (2005). Media, Democracy and the Public sphere. *In*: Hemer and Tufte (*eds.*), Rethinking Communication for Development. Buenos Aires: Publicaciones Cooperativas.

Dudhe, S. (2014). Dalits and Mainstream Media in Maharashtra. Round Table India. Retrieved 16 June 2015 from http://roundtableindia.co.in/index.php?option=com_conent&view=article&id=7595:dalit-and-mainstream-media-2&catid=119;feature&Itemid=132.

Kumar, Ravish (2015). Absent Dalit: The Indian Newsroom. Seminar. Retrieved on 15 December 2015 from http://www.indiaseminar.com/2015/672/672_ravish Jmmar.htm.

Namala, Annie (2007). Killing by Default. Children First. Retrieved on 15 June 2015 from http://www.india-seminar.com/2007/574/574 comment.htm.

Punwani, J. (2015). The Media Short Shrift to Dalits. The Hoot. Retrieved on 16 June 2015 from http://www.thehoot.org/media-watch/.../the-media-s-short-shrift-to-dalits-8275.

Rajan, Nalini (*ed.*) (2007). 21st Century Journalism in India. New Delhi: Sage Publications.

Sen, Amartya (2000). Development as Freedom. USA: Alfred A. Knopf Inc.

Teltumbde, A. (2010). The Persistence of Caste: The Khairlanji Murders and India's Hidden Apartheid. New Delhi: Navyana Publications.

Thorat, S. (*ed.*) (2010). Blocked by Caste: Economic Discrimination in Modern India. New Delhi: Oxford University Press.

Uniyal, B.N. (1996). *In*: Search of a Dalit Journalist. The Pioneer Retrieved on 15 June 2015 from http: // www. chandrabhanprasad. com/My%20 Camp/Dal it%20Journalist, doc.

Varadrajan, S. (2006). Caste Matters in the Indian Media. The Hindu. Retrieved on 15 June 2015 from http://www.thehindu.com/todavs-paper/tp-opinion/caste-niatters-in-the-indian-media/article3114199.ece.

Vij, Shivam (2004). Caste in the Newsroom? The Hoot. Retrieved on 16 June 2015 from http://www.thehoot.org/media-watch/regional-media/caste-in-the-newsroom-1198.

Vundru, Raj Sekhar (2006). Buddha as Untouchable. The Times of India. Retrieved on 15 June 2015 from http://timesofmdia.indiatimes.com/edit-page/Buddha-as-untouchable/articleshow/2169742.cms.

Wayne, M. (2003). Marxism and Media Studies, Key Concepts and Contemporary Trends. Plato Press.

Trupti Ratnaparkhi, Assisttant Professor at Tata Institute of Social Sciences has completed her first post-graduation in English and second in Women's Studies. Currently she is pursuing Ph.D. in English on the Indian English dramatist Poile Sengupta. She has published and presented research papers related to English Literature, Women's Issues etc. Caste system in India is also her favored research area.

Subject Index

T

U

V